D0559195

SOCIAL DEMOCRATIC AMERICA

Social Democratic America

Lane Kenworthy

OXFORD
UNIVERSITY PRESS

Oxford University Press is a department of the University of Oxford.
It furthers the University's objective of excellence in research, scholarship,
and education by publishing worldwide.

Oxford   New York
Auckland   Cape Town   Dar es Salaam   Hong Kong   Karachi
Kuala Lumpur   Madrid   Melbourne   Mexico City   Nairobi
New Delhi   Shanghai   Taipei   Toronto

With offices in
Argentina   Austria   Brazil   Chile   Czech Republic   France   Greece
Guatemala   Hungary   Italy   Japan   Poland   Portugal   Singapore
South Korea   Switzerland   Thailand   Turkey   Ukraine   Vietnam

Oxford is a registered trademark of Oxford University Press
in the UK and certain other countries.

Published in the United States of America by
Oxford University Press
198 Madison Avenue, New York, NY 10016

Library of Congress Cataloging-in-Publication Data
Kenworthy, Lane.
Social democratic America / Lane Kenworthy.
    pages cm
Includes bibliographical references and index.
ISBN 978–0–19–932251–0 (hardback : alk. paper)   1. United States—Social
policy—1993–   2. Public welfare—United States.   3. Democracy—United States.
4. Developed countries—Social policy.   I. Title.
HV95.K38 2014
335.50973—dc23
2013016057

9 8 7 6 5 4 3 2 1
Printed in the United States of America
on acid-free paper

"The moral arc of the universe is long, but it bends toward justice."

—Martin Luther King, Jr.

Contents

1

Toward the Good Society: An American Path

AMERICA IS A very rich nation. And in coming decades we will become richer still. Despite our affluence, however, too few ordinary Americans have adequate economic security, too few who grow up in disadvantaged circumstances are able to reach the middle class, and too few have seen their boat lifted when the economic tide rises.

This book is about how we can do better. The problems we confront are big ones, but they are not intractable. The key to a solution? Government social programs. Social programs function as a safety net, a springboard, and an escalator: they provide economic security, enhance opportunity, and ensure rising living standards. Over the past century, we have gradually expanded the size and scope of such programs. Given recent economic and social shifts, we need to do more. Our history and the experiences of some other affluent nations point us in useful directions, and they suggest we can expand government without destroying liberty, breaking the bank, or wrecking the economy.

Can it happen? The notion that we are likely to further increase the size and scope of our social policy may seem blind to the reality of contemporary American politics. After all, some on the left of the political spectrum feel America's safety net is complete,[1] many in the center favor cutting public spending to reduce our government debt, and many on the right demand lower spending and taxes full stop. But step back and consider the long run. The lesson of the past 100 years is that as the country gets richer, we are willing to spend more in order to safeguard against risk and enhance fairness. Advances in social policy come only intermittently, but they do come. And when they come, they usually last.

Three Failings

From the 1940s to the 1970s, Americans up and down the income ladder enjoyed improved economic security, expanding opportunity, and steadily rising incomes. But since the 1970s, the story has been quite different. Progress has stalled, or even reversed.

Too many Americans have incomes so low that making ends meet is a struggle. Too many experience a sizable income drop at some point during their working career. And too many have no health insurance or inadequate health insurance. This isn't just a function of the 2008–9 economic crisis and its aftermath. It was true before the economy fell apart, and it will still be true once we return to our long-run growth path (and after the 2010 healthcare reform is fully implemented).

In the past half century the United States has made considerable progress in boosting opportunity: most women and many African Americans now have a much better chance to obtain an advanced education and to thrive in the labor market than did their counterparts a generation ago. Yet the story for Americans who grow up poor is much less encouraging. Their odds of climbing into the middle class, already low, have been shrinking.

Since the 1970s, the incomes of households in the middle and below have risen slowly, despite sustained growth in the economy. Income growth has been decoupled from economic growth.

Our Hypercompetitive, Risk-Filled Economy

For society as a whole, competition is a force for immense good, stimulating economic progress and improving living standards. But competition can wreak havoc on the lives of particular individuals. Since the 1970s, competition has become a much more pervasive feature of America's economy. Firms selling goods or services in international markets confront intense foreign rivals. Domestic industries, such as restaurants and hotels, face more competitors too, as technological advances, falling construction and transportation costs, and deregulation have reduced barriers to entry. In addition, shareholders now want rapid appreciation in stock values. Whereas a generation ago they were happy with a consistent dividend payment and some long-term increase in the stock price, they now demand buoyant quarterly profits and constant growth. Robert Reich has an apt label for this new economy: "supercapitalism." American firms, he notes, "now have little choice but to relentlessly pursue profits."[2]

This shift benefits investors, consumers, and some employees. But it encourages companies to resist pay increases, drop health-insurance plans, cut contributions to employee pensions, move abroad, downsize, replace regular employees with temporary ones, and pursue a variety of other cost-cutting strategies that weaken economic security, limit opportunity for the less skilled, and reduce income growth for many ordinary Americans.[3]

For better or worse, the new hypercompetitive, risk-filled economy is here to stay. In coming decades more of us will lose a job or work part-time or irregular hours, fewer of us will get a good healthcare or pension plan from our employer, and more of us will go long stretches without getting a pay increase.

Our Faltering Social Institutions

Families, civic organizations, and labor unions play important roles in a capitalist society. They help give us a good start in life, provide job security and a bigger paycheck, and ensure that if we fall through the cracks, there is someone to help us get back on our feet. But over the past half century, these institutions have been unraveling. Americans marry later and divorce more frequently. Fewer children grow up in a home with both biological parents. Participation in local civic associations has declined. And barely one in ten employed Americans is a union member. Even more problematic, these changes have a class tilt: families, community organizations, and unions have weakened most among those with less education and income.[4]

Some believe the best way to address the stresses and strains of the new economy is to strengthen these institutions. It's a laudable aim. It would be good if more American children grew up in intact families, if unions ensured stable jobs and rising wages for a significant share of workers, and if community organizations provided guidance and support to more people in difficult circumstances. But that's not likely to happen.[5] Advocates of revitalizing these institutions tend to offer lots of hope but little evidence that it can be done. Nor do we find cause for optimism abroad; similar trends are evident in most rich nations.

Even if we could make progress in reversing the decline of families, unions, and community organizations, it wouldn't be good enough. At their best, these institutions leave a significant portion of the population uncovered. There has never been a society in which all children grow up in stable two-parent families, all workers enjoy union-negotiated wages and benefits, and civic associations serve the needs of all the disadvantaged. Only government has the capacity to help all Americans.

Affluence, Insurance, and Government

Most of us try to steer clear of risk events, and we attempt to insure ourselves against potential harm or loss in case we do get hit by one. We save money in case we lose our job or outlive our working years. We bind ourselves in long-term partnerships (marriage) in order to spread childcare duties and safeguard against financial difficulty. We purchase health insurance in case we need expensive medical care. We buy auto insurance in case we get in an accident. We purchase home insurance in case our house is damaged or destroyed.

When our income is low, we can't afford to spend much on insurance, so we often go without. The more income or assets we have, the more insurance we buy. This is true of individuals and of nations. As a person's income or assets increase, she will tend to spend more on insurance. Similarly, as a nation gets richer, it will tend to allocate a larger portion of its income—its gross domestic product (GDP)—to insurance.

For some types of insurance, private markets do an effective job. Auto insurance is a good example; the incidence of accidents and the repair or replacement sums are sufficiently low that private companies can offer insurance at prices most drivers can afford. In other areas, government is a better provider, because it can spread the cost across a larger pool (all citizens), having a single payer reduces administrative costs, and government can insist on cost reductions and safety measures by private actors.[6]

Most of what we call social policy is actually public insurance.[7] Social Security and Medicare insure against the risk of having little or no money in your retirement years. Unemployment compensation insures against the risk of losing your job. Disability payment programs insure against the risk of suffering a physical, mental, or psychological condition that renders you unable to earn a living.

Other public services and benefits also are insurance programs, even if we don't usually think of them as such. Public schools insure against the risk that private schools are unavailable, too expensive, or poor in quality. Special education services insure against the risk of having a disability that inhibits participation in school. Retraining and job-placement programs insure against the risk that market conditions make it difficult to find employment. The

Earned Income Tax Credit (EITC) insures against the risk that your job pays less than what's needed for a minimally decent standard of living. Social assistance programs such as the Supplemental Nutrition Assistance Program (SNAP, or "food stamps") and Temporary Assistance for Needy Families (TANF) insure against the risk that you will find yourself unable to get a job but ineligible for unemployment or disability compensation. Even affirmative action programs are a form of insurance; they insure against the risk of being in a group that is, or formerly was, discriminated against.

Over the past century, the United States, like other rich nations, has created a number of public insurance programs. But we haven't done enough. From our own experience and that of other affluent countries, we know there are significant risks we could insure against but currently don't, and others for which the protection we now provide is inadequate.[8] We need the following:

- Universal health insurance
- One-year paid parental leave
- Universal early education
- Increase in the Child Tax Credit
- Sickness insurance
- Eased eligibility criteria for unemployment insurance
- Wage insurance
- Supplemental defined-contribution pension plans with automatic enrollment
- Extensive, personalized job-search and (re)training support
- Government as employer of last resort
- Minimum wage increased modestly and indexed to prices
- EITC extended farther up the income ladder and indexed to average compensation or GDP per capita
- Social assistance with a higher benefit level and more support for employment
- Reduced incarceration of low-level drug offenders
- Affirmative action shifted to focus on family background rather than race

- Expanded government investment in infrastructure and public spaces
- Increase in paid holidays and vacation time

Now, to some, this will look like a predictable laundry list of left goals. Yet I've arrived at this list not by consulting the latest edition of the "Progressives' Handbook,"[9] but by examining the problems we face and the experiences of the world's rich nations in addressing them. As I explain in chapters 2, 3, and 4, the evidence suggests that we can do better at enhancing economic security, expanding opportunity, and ensuring shared prosperity, and that these policies are the best way to do so. Moreover, you will see, if you read on, that I believe the prevailing wisdom among the American left on some key issues—taxes, regulation, competition in services, wage levels in low-end service jobs, and others—is mistaken.

Government Social Programs Have Economic Costs, but Also Benefits

Of course, spending on insurance has an economic cost. When we allocate funds to insurance, we forgo other uses of the money that might have contributed to economic advance, such as investment in research or new companies or in expansion of existing businesses. Moreover, the existence of insurance increases the incentive for people to engage in risky behavior or to avoid employment. Given these costs, it isn't surprising that some object to the expansion of public insurance.

At the same time, insurance has economic benefits. Schooling and medical insurance improve productivity via better knowledge, creativity, and health. Bankruptcy protection encourages entrepreneurship. Unemployment compensation reduces efforts to restrict employers' flexibility in hiring and firing, and it facilitates employees' skill upgrading and geographic mobility.[10] Programs that boost the income of poor households, such as the Child Tax Credit and the EITC, increase the future employment and earnings of children in those households.[11] Many insurance programs reduce stress and anxiety, enhancing productivity. Insurance also lessens conflict within firms and within society as a whole, contributing to economic stability.[12] Finally, the de facto choice often isn't insurance or no insurance. It's insurance or regulation, and the former interferes with markets and competition less than the latter.[13]

The experience of the world's rich countries over the past century suggests no reason to fear that a rise in the size and scope of public social programs would weaken the economy. In the United States, social policy expenditure has steadily increased, yet the country's rate of economic growth has not slowed.[14] Affluent nations that spend more on public social programs have tended to grow just as rapidly as those that spend less.[15] There surely is a level beyond which public social spending hurts the economy. But the evidence says America hasn't yet reached that level. In fact, we're probably well below it.

Social Democracy

Social democracy originated in the early twentieth century as a strategy to improve rather than replace capitalism. Today, we associate it with European social democratic political parties and the policies they have put in place, particularly in the Nordic nations.[16] I believe our array of social programs will increasingly come to resemble those of the Nordic countries. It is in this sense that I say America's future is a social democratic one.

Let me be clear about what that means. A generation ago, the label "social democratic" referred to policies that make it easier for people to survive with little or no reliance on earnings from employment.[17] Social democracy meant, in effect, a large public safety net. Today that's too narrow a conception. In recent decades the Nordic countries have supplemented generous social insurance programs with services aimed at boosting employment and enhancing productivity, from early education and active labor market programs to public infrastructure and support for research and development.[18] And for the most part, these countries believe in a market-friendly regulatory approach.[19] There are regulations to protect workers, consumers, and the environment, to be sure. But these exist within an institutional context that aims to encourage entrepreneurship and flexibility by making it easy to start or close a business, to hire or fire employees, and to adjust work hours.

In other words, modern social democracy means a commitment to extensive use of government policy to promote economic security, expand opportunity, and ensure rising living standards for all. But it aims to do so while facilitating freedom, flexibility, and market dynamism.

Freedom, flexibility, and market dynamism have long been hallmarks of America's economy. These are qualities worth preserving. The Nordic countries' experience shows us that a nation can successfully embrace both flexibility and security, both competition and social justice. Modern social democracy can give us the best of both worlds.

There are understandable worries about the transportability of Danish or Swedish policies to a large, diverse nation such as the United States. But as I explain in later chapters, the grounds for concern dissolve once we consider specific policies. Indeed, if you look carefully at the policy suggestions listed earlier, you'll notice that many of them are already in place in this country. Getting closer to the good society entails doing more of what we already do, not shifting to something qualitatively different.[20]

Moreover, I'm not suggesting that we copy the Nordic countries' playbook in full. Our future array of public social services and benefits will be broader and more generous than it is now, but it will retain a distinctively American flavor. Indeed, in a few respects, the Nordic and other European nations may come to look more like us.[21]

Expansions in the size and scope of our social programs won't always constitute progress. Policy makers will make some poor choices, and the structure of the US policy-making process ensures that we seldom get optimal policy. But that has always been true, and yet American policy makers have managed to craft a host of programs that work quite well, from Social Security to Medicare to the EITC. As our evidence base grows, and particularly as we learn more about best practice in other nations, there is reason for optimism about the quality of future social policy.

Can We Afford It?

For the past half century, our government has taxed and spent a smaller portion of the country's economic output than have most other affluent nations. In 2007, the peak year of the pre-crash business cycle, government expenditures totaled 37 percent of GDP in the United States. As figure 1.1 shows, in most other rich nations the share was well above 40 percent, and in some it was above 50 percent.

The added cost of the new programs and expansions I recommend plus our existing commitments to Social Security and Medicare is likely to be in the neighborhood of 10 percent of GDP.[22] If that sounds massive, keep in mind two things. First, if our government expenditures rise from around 37 percent of GDP to around 47 percent, we will be only a little above the current norm among the world's rich nations. Second, an increase of 10 percent of GDP would be much smaller than the increase that occurred between 1920 and today.

How can we pay for it? As a technical matter, revising our tax system to raise an additional 10 percent of GDP in government revenue is simple. Adding a national consumption tax could get

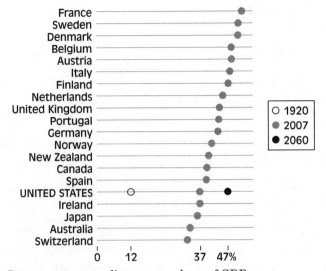

FIGURE 1.1 Government expenditures as a share of GDP
Includes government at all levels: national, regional, local. 2007 is the most recent business cycle peak year. *Data sources:* OECD, stats.oecd.org; Vito Tanzi, *Governments versus Markets*, Cambridge University Press, 2011, table 1. US 47 percent in 2060 is my projection.

us halfway there, and an assortment of relatively minor additions and adjustments would take us the rest of the way.[23]

Since 1980, much of America's left has thought about taxation in terms of its impact on the distribution of income, putting tax progressivity front and center. But we can't get an additional 10 percent of GDP solely from those at the top, even though they are getting a steadily larger share of the pretax income. We would have to increase the effective tax rate paid by the top 1 percent or 5 percent to a level far exceeding what it has been at any point in the past half century.[24] This news may disappoint some. But all rich nations have tax systems that are roughly proportional: households up and down the income ladder pay approximately the same share of their pretax income in taxes. Income redistribution occurs largely via government transfers rather than taxes. The key difference between America's tax system and those of highly redistributive countries such as Denmark and Sweden isn't that ours is less progressive; it's that it raises less revenue.[25]

Are There Better Alternatives?

Some will sympathize with the ends I propose but favor different means. Suggestions include shifting to a smaller and more targeted public safety net, expanding our existing private safety net, privatizing service provision, revitalizing families and communities, putting the brakes on globalization, promoting manufacturing, strengthening unions, expanding profit sharing, mandating a high wage floor, instituting a basic income grant, and facilitating asset building. I consider each of these in chapter 4. Some of them might help. But none, I conclude, would be as effective in addressing economic insecurity, inadequate opportunity, and slow income growth as the public programs I listed earlier.

The Progressive Trajectory of American Social Policy

What about the politics? America has more public insurance than we did a century ago, but given the structure of our political system and the divisiveness of our contemporary politics, is it reasonable to expect that we'll go farther? I believe it is.

Policy makers, drawing on reason and evidence, and perhaps with a push from organized interest groups or the populace, will recognize the benefits of a larger government role in pursuing economic security, opportunity, and rising living standards and will attempt to move the country in that direction. Often they will fail. But sometimes they'll succeed. Progress will be incremental, coming in fits and starts. But it will have staying power. New programs and expansions of existing ones will tend to persist, because programs that work well become popular and because our policy-making process makes it difficult for opponents of social programs to remove them. Small steps and the occasional big leap, coupled with limited backsliding, will have the cumulative effect of significantly increasing the breadth and generosity of government social programs.

This is not a prediction about the timing or conditions under which specific policy advances will occur. It's a hypothesis about a probabilistic process. Over the long run, new programs occasionally will be created and existing ones occasionally will be expanded, and these additions and expansions are unlikely to be reversed.[26]

This is, in fact, an apt description of the history of American social policy over the past century. Many advances occurred when Democrats held the presidency and both houses of Congress, but not all.[27] Some came during bad economic times, others in healthier conditions. In some instances labor unions were strong proponents, in others not. Sometimes support from key sectors of business was critical, but not always. Some changes hinged on interparty compromise, while others didn't.

Two features have been common to all expansions of US social policy. One is problem solving: policy makers attempt to figure out a useful course of action given needs, aims, resources, and available knowledge.[28] The other is policy persistence: policy advances tend to stick, partly because they become popular and partly because the American policy-making process is laden with "veto points" that make it easy for a minority to block proposed policy changes. Problem solving and policy persistence are likely to continue. Over time, they will produce a rise in the size and scope of government social programs in the United States.

There are potential obstacles: Americans don't like big government, the rhetoric used by modern opponents of big government can be persuasive, the left may increasingly struggle to get elected, the balance of organizational power in politics has swung to the right, and the structure of our political system hinders progressive policy change. Given these obstacles, is a social democratic future for the United States just an ivory tower fantasy? I don't think so.

The typical American is ideologically conservative but programmatically progressive. It's true that we aren't fond of the idea of

big government. But when it comes to specific programs, we tend
to be strongly supportive.

Opponents of big government contend that it frequently fails
to achieve its objective, makes things worse, or jeopardizes other
desirable aims. A generous public safety net, they say, makes the
poor worse off in the long run by discouraging employment. High
taxes weaken the economy. These arguments, termed the "rhetoric of reaction" by Albert Hirschman, can seem persuasive. But
they are subject to empirical scrutiny, and their sway is likely to
diminish as scientists expose their flaws with more and better data.

A significant expansion of public social programs in coming
decades hinges on electoral success by Democrats, but some
think their fortunes are dimming. They have lost support among
working-class whites, a key element of the New Deal coalition
that dominated American government from the 1930s through the
1970s. Yet Democratic presidential and congressional candidates
have fared well with a new electoral base of urban professionals,
women, African Americans, and Latinos. Will a flood of private
money into election campaigns, encouraged by the Supreme
Court's 2010 Citizens United v. Federal Election Commission
ruling, doom the Democrats? Maybe, but private campaign contributions have been growing in importance for several decades,
and so far the Democrats have managed to keep up. And while de-
mographics, electoral coalitions, and campaign funding certainly
matter, the state of the economy tends to be the chief determinant
of the outcome of national elections. If Democrats manage the
economy reasonably well when they are in charge, they are likely
to remain electorally competitive.

Some contend that the key determinant of American policy is
the strength of organized interests outside the electoral arena,
where the balance of power has shifted to the right. Businesses
and affluent individuals have mobilized, while the labor movement, the key organized interest group on the left, has steadily
declined in membership and, arguably, in political influence. Yet
this has slowed, not stopped, the advance of social policy. Unless

the balance of power shifts farther to the right, the advance is likely to continue.

Finally, as I noted earlier, the veto-point-heavy structure of America's political system makes it relatively easy for opponents to block policy change. Given this structure, the recent disciplined obstructionist approach by the Republicans is a threat to the forward march of social policy. But only if it continues, and history suggests it won't.

If we extrapolate from the past century, the most likely course for American social policy is continued advance. Political obstacles old and new may slow progress, but they won't halt it.

Will Outcomes Improve?

Economic and social shifts that threaten economic security, opportunity, and shared prosperity are likely to continue. In fact, they may worsen. If that happens, an expansion of social policy won't guarantee improved outcomes. Aggressive government action might not be sufficient to offset these trends. But it will help. Outcomes will be better than if public programs remain in their current state.

The Book

In chapter 2, I examine our failure to ensure economic security, opportunity, and shared prosperity. In chapter 3, I propose a set of policies to address these maladies. In chapter 4, I consider potential objections and alternatives. In chapter 5, I explore the politics.

The book offers an evidence-based case for the desirability and feasibility of an expanded government role in providing economic security, enhancing opportunity, and ensuring rising living standards in the United States. There are grounds for concern but also for optimism. The bad news is that economic and social shifts have made life more difficult than it should be for many ordinary Americans. We aren't doing well enough in protecting against risk, providing everyone with the opportunity to thrive, and ensuring that economic growth benefits us all. The good news is that we can and likely will do better. We know what policies can help, and history suggests we will, in time, make more and better use of them.

2

What's the Problem?

ECONOMIC SECURITY, OPPORTUNITY, and shared prosperity are integral to a good society. We aren't doing as well as we should. In fact, since the 1970s we've been going in the wrong direction.

Too Little Economic Security

To be economically secure is to have sufficient resources to cover our expenses. We achieve economic security with a stable and sizable income, with assets that can be sold or borrowed against, and with insurance.

From the 1930s through the mid-1970s, economic insecurity decreased for virtually all Americans.[1] Incomes grew steadily for most households, reducing the share with low income and facilitating the purchase of private insurance. More Americans became homeowners, thereby accumulating some assets. And a raft of government laws and programs—limited liability law, bankruptcy protection, Social Security old-age benefits, unemployment insurance, statutory minimum wage, AFDC (Aid to Families with Dependent Children, which later became TANF), Social Security disability benefits and Supplemental Security Income (SSI), Medicare and Medicaid, food stamps, EITC, and disaster relief, among others—provided a safeguard against various financial risks, from business failure to job loss to poor health to old age.[2]

Since the 1970s, according to a number of knowledgeable observers, the tide has turned. Economic insecurity has been rising.[3] Paul Osterman sounded the alarm in his 1999 book *Securing Prosperity*, in which he noted the increasing frequency of job loss.[4] In 2006, Louis Uchitelle echoed this argument in his book *The Disposable American*.[5] In *The Great Risk Shift*, published the same year, Jacob Hacker pushed the assessment beyond job loss to suggest that severe income decline has become more common and that private and public insurance against risks such as poor health and old age have weakened.[6] Peter Gosselin reached a similar verdict a few years later in *High Wire*.[7] A survey by the Rockefeller Foundation in early 2007, prior to the 2008–9 "Great Recession," found more than 25 percent of Americans saying they were "fairly worried" or "very worried" about their economic security.[8]

A rise in economic insecurity is what we would expect given the changes in the American economy over the past several decades. Competition among firms has intensified as manufacturing and some services have become internationalized. Competitive pressures have increased even in sectors not exposed to competition from abroad, such as retail trade and hotels, partly due to the emergence of large and highly efficient firms such as Walmart. At the same time, companies' shareholders now demand constant profit improvement rather than steady long-term performance.

These changes force management to be hypersensitive to costs and constraints. One result has been the end of job security, as firms restructure, downsize, move offshore, or simply go under.[9] Another is enhanced management desire for flexibility, leading to greater use of part-time and temporary employees and irregular and unstable work hours. This increases earnings instability for some people and may reduce their likelihood of qualifying for unemployment compensation, paid sickness leave, and other supports. Employers also have cut back on the provision of benefits, including health insurance and pensions.

Private insurance companies are subject to the same pressures. And they now have access to detailed information about the likelihood that particular persons or households will get in a car accident, need expensive medical care, or experience home damage from a fire or a hurricane. As a result, private insurers are more selective about the type and extent of insurance coverage they provide and about the clientele to whom they provide it.

The period since the 1970s also has witnessed commitments by prominent American policy makers to ensure that, in Bill Clinton's expression, "the era of big government is over." From Ronald Reagan to Clinton to George W. Bush and even Barack Obama, recent presidents have expressed a preference for scaling back government expenditures. The 1996 welfare reform, which devolved decision-making authority for America's chief social assistance program to the states and set a time limit on receipt of benefits, embodies this commitment. Tellingly, the number of TANF recipients and the amount they receive have declined sharply since the reform.

Finally, family protections against economic insecurity are weaker for some segments of the American population. Having a second adult who has a paying job (or can get one) in the household is a valuable asset in the event of income loss.[10] Later marriage and more frequent divorce mean that a larger share of Americans has little or no family buffer.

Economic insecurity is a product of low income, significant income decline, or inadequate insurance. To get a complete picture, we would need a single data source that captures each of these elements for a representative sample of American households, and does so consistently over time. Unfortunately, such data don't exist. Instead, the information is available in bits and pieces. In what follows, I put the pieces together to gauge the extent of economic security and its trend over time.

Low Income

As of 2007, the average income of the roughly 25 million house-holds in the bottom 20 percent (quintile) was just $18,000.[11]

Very few of these low-income Americans are destitute. Most have clothing, food, and shelter. Many have a car, a television, heat and air conditioning, and access to medical care.[12] But making ends meet on an income of $18,000 is a challenge. That comes out to $1,500 a month. If you spend $500 on rent and util-ities, $300 on food, and $200 on transportation, you're left with just $500 each month for all other expenses. It's doable. Millions of Americans offer proof of that. But this is a life best described as "scraping by."[13]

Now, there are important caveats. First, income data are never perfect. However, these data, compiled by the Congressional Budget Office (CBO), are quite good. They are created by merging the Census Bureau's annual survey of households with tax records from the Internal Revenue Service (IRS). The income measure includes earnings, capital gains, government transfers, and other sources of cash income. It adds in-kind income (employer-paid health insurance premiums, Medicare and Medicaid benefits, food stamps), employee contributions to 401(k) retirement plans, and employer-paid payroll taxes. Tax payments are subtracted. These data give us a pretty reliable picture of the incomes of American households.

Second, $18,000 is the average among these 25 million house-holds, so some had an income above this amount. According to the CBO's calculations, the highest income among bottom-quintile households with one person was $20,000. For households with four persons, it was $40,000. Making ends meet is a little easier at this income level, but it still isn't easy. And half or more of these 25 million have incomes below the $18,000 average. Some solo adults have to make do with an income of $10,000 or $5,000. Some families with one or more kids have to get by on $20,000 or $15,000 or even less.

Third, some of these households have assets that reduce their expenses or provide a cushion in case expenses exceed income in a particular month or year. Some, for example, are retirees who own a home and therefore have no rent or mortgage payments. But many aren't saved by assets. Asena Caner and Edward Wolff calculate that in the late 1990s, about one-quarter of Americans were "asset poor," meaning they did not have enough assets to replace their income for at least three months.[14]

Fourth, these data very likely underestimate the true incomes of some households at the bottom. The data come from a survey in which people are asked what their income was in the prior year. People in low-income households tend to underreport their income, perhaps out of fear that accurate disclosure will result in loss of a government benefit they receive.[15]

Fifth, some of these 25 million households have a low income for only a short time. Their income may be low one year because the wage earner leaves her job temporarily to have a child, is sick, or gets laid off. By the following year, the earner may be back in paid employment. Some low earners are just beginning their work career. Five or ten years later, their earnings will be higher, or perhaps they will have a partner whose earnings add to household income. Using a panel data set known as the Panel Study of Income Dynamics (PSID), which tracks the same set of households over time, Mark Rank and Thomas Hirschl calculate that by the time Americans reach age 65, fewer than 10 percent will have spent five or more consecutive years with an income below the official poverty line (about $12,000 for a single adult and $23,000 for a household of four as of 2012).[16] On the other hand, some who move up the economic ladder will later move back down. Shuffling in and out of poverty is common. Rank and Hirschl find that if we ask what share of Americans will have spent five or more *total* years below the poverty line upon reaching age 65, the share rises to 25 percent.[17]

Finally, some of these households are made up of immigrants from much poorer nations. Many are better off than they would have been if they had stayed in their native country. But that doesn't change the fact that they are scraping by.

How much should these qualifiers alter our impression of economic insecurity due to low income in the United States? It's difficult to say. Suppose the truly insecure constitute only half of the bottom quintile. That's still 10 percent of American households, much more than we should accept in a nation as rich as ours.

Perhaps we should measure low income in another way. We could, for example, identify the minimum income needed for a decent standard of living and then see how many households fall below this amount. A team of researchers at the Economic Policy Institute did just that, estimating "basic family budgets" for metropolitan and rural areas around the country and calculating the share of families with incomes below these amounts in 1997–99.[18] They concluded that approximately 29 percent of US families could not make ends meet. More recently, researchers with Wider Opportunities for Women and the Center for Social Development at Washington University calculated basic-needs budgets for various household types.[19] They estimate that to meet basic expenses in 2010, a single adult needed, on average, about $30,000, and a household with two adults and two children needed about $68,000. According to their calculations, 43 percent of American households fell below the threshold.

Let's return to low income and consider the trend over time. Is it getting better or worse? Figure 2.1 shows what happened between 1979 and 2007. There was improvement, but only a little. Average income in the bottom fifth rose by just $2,000 over this nearly three-decade period. That's not much, particularly given that the American economy was growing at a healthy clip (a point I expand on later in this chapter). On the other hand, these data don't indicate a rise in insecurity.

One group some believe *has* suffered a rise in insecurity due to low income is the elderly. Now, in one respect elderly Americans have fared well: they are the only age group whose poverty rate has declined since the 1970s.[20] A key reason is Social Security. In

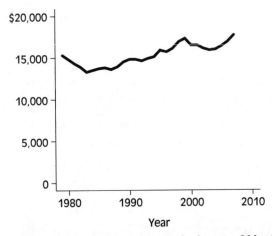

FIGURE 2.1 Average income of households on the bottom fifth of the income ladder Posttransfer-posttax income. The income measure includes earnings, capital gains, government transfers, and other sources of cash income. It adds in-kind income (employer-paid health insurance premiums, Medicare and Medicaid benefits, food stamps), employee contributions to 401(k) retirement plans, and employer-paid payroll taxes. Tax payments are subtracted. The incomes are in 2007 dollars; inflation adjustment is via the CPI-U-RS. *Data source*: Congressional Budget Office, "Average Federal Tax Rates and Income, by Income Category, 1979–2007."

1979, the average recipient of Social Security old-age benefits got about $10,000 (in today's dollars). That average increased steadily over the ensuing three decades, reaching nearly $15,000 as of 2010. During this time, the share of elderly Americans receiving Social Security held steady at around 90 percent.

But Social Security is just the first of three tiers of retirement income security. After all, $15,000 isn't much to live on, even if you don't have a mortgage to pay. The second tier is private—usually employer-based—pensions. The share of people under age 65 who participate in an employer pension plan has remained steady at around 60 percent,[21] but the *type* of plan has changed dramatically. According to the Center for Retirement Research, in the early 1980s nearly 90 percent of Americans with an employer pension plan had a defined-benefit plan. By 2007 that share had shrunk to 36 percent. Defined-benefit pension plans have been replaced by defined-contribution plans such as 401(k)s.

Among those with a pension, defined-contribution plans jumped from 38 percent to 81 percent.[22]

Defined-contribution plans have some advantages: they're portable across employers, the employee has some say in how the money is invested, and a person in financial difficulty prior to retirement age can withdraw some or all of the money, though there is a tax penalty for doing so.[23] The problem is that employees and employers may not contribute enough to defined-contribution plans or keep the money in them long enough to reap the benefits in retirement.[24] If an employee doesn't know about or understand her firm's program, or feels she needs every dollar of her earnings to pay for current expenses, she may go a long time, perhaps even her entire working career, without putting any money into a defined-contribution plan. Employer contributions usually take the form of matching funds, with the amount put in by the employer pegged to the amount put in by the employee. Thus, no employee contribution often means no employer contribution. Moreover, when a person switches employers, she or he can choose to keep the defined-contribution-plan money as is, roll it over into an individual retirement account (IRA), or withdraw it, after a tax penalty is subtracted. Too many people choose to withdraw some or all of the money, leaving them with a lot less, and sometimes nothing at all, for their retirement years.

The third tier of retirement income security is personal savings. It too has weakened. Average household saving as a share of disposable household income fell from 10 percent in the 1970s to 8 percent in the 1980s to 5 percent in the 1990s to 3 percent in the 2000s.[25] And the decline was probably even steeper for households on the lower rungs of the income ladder.

Income Decline

It isn't just a low level of income that threatens economic security. Instability of income does too.

A large income decline can be problematic even if it's temporary. Consider two households with the same average income over ten years. In one, the income is consistent over these years. The other experiences a big drop in income in one of the years, but offsets that drop with higher-than-average income in one or more later years. The latter household may be worse off in two respects. The first has to do with subjective well-being. A loss tends to reduce our happiness more than a gain increases it.[26] The second involves assets. A large decline in income may force a household to sell off some or all of its assets, such as a home, to meet expenses. Even if the income loss is ultimately offset, the household may be worse off at the end of the period due to the asset sell-off.

It turns out, however, that income declines often aren't temporary. Stephen Rose and Scott Winship have analyzed data from the Panel Study of Income Dynamics (PSID) to find out what subsequently happens to households experiencing a significant income decline.[27] According to their calculations, among households that experience a drop in income of 25 percent or more from one year to the next, about one-third do not recover to their prior income level even a full decade later. There are various reasons for this. Some people own a small business that fails and don't manage to get a job that pays as much as they made as entrepreneurs. Others become disabled or suffer a serious health problem and are unable to return to their previous earnings level. Still others are laid off, don't find a new job right away, and then suffer because potential employers view their jobless spell as a signal that they are undesirable employees.

So income decline is a problem for those who experience it. How many Americans are we talking about? Several researchers have attempted to estimate the frequency of sharp income drops. In the study mentioned in the previous paragraph, Rose and Winship find that in any given year, 15 to 20 percent of Americans experience an income decline of 25 percent or more from the previous year.[28] Using a different data source, the Survey of Income and Program Participation (SIPP), Winship estimates that during the 1990s and 2000s approximately 8 to 13 percent of households suffered this fate each year.[29] A study by the CBO matches data from the Survey of Income and Program Participation (SIPP) with Social Security Administration records and gets a similar estimate of approximately 10 percent during the 1990s and 2000s.[30] Finally, a team of researchers led by Jacob Hacker uses a third data source, the Current Population Survey (CPS), covering the mid-1980s through 2009, and comes up with 15 to 18 percent.[31]

These estimates vary, but not wildly. In any given year, approximately 10 to 20 percent of working-age Americans will experience a severe income drop.

Using PSID data, Elizabeth Jacobs has calculated that the share of American households experiencing a severe year-to-year income drop at some point in a ten-year period is roughly twice the share in any given two-year period. If so, the share of working-age Americans who at some point suffer a large income decline is in the neighborhood of 20 to 40 percent.[32]

Has the incidence of large year-to-year income decline increased over time? Yes, according to calculations by Jacob Hacker's team and by Scott Winship. But not a lot. These estimates, shown in figure 2.2, suggest a rise in sharp year-on-year income decline of perhaps three to five percentage points since the 1970s or the early 1980s.[33] Again, though, this might cumulate into a more substantial increase. If we instead focus on the share of Americans experiencing a sharp year-on-year decline at some point over a decade, Elizabeth Jacobs's calculation suggests a rise of seven or eight percentage points from the 1970s to the 1990s.[34]

What's the bottom line? In my read, the data tell us that sharp declines of income among working-age American households are relatively common and that their incidence has increased over the past generation.

We need to keep in mind that some of these declines are (fully or partially) voluntary. A person may leave a job or cut back on work hours to spend more time with children or an ailing relative. A couple may divorce. Someone may quit a job to move to a more

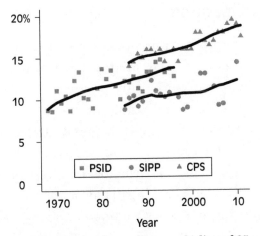

FIGURE 2.2 Households experiencing an income decline of 25 percent or more from one year to the next

The lines are loess curves. PSID and SIPP: posttransfer-pretax income, for households with a "head" aged 25–54. PSID is the Panel Study of Income Dynamics. SIPP is the Survey of Income and Program Participation. *Data source*: Scott Winship, "Bogeyman Economics," *National Affairs*, 2012, figure 1. CPS: posttransfer-pretax income, for households of all ages. CPS is the Current Population Survey. *Data source*: Economic Security Index, www.economicsecurityindex.org, downloaded January 2013.

desirable location without having another lined up. We don't know what portion of income drops are voluntary. But I don't think we should presume that most are.

How should we assess the trend? One perspective is to view it as unavoidable. The American economy has shifted since the 1970s. It's more competitive, flexible, and in flux. Even though this is bad for some households, it can't be prevented unless we seal the country off from the rest of the world and heavily regulate our labor market. In this view, we should be happy that the increase in income volatility hasn't been larger.

I think we should be disappointed. After all, there are ways to insure against income decline. We could have improved our porous unemployment compensation system, added a public sickness insurance program, or created a wage insurance program so that someone who loses a job and gets a new, lower-paying one receives some payment to offset the earnings loss. We could have done more, in other words, to offset the impact of economic shifts.

Large Unanticipated Expense

Low income and a sharp drop in income cause economic in-security because we may have trouble meeting our expenses. A large unanticipated expense can produce the same result, even for those with decent and stable income.

In the United States, the most common large unexpected expense is medical. About one in seven Americans does not have health insurance. Others are underinsured, in the sense that they face a nontrivial likelihood of having to pay out of pocket for health care if they fall victim to a fairly common accident, condition, or disease.

Of course, many of the uninsured and underinsured won't end up with a large healthcare bill. And some who do will be able to pay it (due to high income or to assets that can be sold), or will be allowed to escape paying it because of low income or assets, or will go into personal bankruptcy and have the debt expunged.

Yet in a modern society, we should consider most of the unin-sured and some of the underinsured as economically insecure, in the same way we do those with low income. They are living on the edge to a degree that should not happen in a rich nation in the twenty-first century. After all, every other affluent country manages to provide health insurance for all (or virtually all) its citizens without breaking the bank.

This form of economic insecurity has increased over the past generation, though we don't know exactly how much because we lack a continuous data series on the share of Americans without health insurance. Figure 2.3 shows the information we do have, going back to the late 1970s. Each of the three data series shows a rise in the share without insurance. Over the whole period, the increase is on the order of five percentage points.

Figure 2.3 understates vulnerability to a large medical expense in two respects. First, these data capture the average share of Americans who are uninsured at a *given* point during a year. If we instead ask how many are uninsured at *any* point during a year or

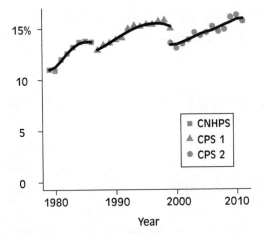

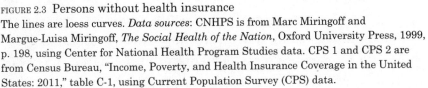

FIGURE 2.3 Persons without health insurance
The lines are loess curves. *Data sources*: CNHPS is from Marc Miringoff and
Margue-Luisa Miringoff, *The Social Health of the Nation*, Oxford University Press, 1999,
p. 198, using Center for National Health Program Studies data. CPS 1 and CPS 2 are
from Census Bureau, "Income, Poverty, and Health Insurance Coverage in the United
States: 2011," table C-1, using Current Population Survey (CPS) data.

two, the figure is larger. The Lewin Group estimates that during
the two-year period of 2007 and 2008, 29 percent of Americans
lacked health insurance at some point.[35]

Second, it isn't only the uninsured who are insecure. Some
Americans have a health insurance policy that is inadequate.
Each year 25 to 30 percent of Americans say they or a member of
their family have put off medical treatment because of the extra
cost they would have to pay.[36] They can indeed end up with a
large out-of-pocket medical expense if they get treated. We know
this from data on bankruptcy filings. Such filings have increased
steadily, from an average of .2 percent of the population each year
in the 1980s to .4 percent in the 1990s to .5 percent in the 2000s.
About one-quarter of Americans who file for bankruptcy do so
mainly because of a large medical bill, and some of them do have
health insurance.[37]

The 2010 healthcare reform is expected to reduce the share of
uninsured Americans from 16 percent to perhaps 7 or 8 percent.
That represents a substantial reduction in economic insecurity,

but it still leaves us well short of where we could be, and where every other affluent nation has been for some time now.

Inadequate Opportunity

Americans believe in equal opportunity. Public opinion surveys consistently find more than 90 percent of Americans agree that "our society should do what is necessary to make sure that everyone has an equal opportunity to succeed."[38]

True equality of opportunity is unattainable. Equal opportunity requires that everyone have equal skills, abilities, knowledge, and noncognitive traits, and that's impossible. Our capabilities are shaped by genetics, developments in utero, parenting styles and traits, siblings, peers, teachers, preachers, sports coaches, tutors, neighborhoods, and a slew of chance events and occurrences. Society can't fully equalize, offset, or compensate for these influences.

Nor do we really want equal opportunity, as it would require genetic engineering and intervention in home life far beyond what most of us would tolerate. Moreover, if parents knew that everyone would end up with the same skills and abilities as adults, they would have little incentive to invest effort and money in their children's development, resulting in a lower absolute level of capabilities for everyone.

What we really want is for each person to have the most opportunity possible. We should aim, in Amartya Sen's helpful formulation, to maximize people's capability to choose, act, and accomplish.[39] Pursuing this goal requires providing greater-than-average help to those in less advantageous circumstances or conditions. This, in turn, moves us closer to equal opportunity, even if, as I just explained, full equality of opportunity is not attainable.

Americans tend to believe that ours is a country in which opportunity is plentiful. This view became especially prominent in the second half of the nineteenth century, when the economy was shifting from farming to industry and Horatio Alger was churning out rags-to-riches tales.[40] It's still present today. On the night of the 2008 presidential election, Barack Obama began his victory speech by saying, "If there is anyone out there who still doubts that America is a place where all things are possible... tonight is your answer."

There is more than a grain of truth in this sentiment. One of the country's major successes in the last half century has been its progress in reducing obstacles to opportunity stemming from gender and race. Today, women are more likely to graduate from college than men and are catching up in employment and earnings.[41] The gap between whites and nonwhites has narrowed as well, albeit less dramatically.[42]

When we turn to family background, however, the news is less encouraging. Americans growing up in less advantaged homes have far less opportunity than their counterparts from better-off families, and the gap is growing.

There is no straightforward way to measure opportunity, so social scientists tend to infer from outcomes, such as employment or earnings. If we find a particular group faring worse than others, we suspect a barrier to opportunity. It isn't proof positive, but it's the best we can do. To assess equality of opportunity among people from different family backgrounds, we look at relative intergenerational mobility—a person's position on the income ladder relative to her or his parents' position. We don't have as much information as we would like about the extent of relative intergenerational mobility and its movement over time. The data requirements are stiff. Analysts need a survey that collects information about citizens' incomes and other aspects of their life circumstances, and then does the same for their children and their children's children, and so on. The best assessment of this type, the PSID, has been around only since the late 1960s.

It is clear, though, that there is considerable inequality of opportunity among Americans from different family backgrounds.[43] Think of the income distribution as a ladder with five rungs, with each rung representing a fifth of the population. In a society with equal opportunity, every person would have a 20 percent chance of landing on each of the five rungs, and hence a 60 percent chance of landing on the middle rung or a higher one. The reality is quite different. An American born into a family in the bottom fifth of incomes between the mid-1960s and the mid-1980s has roughly a 30 percent chance of reaching the middle fifth or higher in adulthood, whereas an American born into the top fifth has an 80 percent chance of ending up in the middle fifth or higher.[44]

Between the mid-1800s and the 1970s, differences in opportunity based on family circumstances declined steadily.[45] As the farming-based US labor force shifted to manufacturing, many Americans joined the paid economy, allowing an increasing number to move onto and up the income ladder. Elementary education became universal, and secondary education expanded. Then, in the 1960s and 1970s, school desegregation, the outlawing of discrimination in college admissions and hiring, and the introduction of affirmative action opened economic doors for many Americans.

But since the 1970s, we have been moving in the opposite direction. A host of economic and social shifts have widened the opportunity gap between Americans from low-income families and those from high-income families.

For one thing, poorer children are less likely to grow up with both biological parents. This reduces their likelihood of succeeding, since children who grow up with both parents tend to fare better on a host of outcomes, from school completion to staying out of prison to earning more in adulthood.[46] For those with higher incomes, there has been far less change in family structure and, as a consequence, less-drastic implications for children's success.[47]

Parenting traits and behaviors have long differed according to parents' education and income, but this difference has increased with the advent of our modern intensive-parenting culture.[48] Low-income parents aren't able to spend as much on goods and services aimed at enriching their children, such as music lessons, travel, and summer camp. They read less to their children and provide less help with schoolwork. They are less likely to set and enforce clear rules and routines. And they are less likely to encourage their children to aspire to high achievement in school and at work.

Differences in out-of-home care also have widened. A generation ago, most preschool-aged children stayed at home with their mothers. Now, many are enrolled in some sort of childcare program. Children of affluent parents attend high-quality, education-oriented preschools, while kids of poorer parents are left with a neighborhood babysitter who plops them in front of the television.

Elementary and secondary schools help equalize opportunity. And in one respect they have become more effective at doing so: funding for public K-12 schools used to vary sharply across school districts, but this has diminished. Even so, there is a large difference in the quality of education between the best and the worst schools, and the poorest neighborhoods often have the weakest schools.

According to data compiled by Sean Reardon, the gap in average test scores between elementary- and secondary-school children from high-income families and low-income families has risen steadily.[49] Among children born in 1970, those from high-income homes scored, on average, about three-quarters of a standard deviation higher on math and reading tests than those from low-income homes. For children born in 2000, the gap has grown to one-and-a-quarter standard deviations. That is much larger than the gap between white and black children.

Partly because they lag behind at the end of high school, and partly because college is so expensive, children from poor backgrounds are less likely than others to enter and complete college.[50] In the past generation this gap has widened. Figure 2.4 shows college completion by parents' income for children growing up in the 1960s and 1970s (birth years 1961–64) and children growing up in the 1980s and 1990s (birth years 1979–82). Among children

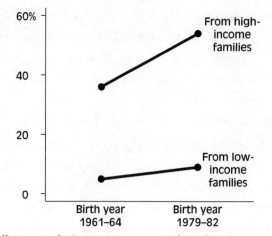

FIGURE 2.4 College completion among persons from low-income and high-income families

College completion: four or more years of college. Low-income family: the person's family income during childhood was on the lowest quarter of the income ladder. High-income family: income during childhood was on the highest quarter. *Data source*: Martha Bailey and Susan Dynarski, "Gains and Gaps: A Historical Perspective on Inequality in College Entry and Completion," in *Whither Opportunity? Rising Inequality, Schools, and Children's Life Chances*, edited by Greg J. Duncan and Richard J. Murnane, Russell Sage Foundation, 2011, figure 6.3, using National Longitudinal Survey of Youth data.

of high-income parents, defined as those with an income in the top quarter of all families, there was a marked increase in the share completing college, from 36 percent of the first cohort to 54 percent of the second. For those from low-income families, the increase was much smaller, from 5 percent to 9 percent.

When it comes time to get a job, the story is no better. Low-income parents tend to have fewer valuable connections to help their children find good jobs. Some people from poor homes are further hampered by a lack of English language skills. Another disadvantage for the lower-income population is that in the 1970s and 1980s, the United States began incarcerating more young men, many for minor offenses. Having a criminal record makes it more difficult to get a stable job with decent pay.[51] A number of developments, including technological advances, globalization, a loss of manufacturing employment, and the decline of unions, have reduced the number of jobs that require limited skills but pay a middle-class wage—the kind of jobs that once lifted poorer Americans into the middle class.[52]

Finally, changes in partner selection have widened the opportunity gap. Not only do those from better-off families tend to end up with more schooling and higher-paying jobs. They also increasingly marry (or cohabit with) others like themselves.[53]

Do we have conclusive evidence of rising inequality of opportunity in earnings and income? Not yet.[54] Existing panel data sets are too young to give us a clear signal. But given the large increases in inequality of test scores and college completion between children from low-income families and those from high-income families, it is very likely that the same will be true, and perhaps already is true, for their earnings and incomes when they reach adulthood.

Slow Income Growth

As a society gets richer, the living standards of its households should rise.[55] The poorest needn't benefit the most; equal rates of improvement may be good enough. We might not even mind if the wealthiest benefit a bit more than others; a little increase in income inequality is hardly catastrophic. But in a good society, those in the middle and at the bottom ought to benefit significantly from economic growth. When the country prospers, everyone should prosper.

In the period between World War II and the mid-to-late 1970s, economic growth was good for Americans in the middle and below. Figure 2.5 shows that as GDP per capita increased, so did family income at the fiftieth percentile (the median) and at the twentieth percentile. Indeed, they moved virtually in lockstep. Since then, however, household income has been decoupled from economic growth. As the economy has grown, relatively little of that growth has reached households in the middle and below.

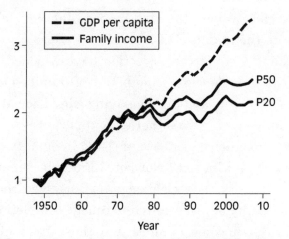

FIGURE 2.5 GDP per capita and the incomes of lower-half families
P50 is the fiftieth percentile (median) of the income ladder; P20 is the twentieth
percentile. Each series is displayed as an index set to equal 1 in 1947. The family
income data are posttransfer-pretax. Inflation adjustment for each series is via the
CPI-U-RS. *Data sources:* Bureau of Economic Analysis, "GDP and the National Income
and Product Account Historical Tables," table 1.1.5; Council of Economic Advisers,
Economic Report of the President, table B-34; Census Bureau, "Historical Income
Tables," tables F-1 and F-5.

Why has this happened? Rising inequality. Since the 1970s, a
larger and larger share of household income growth has gone to
Americans at the very top of the ladder—roughly speaking, those
in the top 1 percent. The income pie has gotten bigger, and everyone's slice has increased in size, but the slice of the richest has
expanded massively while that of the middle and below has gotten
only a little bigger.

Figure 2.6 shows average incomes among households in the top
1 percent and in the bottom 60 percent.[56] The years 1979 and 2007
are business-cycle peaks, so they make for sensible beginning and
ending points. Average income for households in the top 1 percent soared from $350,000 in 1979 to $1.3 million in 2007. For the
bottom 60 percent the rise was quite modest, from $30,000 in 1979
to $37,000 in 2007.

This is a disappointing development. But does the trend in
lower-half incomes paint an accurate picture of changes in living
standards?

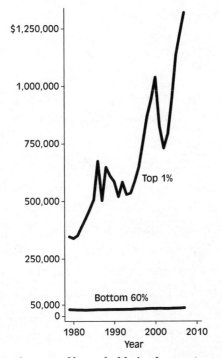

FIGURE 2.6 Average income of households in the top 1 percent and bottom 60 percent

Posttransfer-posttax income. The income measure includes earnings, capital gains, government transfers, other sources of cash income, in-kind income (employer-paid health insurance premiums, Medicare and Medicaid benefits, food stamps), employee contributions to 401(k) retirement plans, and employer-paid payroll taxes. Tax payments are subtracted. The incomes are in 2007 dollars; inflation adjustment is via the CPI-U-RS. *Data source*: Congressional Budget Office, "Average Federal Tax Rates and Income, by Income Category, 1979–2007."

"It's Better Than It Looks"

To some, the picture conveyed by figure 2.5 is too pessimistic. They argue that incomes or broader living standards have grown relatively rapidly, keeping pace with the economy.[57] There are eight variants of this view. Let's consider them one by one.

1. *The income data are too thin.* The data for family income shown in figure 2.5 don't include certain types of government transfers or the value of health insurance contributions from employers or (in the case of Medicare and Medicaid) from government. And they don't subtract taxes. If these sources of income

have risen rapidly for middle-class households, or if taxes have fallen sharply, the story conveyed by figure 2.5 will understate the true rate of progress.

Happily, we have a good alternative source of information: the data compiled by the CBO used in figure 2.6. I didn't use these data in figure 2.5 because they don't begin until 1979. But if figure 2.5 is replicated using the CBO data for average income in the middle or lower quintiles of households instead of median or p20 family income, the trends since the 1970s look similar.[58]

2. *The income data miss upward movement over the life course.* The family income data shown in figure 2.5 are from the Current Population Survey. Each year a representative sample of American adults is asked what their income was in the previous year. But each year, the sample consists of a new group; the survey doesn't track the same people as they move through the life course.

If we interpret figure 2.5 as showing what happens to typical American families over the life course, we conclude that they see very little increase in income as they age. But that's incorrect. In any given year, some of those with below-median income are young. Their wages and income are low because they are in the early stages of the work career and/or because they're single. Over time, many will experience a significant income rise, getting pay increases or partnering with someone who also has earnings, or both. Figure 2.5 misses this income growth over the life course.

Figure 2.7 illustrates this. The lower line shows median income among families with a family "head" aged 25 to 34. The top line shows median income among the same cohort of families twenty years later, when their heads are aged 45 to 54. Consider the year 1979, for instance. The lower line tells us that in 1979 the median income of families with a 25- to 34-year-old head was about $54,000 (in 2010 dollars). The data point for 1979 in the top line looks at the median income of that same group of families in 1999, when they are 45 to 54 years old. This is the peak earning stage for most people, and their median income is now about $85,000.

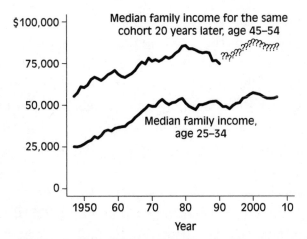

FIGURE 2.7 Median income within and across cohorts
For each year, the lower line is median income among families with a "head" aged 25–34, and the top line is median income for the same cohort of families twenty years later. In the years for which the calculation is possible, 1947 to 1990, the average increase in income during this two-decade portion of the life course is $30,500. The data are in 2010 dollars; inflation adjustment is via the CPI-U-RS. *Data source*: Census Bureau, "Historical Income Tables," table F-11.

In each year, the gap between the two lines is roughly $30,000. This tells us that the incomes of middle-class Americans tend to increase substantially as they move from the early years of the work career to the peak years.

Should this reduce our concern about the over-time pattern shown in figure 2.5? No, it shouldn't. Look again at figure 2.7. Between the mid-1940s and the mid-1970s, the median income of families in early adulthood (the lower line) rose steadily. In the mid-1940s median income for these young families was around $25,000; by the mid-1970s, it had doubled to $50,000. Americans during this period experienced income gains over the life course, but they also tended to have higher incomes than their predecessors, both in their early work years and in their peak years. That's because the economy was growing at a healthy clip and the economic growth was trickling down to Americans in the middle.

After the mid-1970s, this steady gain disappeared. From the mid-1970s to 2007, the median income of families with a 25- to 34-year-old head was flat. They continued to achieve income gains during the life course. (Actually, we don't yet know about those who started out in the 1990s and 2000s because they are just now beginning to reach ages 45 to 54. The question marks in the chart show what their incomes will be if the historical trajectory holds true.) But the improvement across cohorts that characterized the period from World War II through the 1970s—each cohort starting higher and ending higher than earlier ones—disappeared.

For many Americans, income rises during the life course, and that fact is indeed hidden by charts such as figure 2.5. But that shouldn't lessen our concern about the decoupling of household income growth from economic growth that has occurred over the past generation. We want improvement not just within cohorts, but also across them.

3. *Families have gotten smaller.* The size of the typical American family and household has been shrinking since the mid-1960s, when the baby boom ended. Perhaps, then, we don't need income growth to be so rapid any more.

Let me pause briefly to explain why figure 2.5 shows the income trend for families rather than households. The household is the better unit to look at. A "family" is defined by the Census Bureau as a household with two or more related persons. Families therefore don't include adults who live alone or with others to whom they aren't related. It's a bit silly to exclude this group, but that's what the Census Bureau did until 1967. Only then did it begin tabulating data for all households. I use families in figure 2.5 in order to begin earlier, in the mid-1940s. As it happens, though, the trends for households since the mid-1970s have been virtually identical to the trends for families.

Should the shrinkage in family size alter our interpretation of slow income growth? No. As noted earlier, incomes have become decoupled from economic growth because a steadily rising share of economic growth has gone to families or households at the top of the ladder. But family size has decreased among the rich, too; they don't need the extra income more than those in the middle and below do.

4. *More people are in college or retired.* The income data in figure 2.5 are for families with a "head" aged 15 or older. However, the share of young Americans attending college has increased since the 1970s, and the share of Americans who are elderly and hence retired has risen. Because of these developments, the share of families with an employed adult head may be falling. Does this account for the slow growth of family income relative to the economy? No, it does not. The trend in income among families with a head aged 25 to 54, in the prime of the work career, is very similar to that for all families.[59]

5. *There are more immigrants.* Immigration into the United States began to increase in the late 1960s. The foreign-born share of the American population, including both legal and illegal immigrants, rose from 5 percent in 1970 to 13 percent in 2007.[60] Many immigrants arrive with limited labor market skills and little or no English, so their incomes tend to be low. For many such immigrants, a low income in the United States is a substantial improvement over what their income would be in their home country. So if this accounts for the divorce between economic growth and median income growth over the past generation, it should allay concern.

Immigration is indeed part of the story. But it is a relatively small part. The rise in lower-half family income for non-Hispanic whites, which excludes most immigrants, has been only slightly greater than the rise in lower-half income for all families shown in figure 2.5.[61]

6. *Consumption has continued to rise rapidly.* Some consider spending a better indicator of standard of living than income. Even though the incomes of middle- and low-income Americans have grown slowly, they may have increased their consumption more rapidly by drawing on assets (equity in a home, savings) and/or debt.

But that is not the case. According to the best available data, from the Consumer Expenditures Survey (CES), median family expenditures rose at the same pace as median family income in the 1980s, 1990s, and 2000s.[62]

7. *Wealth has increased sharply.* Maybe the slow growth of income has been offset by a rapid growth of wealth (assets minus debts). Perhaps many middle- and low-income Americans benefited from the housing boom in the 1990s and 2000s. In this story, their income and consumption growth may have lagged well behind growth of the economy, but they got much richer due to appreciation of their assets.

This is true, but only up to 2007. We have data on wealth from the Survey of Consumer Finances (SCF), administered by the Federal Reserve every three years. Figure 2.8 shows the trend in median family wealth along with the trend in median family income (the same as in figure 2.5). The wealth data are first available in 1989. What we see is a sharp upward spike in median wealth in the 1990s and much of the 2000s. The home is the chief asset of most middle-class Americans, and home values jumped during this period. But then the housing bubble burst, and between 2007 and 2010 median family wealth fell precipitously, erasing all the gains of the preceding two decades.[63] And for those who lost their home, in foreclosure, things are worse than what's conveyed by these data.

In fact, even before the bubble burst, not everyone benefited. Of the one-third of Americans who don't own a home, many are on the lower half of the income ladder. For them, the rise in home values in the 1990s and 2000s did nothing to compensate for the slow growth of income since the 1970s.

8. *There have been significant improvements in quality of life.* The final variant of the notion that income data understate the degree of advance in living standards focuses on improvements in the quality of goods, services, and social norms. It suggests that adjusting the income data for inflation doesn't do justice to the enhancements in quality of life that have occurred in the past generation.

Fewer jobs require hard physical labor, and workplace accidents and deaths have decreased. Life expectancy rose from 74 years in 1979 to 78 years in 2007. Cancer survival is up. Infant mortality is down. An array of new pharmaceuticals now help relieve various

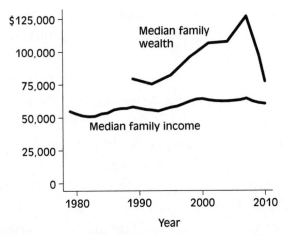

FIGURE 2.8 Median family income and median family wealth

The wealth measure is "net worth," calculated as assets minus liabilities. The wealth data are available beginning in 1989. The income data are the same as those shown in figure 2.5. Both series are in 2010 dollars; inflation adjustment is via the CPI-U-RS. *Data sources*: Jesse Bricker et al., "Changes in U.S. Family Finances from 2007 to 2010: Evidence from the Survey of Consumer Finances," *Federal Reserve Bulletin*, June 2012; Federal Reserve, *2007 SCF Chartbook*; Census Bureau, "Historical Income Tables," table F-5.

conditions and ailments. Computed tomography (CT) scans and other diagnostic tools have enhanced physicians' ability to detect serious health problems. Organ transplants, hip and knee replacements, and lasik eye surgery are now commonplace. Violent crime has dropped to pre-1970s levels. Air quality and water quality are much improved.

We live in bigger houses; the median size of new homes rose from 1,600 square feet in 1979 to 2,300 in 2007. Cars are safer and get better gas mileage. Food and clothing are cheaper. We have access to an assortment of conveniences that didn't exist or weren't widely available a generation ago: personal computers, printers, scanners, microwave ovens, TV remote controls, TIVO, camcorders, digital cameras, five-blade razors, home pregnancy tests, home security systems, handheld calculators. Product variety has increased for almost all goods and services, from cars to restaurant food to toothpaste to television programs.

We have much greater access to information via the Internet, Google, cable TV, travel guides, Google Maps and GPS, smartphones, and tablets. We have a host of new communication tools: cell phones, call waiting, voicemail, e-mail, social networking websites, Skype. Personal entertainment sources and devices have proliferated: cable TV, high-definition televisions, home entertainment systems, the Internet, MP3 players, CD players, DVD players, Netflix, satellite radio, video games.

Last, but not least, discrimination on the basis of sex, race, and more recently, sexual orientation have diminished. For women, racial and ethnic minorities, and lesbian and gay Americans, this may be the most valuable improvement of all.

There is no disputing these gains in quality of life. But did they occur because income growth for middle- and low-income Americans lagged well behind growth of the economy? In other words, did we need to sacrifice income growth to get these improved products and services?

Some say yes, arguing that returns to success soared in such fields as high tech, finance, entertainment, and athletics, as well as for CEOs. These markets became "winner take all," and the rewards reaped by the winners mushroomed. For those with a shot at being the best in their field, this increased the financial incentive to work harder or longer or to be more creative. This rise in financial incentives produced a corresponding rise in excellence—new products and services and enhanced quality.

Is this correct? Consider the case of Apple and Steve Jobs. Apple's Macintosh, iPod, iTunes, MacBook Air, iPhone, and iPad were so different from and superior to anything that preceded them that their addition to living standards isn't likely to be adequately measured. Did slow middle-class income growth make this possible? Would Jobs and his teams of engineers, designers, and others at Apple have worked as hard as they did to create these new products and bring them to market in the absence of massive winner-take-all financial incentives?

It's difficult to know. But Walter Isaacson's comprehensive biography of Steve Jobs suggests that he was driven by a passion for the products, for winning the competitive battle, and for status among peers.[64] Excellence and victory were their own reward, not a means to the end of financial riches. In this respect, Jobs mirrors scores of inventors and entrepreneurs over the ages. So, while the rise of winner-take-all compensation occurred simultaneously with surges in innovation and productivity in certain fields, it may not have caused those surges.

For a more systematic assessment, we can look at the preceding period—the 1940s, 1950s, 1960s, and early 1970s.[65] In these years, lower-half incomes grew at roughly the same pace as the economy and as incomes at the top. Did this squash the incentive for innovation and hard work and thereby come at the expense of broader quality-of-life improvements?

During this period, the share of Americans working in physically taxing jobs fell steadily as employment in agriculture and manufacturing declined. Life expectancy rose from 65 years in 1945 to 71 years in 1973. Antibiotic use began in the 1940s, and open-heart bypass surgery was introduced in the 1960s.

In 1940, only 44 percent of Americans owned a home; by 1970 the number had jumped to 64 percent. Home features and amenities changed dramatically, as the following list makes clear. Running water: 70 percent in 1940, 98 percent in 1970. Indoor flush toilet: 60 percent in 1940, 95 percent in 1970. Electric lighting: 79 percent in 1940, 99 percent in 1970. Central heating: 40 percent in 1940, 78 percent in 1970. Air conditioning: very few (we don't have precise data) in 1940, more than half of homes in 1970. Refrigerator: 47 percent in 1940, 99 percent in 1970. Washing machine: less than half of homes in 1940, 92 percent in 1970. Vacuum cleaner: 40 percent in 1940, 92 percent in 1970.

In 1970, 80 percent of American households had a car, compared to just 52 percent in 1940. The interstate highway system was built in the 1950s and 1960s. In 1970, there were 154 million air passengers versus 4 million in 1940. Only 45 percent of homes had a telephone in 1945; by 1970, virtually all did. Long-distance phone calls were rare before the 1960s. In 1950, just 60 percent of employed Americans took a vacation; in 1970 the number had risen to 80 percent. By 1970, 99 percent of Americans had a television, up from just 32 percent in 1940. In music, the "album" originated in the late 1940s, and rock 'n' roll began in the 1950s. Other innovations that made life easier or more pleasurable include photocopiers, disposable diapers, and the bikini.

The Civil Rights Act of 1964 outlawed gender and race discrimination in public places, education, and employment. For women, life changed in myriad ways. Female labor force participation rose from 30 percent in 1940 to 49 percent in 1970. Norms inhibiting divorce relaxed in the 1960s. The pill was introduced in 1960. Abortion was legalized in the early 1970s. Access to college increased massively in the mid-1960s.

Comparing these changes in quality of life is difficult, but I see no reason to conclude that the pace of advance, or of innovation, has been more rapid in recent decades than before.[66]

Yes, there have been significant improvements in quality of life in the United States since the 1970s. But that shouldn't lessen our disappointment in the fact that incomes have grown far more slowly than the economy.

"It's Worse Than It Looks"

Rather than understate the true degree of progress for middle- and low-income Americans, the income trends shown in figure 2.5 might overstate it, for the following reasons.[67]

1. *Income growth is due mainly to the addition of a second earner.* The income of American households in the lower half has grown slowly since the 1970s. But it might not have increased at all if not for the fact that more households came to have two earners rather than one. From the 1940s through the mid-1970s, wages rose steadily. As a result, the median income of most

families, whether they had one earner or two, increased at about the same pace as the economy.[68] Since then, wages have barely budged.[69]

It's important to emphasize that most of this shift from one earner to two has been voluntary. A growing number of women seek employment, as their educational attainment has increased, discrimination in the labor market has dissipated, and social norms have changed. The transition from the traditional male-breadwinner family to the dual-earner one isn't simply a product of desperation to keep incomes growing.

Even so, the fact that income growth for lower-half households has required adding a second earner has two problematic implications. First, single-adult households have seen no income rise at all.[70] Second, as more two-adult households have both adults in employment, more struggle to balance the demands of home and work. High-quality childcare and preschools are expensive, and elementary and secondary schools are in session only 180 of the 250 weekdays each year. The difficulty is accentuated by the growing prevalence of long work hours, odd hours, irregular hours, and long commutes. By the early 2000s, 25 percent of employed men and 10 percent of employed women worked fifty or more hours per week.[71] And 35 to 40 percent of Americans worked outside regular hours (9 a.m. to 5 p.m.) and/or days (Monday to Friday).[72] Average commute time rose from forty minutes in 1980 to fifty minutes in the late 2000s.[73]

2. *The cost of key middle-class expenses has risen much faster than inflation.* The income numbers in figure 2.5 are adjusted for inflation. But the adjustment is based on the price of a bundle of goods and services considered typical for American households. Changes in the cost of certain goods and services that middle-class Americans consider essential may not be adequately captured in this bundle. In particular, because middle-class families typically want to own a home and to send their kids to college, they suffered more than other Americans from the sharp rise in housing prices

and college tuition costs in the 1990s and 2000s. Moreover, as middle-class families have shifted from having one earner to two, their spending needs may have changed in ways that adjusting for inflation doesn't capture. For example, they now need to pay for childcare and require two cars rather than one.[74]

Consider a four-person family with two adults and two preschool-age children. In the early 1970s, one of the adults in this family was probably employed, and the other stayed at home. By the mid-2000s, it's likely that both were employed. Here is how their big-ticket expenses might have differed.[75] Childcare: $0 in the early 1970s, $12,500 in the mid-2000s. Car(s): $5,800 for one car in the early 1970s, $8,800 for two cars in the mid-2000s. Home mortgage: $6,000 in the early 1970s, $10,200 in the mid-2000s. When the children reach school age, the strain eases. But when they head off to college it reappears; the average cost of tuition, fees, and room and board at public four-year colleges rose from $6,500 in the early 1970s to $12,000 in the mid-2000s.[76]

Overall, among American households, debt as a share of personal disposable income jumped from 74 percent in 1979 to 138 percent in 2007.[77] The confluence of slowly rising income and rapidly rising big-ticket costs is part of the reason why.[78]

We Can Do Better

In the past generation, ordinary Americans have had less economic security, less opportunity, and less income growth than should be the case in a country as prosperous as ours. Can we do better? Yes. In the next chapter I explain how.

3

How Can We Fix It?

AMERICA'S EXISTING INSTITUTIONS and policies aren't doing well enough in providing economic security, in promoting capabilities and opportunity, and in ensuring rising living standards for households in the lower half. We can do better. In this chapter, I describe how.

Happily, for the most part we aren't in need of new ideas. We have good programs in place that we can build on, and other rich nations have some that we could adopt. We can go a long way toward a good society via programs already in existence here or abroad.

How to Enhance Economic Security

What can be done to reduce economic insecurity? In chapter 2, I highlighted three sources of insecurity: low income, large income declines, and unexpected large expenses. Let's consider these in reverse order.

First, unexpected expenses. The most common large unanticipated expense Americans face is a medical bill. The remedy here is simple and straightforward: universal health insurance.

Who should provide this insurance? Currently, more than half of Americans get their health insurance via an employer-based program. Another third are insured through a government program (Medicare, Medicaid, or the Veteran's Administration), and the remainder purchase health insurance directly or are not insured.[1] Our employer-centered health insurance system was a historical accident. It originated in World War II, when wage controls led firms to offer health insurance in order to attract employees. After the war, encouraged by a new tax break, this practice proliferated, and it has remained in place ever since. In a society in which people switch jobs frequently, it makes little sense for insurance against a potentially major and very costly risk such as medical problems to be tied to employment. Moreover, growing numbers of employers have cut back on or dropped their health insurance plans, and that's likely to continue.[2]

This is a problem, but it's also an opportunity. As fewer Americans in coming decades have access to affordable private health insurance, we should allow them to shift into Medicare or Medicaid (and eventually combine these two programs). This will free employers from having to deal with the cost and hassle of health insurance and free employees to move more readily from job to job. And it will give Medicare and Medicaid more leverage to impose cost controls on healthcare providers.[3]

Can the country afford universal health insurance? Containing the growth of health-care costs is vital, and there is disagreement about the best way to do it.[4] The good news is that we can go a long way simply by learning from other rich nations.[5] As figure 3.1 shows, health expenditures in the United States have risen much faster than in other affluent nations, yet we've achieved less improvement in life expectancy. This is a big challenge, but it's a manageable one.

Next, large involuntary declines in income. Here, four changes are needed. One is sickness insurance. We are the only rich nation without a public sickness insurance program.[6] Though many large private-sector firms offer employees some paid sickness days, and a few cities and states have a public program, one in three employed Americans gets zero days of paid sick leave.[7]

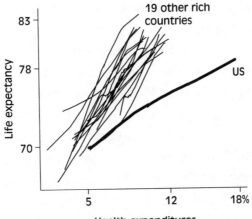

FIGURE 3.1 Health expenditures and life expectancy, 1960–2010
The data points are years. The lines are loess curves. Life expectancy: years at birth.
Health expenditures: public plus private, as percent of GDP. The other countries are
Australia, Austria, Belgium, Canada, Denmark, Finland, France, Germany, Ireland,
Italy, Japan, the Netherlands, New Zealand, Norway, Portugal, Spain, Sweden,
Switzerland, and the United Kingdom. *Data source*: OECD, stats.oecd.org.

A second is paid parental leave. A 1993 law, the Family and
Medical Leave Act, requires firms with fifty or more employees
to provide twelve weeks of leave to employees having a child or
caring for a sick relative. But that isn't much time, and there
is no requirement that the leave be paid. Consequently, many
Americans in low-income households take little time off. That's
bad for newborn children. Outcomes for children tend to be best
when they are with their parent(s) throughout the first year of
life.[8] Swedish policy gets it right. Parents of a newborn child have
thirteen months of job-protected paid leave, with the benefit level
set at approximately 80 percent of earnings. (Two of those months
are "use it or lose it" for the father; if he doesn't use them, the
couple gets eleven months instead of thirteen.) In addition, parents can take four months off per year to care for a sick child up to
age twelve, paid at the same level as parental leave.[9]

A third change needed to reduce large income declines is to
expand access to unemployment insurance.[10] Only about 40 percent of unemployed Americans qualify for compensation.[11]

Fourth, we should add a new wage insurance program.[12] Flexibility is a hallmark of America's economy. It's a feature worth preserving and enhancing. Some Americans who get laid off from a job cannot find another one that pays as well and are forced to settle for one that pays less. For a year or two, wage insurance would fill half the gap between the former pay and the new lower wage. This would enhance economic security. It would also ease resistance to globalization and to technological advance, both of which are beneficial for the whole but result in job loss for some.

Finally, we come to the question of low income. For the bulk of working-age Americans, the problem of too-low household income can be addressed via two simple steps. First, increase the statutory minimum wage and index it to inflation. Second, increase the EITC benefit level, particularly for households without children, for whom the EITC currently provides only a small amount. These two steps would boost the incomes of working-age households that have someone employed.[13]

But this leaves out working-age households in which no one is employed. What to do about such households has long been the thorniest question in American social policy.[14] There is no optimal solution. If we are generous, some will cheat the system. If we are stingy, we cause avoidable suffering. Given this tradeoff, the best approach is a policy that vigorously promotes employment for those who are able to work, provides a decent minimum for those who aren't, and deals on a case-by-case basis with those who can work but don't.[15]

Such a policy would require four modifications to what we have now. First, we should alter our approach to caseworkers and the assistance they provide. In theory, caseworkers help TANF recipients find jobs, but in reality many caseworkers are undertrained, overworked, and have limited means to provide real help.[16] We need a unified active labor market policy. Let me explain what I mean. For some Americans at the low end of the labor market, adulthood is a series of transitions, in which they move in and out of part-time or full-time employment, off-the-books work, receipt of government benefits, romantic relationships, child rearing, drug or alcohol addiction, and time in jail.[17] The best thing we can do is to provide help, support, cajoling, pushing, and the occasional threat. People who struggle to find a job after leaving school (whether at age 22, 18, or earlier) should immediately get individualized help.[18] This may include temporary cash support, a push into a training program, and/or a push into counseling. Strugglers should be monitored as they move along in life. For this to be effective, we need caseworkers who are well trained, connected to local labor market needs, committed to their job, and not swamped with clients. They must be able to make realistic judgments about when clients can make it in the workforce and when the best solution is simply to help them survive.

Second, government should act as an employer of last resort. Make-work has a mixed history in the United States. It played a prominent role in the 1930s, and subsequent smaller-scale programs have boosted the employment rates of low-end workers.[19] Although these programs don't tend to provide a ladder to a permanent, high-paying job, that shouldn't discourage us. The point is to ensure that there is a job for anyone able and willing to work.

Third, restrictions on receipt of TANF should be eased. In bad economic times, such as the 2008–9 recession and its aftermath, the five-year lifetime limit instituted in the mid-1990s has proved too strict, causing needless hardship and suffering.[20] We should allow more exemptions to this limit during economic downturns.

Fourth, the benefit amounts should be increased and eligibility criteria eased for our key social assistance programs—TANF, general assistance, food stamps, housing assistance, and energy assistance. Given the time limit on receipt of TANF benefits, a generous benefit level is unlikely to be a deterrent to employment.

Of course, there are a variety of circumstances in which we don't expect working-age adults to be in a job: unemployment (actively seeking work but unable to find it), disability, sickness, and childbirth. Financial assistance for these people comes from other programs discussed earlier in this section.

What about the elderly? Social Security is a very good program, and one that's in solid shape. With a few tweaks, it will be solvent and effective for generations to come.[21] But we need to shore up retirement income security's second tier: private pensions. There is no going back to the defined-benefit past; for most Americans, a private pension in the future will be a defined-contribution one. Rather than allow Americans who are employed full-time to contribute to defined-contribution plans if their employer offers one, if they are aware of it, and if they feel they can afford to put some of their earnings in it, we should make contributing the default option and make it available to everyone.[22] Employers with an existing plan could continue it, but they would have to automatically enroll all employees and deduct a portion of their earnings unless the employee elects to opt out. Employers without an existing plan could participate in a new universal retirement fund, which would automatically enroll every employee. Workers whose employer does not match their individual contributions would be eligible for matching contributions from the government.

The final piece of the economic security puzzle is public goods, services, spaces, and mandated free time—including childcare, roads and bridges, healthcare, holidays and vacations, and paid parental leave. These increase the sphere of consumption for which the cost to households is zero or minimal. They lift the living standards of households directly and free up income for purchasing other goods and services.[23]

Figure 3.2 displays two measures of material well-being for households at the low end. The horizontal axis shows income for households at the tenth percentile as of the mid-2000s. On the vertical axis is a measure of material deprivation, a more direct indicator of living standards. Two OECD researchers, Romina Boarini and Marco Mira d'Ercole, have compiled material deprivation data from surveys in various nations.[24] Each survey asked identical or very similar questions about seven indicators of material hardship: inability to adequately heat one's home, constrained food choices, overcrowding, poor environmental conditions (noise,

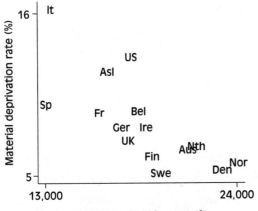

FIGURE 3.2 Low-end household incomes and material deprivation
P10 household income: posttransfer-posttax income of households at the tenth percentile
of the income distribution. Measured in 2005 or as close to that year as possible. Incomes
are adjusted for household size (the numbers shown here are for a household with three
persons) and converted into US dollars using purchasing power parities (PPPs). *Data
sources:* Luxembourg Income Study, www.lisdatacenter.org, series DPI; OECD, stats.
oecd.org. Material deprivation rate: share of households experiencing one or more of the
following: inability to adequately heat home, constrained food choices, overcrowding,
poor environmental conditions (e.g., noise, pollution), arrears in payment of utility bills,
arrears in mortgage or rent payment, difficulty in making ends meet. Measured in 2005.
Data sources: OECD, *Growing Unequal?*, 2008, pp. 186–188, using data from the Survey
on Income and Living Conditions (EU-SILC) for European countries, the Household
Income and Labour Dynamics in Australia survey (HILDA) for Australia, and the Survey
of Income and Program Participation (SIPP) for the United States. "Asl" is Australia;
"Aus" is Austria.

pollution), arrears in payment of utility bills, arrears in mortgage or rent payments, and difficulty making ends meet. Boarini
and Mira d'Ercole create a summary measure of deprivation by
averaging, for each country, the shares of the population reporting
deprivation in each of these seven areas.

The income of a typical low-end household in the United States is
similar to that in many rich countries, albeit lower than in Norway,
Sweden, Denmark, and Finland. Our rate of material deprivation,
by contrast, is higher than in all but one of the other nations, and
by a relatively large margin. This difference is most likely due to
our limited public provision of services. Services enhance access to
medical care, childcare, and housing, and allow poor households to
spend their limited income on other necessities.

To reduce economic insecurity, we need to make a number of policy changes. But none are radical, and most build on programs we already have in place. This is quite doable.

How to Expand Opportunity

Inequality of opportunity is increasing. But all hope is not lost. We know this because many other rich nations do better. The best indicator when comparing countries is relative intergenerational mobility, and data exist for ten of our peer nations. As figure 3.3 shows, the United States has less equality of opportunity than eight of them, and the same amount as the other two.

What can we do to address this problem? Genetics, families, friends, and neighborhoods influence capability development, but we don't want government intervening directly in family life or telling us where we should live. We therefore rely heavily on schools. School is especially valuable for children from less

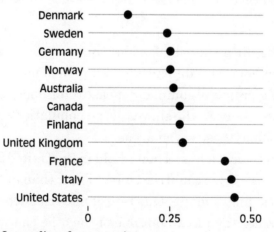

FIGURE 3.3 Inequality of opportunity
Correlation between the earnings of parents and those of their children. A higher score indicates less relative intergenerational mobility and hence more inequality of opportunity. *Data source*: John Ermisch, Markus Jäntti, and Timothy Smeeding, eds., *From Parents to Children: The Intergenerational Transmission of Advantage*, Russell Sage Foundation, 2012, figure 1.1.

advantaged circumstances. We know this in two ways. First, children from poor homes tend to have significantly lower cognitive and noncognitive skills than children from affluent homes when they enter kindergarten, and the size of that gap is about the same when they finish high school.[25] Given the huge differences in home and neighborhood circumstances, this suggests that schools have an equalizing effect. Second, during summer vacations, when children are out of school, the gap in cognitive ability increases.[26]

Let's begin with college. Figure 3.4 shows rates of college entry and completion by family income for Americans growing up in the 1980s and 1990s. On average, about two-thirds of a typical cohort enter college and about one-third end up with a four-year degree. But both entry and completion vary starkly by family income. For those whose parents' income is in the bottom quarter, only 30 percent begin college and only 10 percent get a four-year degree. Moreover, the increase over the past generation has been minimal (see figure 2.4).

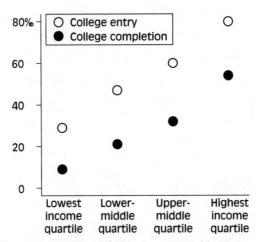

FIGURE 3.4 College entry and completion by parents' income
Persons born 1979–82. College entry: includes all two-year and four-year postsecondary institutions. College completion: four or more years of college. *Data source*: Martha Bailey and Susan Dynarski, "Gains and Gaps: A Historical Perspective on Inequality in College Entry and Completion," in *Whither Opportunity? Rising Inequality, Schools, and Children's Life Chances*, edited by Greg J. Duncan and Richard J. Murnane, Russell Sage Foundation, 2011, figures 6.2 and 6.3, using National Longitudinal Survey of Youth data.

How can we help more Americans from low-income families start and finish college?[27] One suggestion is to improve prior schooling. Better preparation in elementary and secondary school, in this view, will encourage more low-income kids to go to college and enable them to succeed once there. A second approach stresses improving performance and retention among less advantaged youth who enter college through better instruction, advising, support, and close monitoring. A third emphasizes cost. Now, the actual cost of college sometimes is overstated. If we take into account grants and financial aid, instead of looking simply at the "sticker price" of tuition and room and board, the average cost per year for a public four-year university was $11,500 in 2011–12, and for low-income families the cost often is less than this. But the average income among families in the bottom fifth of incomes is just $18,000 (see chapter 2), and at that income, even $5,000 a year for college may be too much.

All three strategies—improving preparation, enhancing retention, and reducing cost—would help. But where do we start? Christopher Jencks offers the following sensible advice: "Making college a lot more affordable is a challenge governments know how to meet, while making students learn a lot more is a challenge we do not currently know how to meet. Under those circumstances, starting with affordability is probably the best bet."[28]

In Denmark, Finland, Norway, and Sweden, attending a four-year public university is free. In those countries the odds that a person whose parents didn't complete high school will attend college are between 40 percent and 60 percent, compared to just 30 percent in the United States.[29]

Some feel it makes no sense to try to increase college attendance and completion.[30] After all, there is a limited supply of high-skill jobs, so some graduates will end up in jobs that don't require anything near college-level skills. Yet if our aim is to maximize capabilities, including the ability to make informed preferences, we must help more Americans from low-income families into and through college. In addition to providing a vocational skill and a valuable job-market credential, a college education can aid in the development of general skills, such as complex reasoning, critical thinking, and written and verbal communication.

Moving backward through the education system, what about K-12? After rising steadily for a century, the share of Americans completing secondary school has been stuck at 75 percent for several decades.[31] Social and economic shifts are partly to blame: there are more students for whom English is not the principal language at home, more children grow up in unstable families, and the incomes of low-income households have barely budged. Despite these obstacles, or perhaps because of them, we need schools to do better.

A generation ago many blamed the huge inequality of school resources, a product of our decentralized, property-tax-based system of school funding.[32] Some of that inequality has been rectified, as state governments now contribute a larger share of funds to schools and distribute them to offset the unequal distribution of local property values.[33] While funding inequality across states remains substantial, overall the situation is better.

Some believe the problem lies in lack of competition among public schools. If competition works, it is in one respect an ideal policy strategy: it requires little or no understanding of why some schools perform well while others don't. Customers (parents) simply choose the effective schools, and the bad ones go out of business. Choice is a good thing in and of itself. We want to be able to choose our doctor, after all, so why not our children's school? Social democratic Sweden introduced choice into its school systems in the mid-1990s.

But so far our experience in the United States suggests that whatever its intrinsic merit, choice may not improve schooling. Charter schools—publicly funded elementary and secondary schools that are allowed considerable leeway in determining procedures and practices and that compete with regular public schools—have not, on average, boosted student performance.[34] In any case, transportation barriers, friendship ties, and other factors cause many children who might benefit from switching to a better school to remain at their nearby school instead.[35]

The federal government's 2001 No Child Left Behind reform mandated regular standardized testing in America's elementary and secondary schools. This is a useful means of improving information about school effectiveness. But it is not in and of itself a strategy for making schools better.

Evidence from a variety of sources—standardized tests in the United States, international tests, quasi-experimental studies, and a host of qualitative analyses—suggests that teachers are a key ingredient in effective K-12 schooling.[36] We should do more to attract, retain, and support good teachers. That means more-rigorous training, better efforts to identify effective teachers, higher pay, improved working conditions, and reduced restrictions on firing less effective teachers.[37]

Of the various things we can do to improve American schooling, the most valuable would be to introduce universal high-quality affordable early education. Here, too, we can learn from the Nordic countries. Beginning in the 1960s, these countries introduced and steadily expanded paid maternity leave and publicly funded childcare and preschool. Today, Danish and Swedish parents can take a paid year off work following the birth of a child. After that, parents can put the child in a public or cooperative early education center. Early education teachers receive training and pay comparable to that of elementary school teachers. Parents pay a fee, but the cost is capped at around 10 percent of household income. In these countries, the influence of parents' education, income, and parenting practices on their children's cognitive abilities, likelihood of completing high school and college, and labor market success is weaker than elsewhere.[38] Evidence increasingly suggests that the early years of a child's life are the most important ones for developing cognitive and noncognitive skills, so the Nordic countries' success in equalizing opportunity very likely owes partly, perhaps largely, to early education.[39]

Early education also facilitates employment of parents, especially mothers, thereby enhancing women's economic opportunity and boosting family incomes.[40] In a country that values employment, that wants to facilitate and promote work, this is the type of service our government should support. About half of preschool-age American children already are in out-of-home care, but much of it is unregulated and therefore of uneven quality.[41] While some parents can pay for excellent care, many cannot. Universal early education would change that.

When someone suggests borrowing a policy or institution from the Nordic countries, skeptics immediately point out that these countries are very different from the United States. They're small, they're more ethnically and racially homogenous, and their cultures and histories are quite distinct from ours. What works there, in other words, won't necessarily work here.

That's true. But it doesn't justify blanket skepticism about borrowing. We have to consider the particulars of the policy in question. There is no reason to think a system of public, or at least publicly funded, early-education centers (schools) can function effectively only in a small homogenous country. France has this kind of system, even though it's a pretty large nation. Belgium does, too, despite its diversity. And we do a reasonably good job with our kindergartens and elementary schools. Education experts and ordinary Americans routinely profess dissatisfaction with our K-12 public schools. But recall the evidence from summer vacations: children from less advantaged homes lose substantial ground when they aren't in school. American schools could be better, to be sure, but for less advantaged children they are, even in their current condition, far better than the likely alternative.

Why should early education be universal? Why not just expand Head Start, our existing public pre-K program for low-income children? The reason is that development of both cognitive and, especially, noncognitive skills is helped by peer interaction. Children from less advantaged homes gain by mixing with kids from middle-class homes, which doesn't happen in a program that exclusively serves the poor.[42]

I've focused on schools because they are our principal lever for enhancing opportunity. But they aren't the only one. Three other strategies are worth pursuing.[43] First, we could get more money into the hands of low-income families with children. Greg Duncan, Ariel Kalil, and Kathleen Ziol-Guest have found that for American children growing up in the 1970s and 1980s, an increase in family income of a mere $3,000 during a person's first five years of life was associated with nearly 20 percent higher earnings later in life.[44] Most other affluent countries, including those that do better on equality of opportunity, offer a universal "child allowance." In Canada, for instance, a family with two children receives an annual allowance of around $3,000, and low-income families with two children might receive more than $6,000.[45] We have a weaker version, the Child Tax Credit, which doles out a maximum of $1,000 a year per child. Moreover, receipt of the money is contingent on filing a federal tax return, which not all low-income families do.

Second, in the 1970s and 1980s, the United States began incarcerating more young men, including many for minor offenses. Having a criminal record makes it difficult to get a stable job with decent pay, dooming many offenders to a life of low income.[46] We should rethink our approach to punishment for nonviolent drug offenders. States that have reduced imprisonment, turning to alternative punishments such as fines and community corrections programs, have experienced drops in crime similar to those in states that have increased imprisonment.[47] If more states followed suit, we could avoid needlessly undermining the employment opportunities of a significant number of young men from less advantaged homes.

Third, since the late 1960s, affirmative action programs for university admissions and hiring have promoted opportunity for women and members of racial and ethnic minority groups.[48] Affirmative action should continue, but with family background as the focal criterion.[49]

How to Ensure Shared Prosperity

In chapter 2, I described the slow growth of income among lower-half American households since the 1970s. But what if there is no alternative? Do globalization, heightened competition, computerization, and manufacturing decline make it impossible for more than a little of our economic growth to trickle down to households on the middle and lower rungs of the income ladder? To assess this hypothesis, we can look at the experiences of other rich nations. Have they suffered the same decoupling of household income growth from economic growth?

Some have, but many haven't. In fact, in quite a few other affluent countries we see a healthy relationship between economic growth and household income growth since the 1970s. Figure 3.5 shows the pattern in the United States and fourteen other nations. The horizontal axis shows change in GDP per capita, and the vertical axis shows change in average income among households on the lower half of the income ladder. The United States is one of the lowest on the vertical axis; the incomes of lower-half American households increased less than in most of the other nations. In some cases, such as Finland and Austria, that's because their economy grew more rapidly than ours did. But a number of countries, including Denmark and Sweden, achieved larger increases in household incomes despite increases in GDP per capita very similar to America's. Too little of our economic growth trickled down.[50]

Why did some countries do better than others? Lower-half households have two principal sources of income: earnings and net government transfers. Earnings are wage or salary income from employment. Net government transfers are cash and near-cash benefits a household receives from government programs minus taxes it pays. Figure 3.6 shows the contribution to household income growth from each of these two sources. Data are available for twelve countries. Here I separate households in the bottom

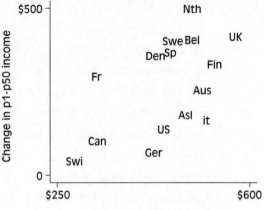

FIGURE 3.5 Economic growth and lower-half households' income growth, 1979–2005

Change is per year on both axes. The actual years vary somewhat depending on the country. Household incomes are posttransfer-posttax, adjusted for household size (the amounts shown are for a household with four persons). The income data are averages for households in the lower half of the income distribution. Household incomes and GDP per capita are adjusted for inflation using the CPI and converted to US dollars using purchasing power parities. "Asl" is Australia; "Aus" is Austria. Ireland and Norway are omitted; both would be far off the plot in the upper-right corner. *Data sources*: OECD, stats.oecd.org; Luxembourg Income Study, www.lisdatacenter.org.

quarter of incomes from those in the lower-middle quarter (together these make up the lower half). Among households in the bottom quarter, rising income came mostly from increases in net government transfers. Among those in the lower-middle quarter, rising income stemmed from improvement in both earnings and net government transfers.[51] In America, neither earnings nor net government transfers increased much. That's why we observe the decoupling of economic growth and lower-half household income growth in the United States in figure 3.5 (also figure 2.5).

What are the prospects for earnings going forward? Household earnings can rise in two ways: higher wages and more employment. From the 1940s through the mid- to late-1970s, much of the growth in household incomes for working-age Americans came from rising wages.[52] But as figure 3.7 shows, since the late 1970s inflation-adjusted wages in the bottom half have barely budged.

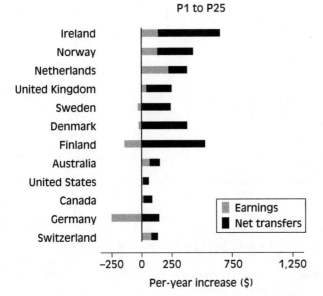

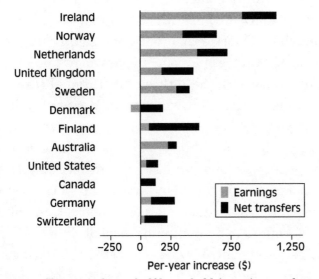

FIGURE 3.6 Change in lower-half households' earnings and net government transfers, 1979–2005
Earnings and net transfers are adjusted for inflation using the CPI and converted to US dollars using purchasing power parities. *Data source*: Luxembourg Income Study, www.lisdatacenter.org.

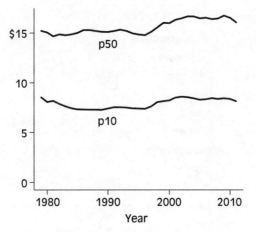

FIGURE 3.7 Wages
Hourly wage at the fiftieth (median) and tenth percentiles of the wage distribution. 2011 dollars; inflation adjustment is via the CPI-U-RS. *Data source*: Lawrence Mishel et al., *The State of Working America*, stateofworkingamerica.org, "Hourly wages of all workers, by wage percentile," using Current Population Survey (CPS) data.

In the post-World War II golden age, many American firms faced limited product market competition, limited pressure from shareholders to maximize short-term profits, and significant pressure from unions (or the threat of unions) to pass on a "fair" share of profit growth to employees. These three institutional features are gone, and it's unlikely that they will return. Moreover, a host of additional developments now push against wage growth: technological advances (computers and robots), the continuing decline of manufacturing jobs, new opportunities to offshore mid-level service jobs, an increase in less-skilled immigrant workers, the growing prevalence of winner-take-all labor markets, a shift toward pay for performance, and minimum wage decline.

In the one brief period of nontrivial wage growth in the past generation, the late 1990s, the key seems to have been a tight labor market.[53] The unemployment rate dipped below 4 percent, the lowest since the 1960s. It would be good to repeat this, but I suspect it won't happen. The next time our unemployment rate gets near 4 percent, the Federal Reserve is more likely to slam on the brakes by raising interest rates. In the late 1990s, Fed chair Alan Greenspan held interest rates low despite opposition from other

Fed board members who worried about potential inflationary consequences of rapid growth, rising wages, and the Internet stock
market bubble. Greenspan's belief in the self-correcting nature of
markets led him to worry less than others. Given the painful consequences of the 2000s housing bubble, the Fed is highly unlikely
to repeat that approach.

So for Americans in middle- and lower-paying jobs, prospects
for rising wages going forward are slim.

Employment is the other potential source of rising earnings.
Indeed, as I noted in chapter 2, it's the chief reason there has been
any increase at all in household incomes since the 1970s. We also
need employment to fund generous social programs. Tax rates
need to increase, as I discuss in chapter 4, but we also need a larger
tax base, in the form of more people employed.[54] About 85 percent
of prime-working-age males and 70 percent of prime-working-age
females were employed as of 2010. We may see no further increase
among prime-age men, but among women and the near elderly
(aged 55–64) there is substantial room for growth.

The United States has a set of institutions and policies that in
theory should be conducive to rapid employment growth: a low
wage floor, limited labor market regulation, relatively stingy government benefits, and low taxes. Up to the turn of the century,
we were comparatively successful. As figure 3.8 shows, during the
1980s and 1990s the employment rate among 25- to 64-year-olds
rose by seven percentage points—better than most other rich
nations.[55] Some commentators labeled our economy the "great
American jobs machine."

But in the 2000s the bloom fell off the rose.[56] The early years
of recovery after the 2001 recession featured feeble job growth,
and things didn't improve much after that. By the peak year of
the 2000s business cycle, 2007, the employment rate had not yet
reached its prior peak.[57] And during the subsequent economic
crash nearly all the progress of the 1980s and 1990s was erased.

What happened? We don't know. It may be that economic and
institutional forces—strong competition, the shareholder value

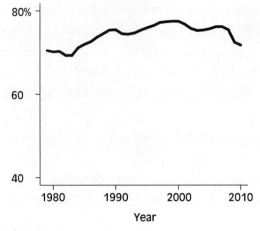

FIGURE 3.8 Employment rate
Employed share of persons aged 25 to 64. The vertical axis does not begin at zero. *Data source*: OECD, stats.oecd.org.

orientation in corporate governance, Wall Street's appetite for downsizing, weakened unions—have made management reluctant to hire.[58] Perhaps it was manufacturing jobs fleeing to China and service jobs shifting to India.[59] Or perhaps the computer-robotics revolution finally began to hit full force.[60] Maybe it was a combination of these and other factors. Whatever the cause, it doesn't bode well for employment going forward.

So there is reason to worry about both wages and jobs. What can we do? Let's begin with employment.[61] First, adequate demand is essential. When our economy finally emerges from the aftermath of the great recession, it may struggle in the absence of a 1990s- or 2000s-style stock market or housing bubble to fuel consumer spending. Rising living standards in developing nations should help by boosting American exports, and government job creation can enhance domestic spending. But demand is a significant question mark going forward. Second, as I suggested earlier, high-quality, affordable early education would help by facilitating mothers' employment. Third, we would do well to expand provision of individualized assistance for those who struggle in the labor market. This is expensive, but it helps.[62] Fourth, government can directly promote job creation by subsidizing private-sector job growth and creating public-sector jobs.[63]

The better our educational system, the more Americans are likely to work in professional analytical jobs. But a nontrivial share of the jobs in our future economy will be low-end ones.[64] Rather than fight this, we should embrace it. As we get richer, most of us are willing to outsource more tasks we don't have the time or expertise or desire to do ourselves—changing the oil in the car, mowing the lawn, cleaning, cooking, caring for children and other family members, and much more. This can be a win-win proposition if we approach it properly. We need more Americans teaching preschool children, helping people find their way in the labor market and transition to a new career in midlife, and caring for the elderly.[65] Improved productivity and lower wage costs abroad reduce the price we pay for manufactured goods and some services. This enables us to purchase more helping-caring services and more of us to work in helping-caring service jobs.[66]

But some of these jobs, perhaps many of them, won't pay enough to ensure a good standard of living. And as I've noted, the experience of the past several decades suggests that pay likely won't improve over time.

The solution has two parts. First, we should increase the minimum wage a bit and, more important, index it to prices so that it keeps pace with the cost of living.

The second element is a government program that can compensate for stagnant or slowly-rising wages in a context of robust economic growth—insurance against decoupling, if you will.[67] We could do this by building on the EITC. The ideal, in my view, would be to give it to individuals rather than households, increase the benefit amount for those with no children, give it to everyone with earnings rather than only to those with low income, and tax it if household income is relatively high. Most important, we could index it to average compensation or to GDP per capita.[68] This would help restore the link between growth of the economy and growth of household incomes.[69]

The real value of the minimum wage and the restructured EITC will need to be adjusted periodically. Rather than relying on Congress and the president to come to agreement, I recommend delegating this task to an independent board, similar to the Federal Reserve board and the new Independent Payment Advisory Board for Medicare in that its members would be nominated by the president and confirmed by the Senate but it would have independent decision-making authority.

Policies That Can Help

I've outlined a number of new programs and some expansions of existing ones that would enhance economic security, expand opportunity, and ensure rising living standards for Americans. They include the following:

- Universal health insurance
- One year of paid parental leave
- Universal early education
- Increased Child Tax Credit
- Sickness insurance
- Eased eligibility criteria for unemployment insurance
- Wage insurance
- Supplemental defined-contribution pension plans with automatic enrollment
- Extensive, personalized job search and (re)training support
- Government as employer of last resort
- Minimum wage increased modestly and indexed to prices
- EITC extended farther up the income ladder and indexed to average compensation or GDP per capita
- Social assistance with a higher benefit level and more support for employment
- Reduced incarceration of low-level drug offenders
- Affirmative action shifted to focus on family background rather than race

- Expanded government investment in infrastructure and public spaces
- More paid holidays and vacation time

The American economy's performance in coming decades is likely to be similar to what we've experienced since the 1970s: reasonably healthy economic growth, a modest increase in the employment rate, a rise in the likelihood of losing a job, little or no improvement in inflation-adjusted wages for earners in the lower half, growing inequality of market household incomes, and little rise in wealth for middle- and low-income households. Economic pressures will continue to intensify. Risks will continue to grow. Families, civic organizations, and unions will remain weak. In this context, the policies I've recommended here won't eliminate the problems of economic insecurity, inadequate opportunity, or slow income growth. In fact, they might not fully compensate for these adverse shifts in our economy and society. Better policies won't guarantee better outcomes.

But these policies will help. Americans from less advantaged homes will have cognitive skills and noncognitive traits that give them a better shot at successfully entering and staying in the labor market and at having a long-lasting family relationship. Those who lose a job will have a stronger incentive to take another job even if it pays less, and they will have more help in finding one. Individuals unable to function effectively or continuously in the labor market, whether working age or elderly, will have a higher income. No one will have to fear lack of access to medical care, and fewer will face a massive out-of-pocket expense resulting from such care. Expanded provision of public goods and services will enhance economic security and take the edge off rising income inequality for those at the low end of the scale. A steady rise in the EITC will ensure that more of our economic growth reaches households in the middle and below.

How much will all this cost? That depends on the structure and generosity of the policies, and it isn't my aim to offer

recommendations at that level of specificity. As a ballpark estimate, I suggest we think in terms of 10 percent of GDP to cover
the cost of new programs, the expansion of existing ones, and the
rise in the cost of Social Security and Medicare that will come from
population aging.

Can we afford it? Will this "social democratic" approach require
sacrificing other elements of a good society? Are there attractive alternatives? Can these proposals get passed in our political
system? I answer these questions in chapters 4 and 5.

4

Objections and Alternatives

SOME WILL SYMPATHIZE with the ends I have laid out— improving economic security, expanding opportunity, and ensuring shared prosperity—but disagree with the means. One objection, common among those on the right side of the political spectrum, is that bigger government will lead to greater public debt, slower economic growth, less employment, restricted liberty, and diminished self-reliance, so we might do better to rely on private institutions such as families and communities. On the left, many favor stronger labor unions, promotion of manufacturing jobs, a higher wage floor, or perhaps a basic income grant. In this chapter I address these objections and alternatives along with a number of others.

Can We Pay for It?

Suppose we need, as I suggest in chapter 3, an additional 10 percent of GDP to fund new social programs, expansion of existing ones, and demography-imposed increases in the cost of Social Security and Medicare. Is that feasible? If so, what's the best way to do it?

Let's begin with feasibility. Is heavy taxation still possible in a world where firms, institutions, and wealthy individuals can move their money anywhere they like? The answer, at least so far, is yes. Globalization has not induced a race to the bottom in taxation. Many rich nations have reduced their top statutory rates, but they've offset this by reducing tax exemptions and deductions. Effective tax rates have therefore changed little, and taxes as a share of GDP have not fallen.[1]

Indeed, the rich nations with big governments are no more likely than others to have large public deficits and debt. As figure 4.1 shows, the social democratic Nordic countries have comparatively low levels of government debt. (Norway's oil resources account for its outlying position.) They spend a lot, but they generate enough tax revenues to pay for that spending.

How, then, should the United States go about taxing? Before answering, let me pause for a moment to define some basic terms. When those with high incomes pay a larger share of their income in taxes than those with low incomes, we call the tax system "progressive." When the rich and poor pay a similar share of their incomes, the tax system is termed "proportional." When the poor pay a larger share than the rich, the tax system is "regressive."

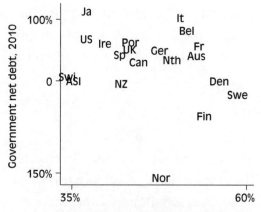

FIGURE 4.1 Government spending and government debt
Higher on the vertical axis indicates larger debt. Government net debt: government financial liabilities minus government financial assets, measured as a share of GDP. The pattern is similar for gross debt (government financial liabilities). Government expenditures are measured as a share of GDP. *Data source:* OECD, stats.oecd.org. The correlation is −.25 (with Norway excluded). "Asl" is Australia; "Aus" is Austria.

The US tax system as a whole—taxes of all types and at all levels of government—is roughly proportional. The key measure is the effective tax rate, which is calculated as tax payments divided by pretax (and pre-government-transfer) income. According to the best data we have, the effective tax rate is about the same whether one's income is high, middle, or low.[2] Federal income taxes are progressive; the rich pay at a higher rate than the poor. But that progressivity is largely offset by regressive payroll taxes and sales taxes.

America is not unique in this. In all rich nations for which we have data, the tax system does little to alter the distribution of pretax income. In fact, if anything, our tax system is a bit less regressive than those of other affluent countries, because most of them have heavier consumption and payroll taxes than we do.[3]

For the past generation, America's left has focused on the progressivity of federal income taxes, viewing taxes through a lens that emphasizes fairness and redistribution. But if your concern is income redistribution, your focus should be on transfers. It is transfers that do the bulk of the redistributive work in affluent countries.[4]

Taxes matter mainly because they provide the funds for public goods, services, and transfers, and our tax system provides much less revenue than most other rich countries. This brings us back to the question of how to increase revenues in the United States.

As a candidate for president in 2008, Barack Obama pledged to not increase tax rates for the bottom 95 percent of American households, and as president he has held to this promise.[5] There is some sense in focusing on those at the top in the search for more revenue. The chief rationale for progressive taxation is that those with more income can afford to pay a larger share of that income than those with less.[6] The incomes of Americans in the middle and below have risen slowly over the past few decades. Meanwhile, the incomes of those at the top have soared, so they're now able to pay a larger share of those incomes.

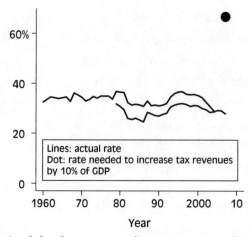

FIGURE 4.2 Effective federal tax rate on the top 5 percent of incomes
Effective tax rate: tax payments as a share of pretax income. Federal taxes include personal income, corporate income, payroll, and excise. The chart has two estimates of the
actual rate. *Data sources*: for the top line, Thomas Piketty and Emmanuel Saez, data set
for "How Progressive Is the U.S. Federal Tax System?" *Journal of Economic Perspectives*,
2007, available at elsa.berkeley.edu/~saez; for the lower line, Congressional Budget
Office, "Average Federal Tax Rates and Income, by Income Category, 1979–2007." See the
notes for calculation of the rate needed to increase tax revenues by 10 percent of GDP.

To get a *lot* more revenue, however, we have to go beyond the
rich. Suppose we need an additional 10 percent of GDP, as I suggest in chapter 3. Figure 4.2 shows the effective federal tax rate on
the top 5 percent of households going back to 1960. This includes
all types of federal taxes—personal income, corporate income,
payroll, and excise. We have two estimates of this tax rate, one
beginning in 1960 and the other in 1979. The dot for the year 2007
indicates what the effective tax rate on this group would need to
have been in 2007 to increase tax revenues by 10 percent of GDP.[7]
This is far above the actual rate at any point in the past half century. Whether desirable or not, an increase of this magnitude
won't find favor among policy makers.

If getting the needed revenues solely from the rich is unlikely,
where *can* we get it? To raise the 10 percent of GDP in additional
tax revenues that we need, a multipronged approach is required.
Figure 4.3 shows one way to do it.

It begins with a national consumption tax. Limited use of consumption taxation is the main feature of the US tax system that separates us from other rich nations. Currently, we collect only about 5 percent of GDP in consumption taxes, almost entirely at the state and local levels. Most other affluent countries collect 10 percent or more.[8] A value-added tax (VAT) at a rate of 12 percent, with limited deductions, would likely bring in about 5 percent of GDP in revenue.[9]

The idea of a large consumption tax has yet to be embraced by America's left, which objects to its regressivity. The degree of regressivity can be reduced by exempting more items from the tax;[10] but the greater the exemptions, the less revenue the tax will bring in. A better strategy is to offset the regressivity of a new consumption tax with other changes to the tax system, including some of those listed in figure 4.3.

The right tends to object to a VAT for fear it will become a "money machine"—a tax that can be steadily increased over time. But this fear is based on a misreading of the experience of other rich nations. Some countries have decreased their VAT rate, some have held it constant, and most of those that have increased it did so mainly in the 1970s and early 1980s, when high inflation made such increases less noticeable.[11] Some argue that tax increases in rich countries since the 1960s have come mainly via

5.0%	National consumption tax (VAT) at a rate of 12%, with limited deductions or a small flat rebate
2.0	Return to the 2000 (pre-Bush) federal income tax rates
0.7	Several new federal income tax rates for households in the top 1%, increasing the average effective tax rate for this group by an additional 4.5 percentage points
0.6	End the mortgage interest tax deduction
0.7	Carbon tax
0.5	Financial transactions tax of 0.5% on trades
0.2	Increase the cap on the Social Security payroll tax so the tax covers 90% of total earnings, as it did in the early 1980s
0.3	Increase the payroll tax by 1 percentage point

FIGURE 4.3   How to increase tax revenues by 10 percent of GDP

The numbers are percentages of GDP. They total 10 percent. All are estimates.

VAT increases; in fact, they have come as much or more from increases in income and payroll taxes.[12]

It may be a while yet before political leaders on America's left and right come to agreement that a VAT has considerable advantages and few drawbacks. But eventually it will happen.

Second, we should return to the pre-Bush income tax rates for everyone. This would increase revenues by about 2 percent of GDP.[13]

Third, we can raise income tax rates for those in the top 1 percent a bit more.[14] Increasing the average effective tax rate for this group by 4.5 percentage points would generate about .7 percent of GDP. The 2012 tax deal will return the effective tax rate on the top 1 percent to around its pre-Bush level of 33 percent. An increase of four to five percentage points, to a 37–38 percent effective rate, would hardly be confiscatory.

Fourth, we can get rid of the tax deduction for interest paid on mortgage loans. This would increase revenues by about .6 percent of GDP. The aim of the mortgage interest deduction is to boost home ownership, but other affluent nations, such as Australia and Canada, have homeownership rates comparable to ours or higher without a tax incentive. Moreover, most of this deduction goes to households in the top fifth of incomes.[15] Few in the middle or below benefit from it.

Fifth, we need a carbon tax. This would generate about .7 percent of GDP in revenues. We should have a carbon tax regardless of its impact on government revenue, to shift resources away from activities that contribute to climate change.

Sixth, we could impose a modest tax on financial transactions, such as purchases of stock shares, which would bring in about .5 percent of GDP. Opponents warn that it might cause trading to flee to other financial centers that don't have such a tax, but the United Kingdom has long had a financial transactions tax without any apparent damage.

Seventh, we can increase the cap on earnings that are subject to the Social Security payroll tax. A person's earnings above $114,000 are not subject to the tax (as of 2013). Because a growing share of total earnings in the US economy has gone to those at the top in recent decades, a growing share has been exempt from the tax. In the early 1980s, about 90 percent of earnings was subject to the Social Security payroll tax; as of 2012 this had dropped to 84 percent.[16] Raising the cap to get back to 90 percent would increase tax revenues by about .2 percent of GDP.

Finally, to get an additional .3 percent of GDP, bringing the total to 10 percent, we could increase the payroll tax by one percentage point (half a percentage point on employees and half a point on employers).[17] This would leave the payroll tax rate well below what it is in many European countries, and almost certainly below the level at which it would be a significant deterrent to employment.

Figure 4.3 offers only one way to increase tax revenues. There are other options. The point is that the technical details of getting an additional 10 percent of GDP are not difficult.

Let's return now to progressivity and redistribution. Some egalitarian readers may be incredulous. Why would I say that America's tax system currently is not very progressive and then recommend changes that might make it even less so?

Keep in mind that the principal objectives of government social programs are to enhance economic security and opportunity and to ensure rising living standards. Redistribution of income is not the chief aim. And yet, in doing these things, social policy does achieve a good bit of redistribution. Let me spell out how this works.

Figure 4.4 shows a hypothetical distribution of tax payments and receipt of government goods, services, and transfers. Households are separated into quintiles based on their pretax income. The light bars in the chart show the share of dollars paid in taxes by households in each quintile. The tax system in this illustration is proportional; households pay the same effective tax rate regardless of their pretax income. Although everyone has the same tax *rate*, those with higher pretax income pay more in tax *dollars* because their pretax income is higher. The richest fifth of households get 56 percent of all pretax income, so they pay 56 percent of the tax dollars in this illustration.[18] The poorest fifth of households get

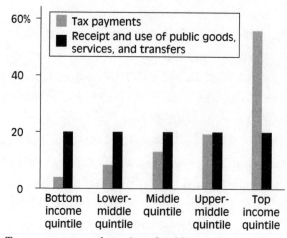

FIGURE 4.4 Tax payments and receipt of public goods, services, and transfers by income quintile
These shares are hypothetical. They assume all households pay the same effective tax rate (proportional tax system). And they assume all households receive or use the same quantity (dollar value) of public goods, services, and transfers.

4 percent of the pretax income, so they pay 4 percent of the tax dollars.

The dark bars in the chart show the estimated value of the government goods, services, and transfers received and used by households in each group. I assume this value to be equal for all groups; in other words, households at each point on the income ladder get about the same amount of services, public goods, and cash and near-cash transfers. This is fairly close to the truth for public goods such as roads and parks and for public services such as schooling and healthcare. It's less likely to be true for transfers. But let's suppose, for this illustration, that it's accurate for the total of services, goods, and transfers doled out by the government.

What we see in the chart is that even with a tax system that is proportional rather than progressive, government social programs are fairly heavily redistributive. Those with high pretax incomes pay far more in tax dollars than they receive in government goods, services, and transfers. Those with low pretax incomes receive much more than they pay in taxes. Although redistribution is not the chief aim, it is a result nonetheless.

Much of this redistributive impact is hidden. We can't see it in income statistics. A lot of government social expenditure is on public services and goods, and their value isn't included in household income measures. But that doesn't mean it isn't real.

One final point: while increasing tax revenues by 10 percent of GDP would be a significant change, it isn't unprecedented. Over the course of the twentieth century, revenues' share of our GDP rose by about twenty-five percentage points. And an increase of 10 percent would put the United States merely in the middle of the pack—not at the front—among the world's rich countries.

The bottom line: we *can* pay for bigger government.

Is Big Government Bad for Economic Growth?

If our government gets bigger, will our economy suffer? It's easy to understand why some think so. After all, an increase in taxes reduces the financial incentive to work harder or longer, invest in acquiring more skills, start a new company, or expand an existing one. And when governments provide goods and services, they inevitably waste some resources, particularly when they face no competition.

But that's too simplistic.[19] The incentive effect of higher taxes can also work in the other direction; if tax rates go up, I may work more in order to end up with the same after-tax income I had before. Moreover, some of what government does helps the economy.[20] When government protects people's safety and property and enforces contracts, it facilitates business activity. Enforcement of antitrust rules enhances competition. Schools boost human capital. Roads, bridges, and other infrastructure grease the wheels of business activity. Limited liability and bankruptcy provisions encourage risk taking. Affordable high-quality childcare increases parental employment and boosts the capabilities of less advantaged kids. Access to medical care improves health and reduces anxiety. Child labor restrictions, antidiscrimination laws, minimum wages, job safety regulations, consumer safety protections, unemployment insurance, and a host of other policies help to ensure social peace.

There surely is a tipping point at which government taxing and spending begins to harm the economy. But where are we in relation to that point? We have the experiences of the world's rich countries to draw upon in answering this question. This evidence doesn't give us a full and final answer, but it strongly suggests that America hasn't reached the tipping point. Indeed, we might be far below it.

A useful measure of the size of government is government revenues as a share of GDP. Data for the United States are available going back to the early 1900s. These data include the federal government and state and local governments. Most of the revenues, though not all, are from taxes. The chart on the left in figure 4.5 shows that revenues rose from the 1910s through the 1990s and then leveled off. All told, government revenues increased by approximately twenty-five percentage points, from less than 10 percent of GDP to around 35 percent.

The chart on the right in figure 4.5 shows GDP per capita all the way back to 1890. I display the data in log form in order to focus on the rate of growth. The straight line represents what the data would look like if the economic growth rate had been perfectly constant. The actual data points hug this line. In other words, despite occasional slowdowns and speedups, the rate of per capita GDP growth in the United States has essentially been constant for the past 120 years.[21] We've gone from being a country with a relatively small government to one with a medium-size government, and in doing so we've suffered no slowdown in economic growth.[22]

Now let's look at two big-government countries: Denmark and Sweden. Figure 4.6 shows trends in government revenues and in economic growth for these two nations. In both, government revenues jumped sharply, especially in the decades after World War II. Revenues stopped rising around 1990, flattening out in Denmark and falling back a bit in Sweden. Like the United

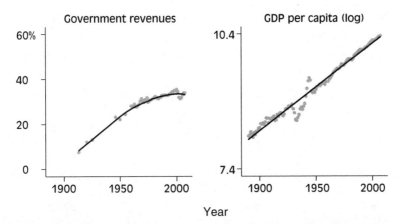

FIGURE 4.5 Government revenues and economic growth in the United States
Government revenues: Government revenues as a share of GDP. Includes all levels
of government: federal, state, and local. The line is a loess curve. *Data sources*: for
1960–2007, OECD, stats.oecd.org; for 1946–55, *Economic Report of the President* 2011,
tables B-79, B-86; for 1913–25, Vito Tanzi *Government versus Markets*, Cambridge
University Press, 2011, pp. 9, 92, with a minor adjustment. GDP per capita: Natural log
of inflation-adjusted GDP per capita. A log scale is used to focus on rates of change. The
vertical axis does not begin at zero. The line is a linear regression line; it represents a
constant rate of economic growth. *Data source*: Angus Maddison, www.ggdc.net/maddison/
historical_statistics/vertical-file_02-2010.xls.

States, these two countries have had a nearly constant rate of
economic growth since the late 1800s. A very large increase
in the size of government didn't knock either country off its
growth path.

A possible exception is what happened in Sweden around 1990.
At the end of the 1980s, government revenues in Sweden reached
65 percent of GDP. Shortly thereafter, the country experienced a
severe economic downturn. By 1995, revenues dropped to 60 percent of GDP, and the economy returned to its long-run growth
path. The onset of the early-1990s crisis stemmed mainly from the
deregulation of Swedish financial markets and the government's
pursuit of fiscal austerity during the downturn. Given that the
economic downturn coincided with a high point in government
revenues, it could be argued that government taxing and spending
at 65 percent of GDP is too high. Maybe that's correct. If we follow
that logic, however, then we must conclude that 60 percent of GDP,

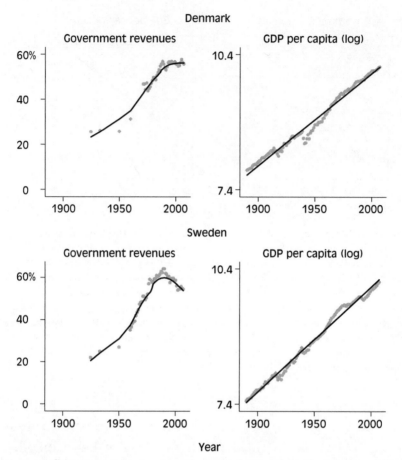

FIGURE 4.6 Government revenues and economic growth in Denmark and Sweden
Government revenues: Government revenues as a share of GDP. Includes all levels of
government: central, regional, and local. The lines are loess curves. *Data sources*: for
1960–2007, OECD, stats.oecd.org; for pre-1960, Vito Tanzi, *Government versus
Markets*, Cambridge University Press, 2011, table 13.2, with a minor adjustment. GDP
per capita: Natural log of inflation-adjusted GDP per capita. A log scale is used to focus
on rates of change. The vertical axis does not begin at zero. The lines are linear regression lines; they represent a constant rate of economic growth. *Data source*: Angus
Maddison, www.ggdc.net/maddison/historical_statistics/vertical-file_02-2010.xls.

the level of government revenues when the Swedish economy
returned to solid growth, is not too high.

When the United States is compared to countries like Denmark
and Sweden, a common objection is that the latter are small and
homogenous.[23] But the point here has nothing to do with simi-
larities or differences between these three countries. The point is

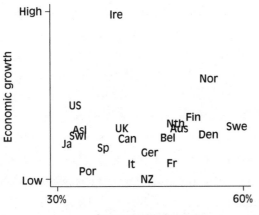

FIGURE 4.7 Government revenues and economic growth, 1979–2007
Government revenues: Average level of government revenues as a share of GDP, 1979–
2007. Includes all levels of government: central, regional, and local. *Data source*: OECD,
stats.oecd.org. Economic growth: Average annual rate of change in GDP per capita,
adjusted for initial level (catch-up), 1979–2007. *Data source*: OECD, stats.oecd.org. The
correlation is .11 (with Ireland and Norway excluded). "Asl" is Australia; "Aus" is Austria.

that developments over time *within* each of the three countries
tell a similar tale. In each, government taxing and spending rose
substantially—in the United States to about 35 percent of GDP,
in Denmark and Sweden as high as 60 percent—with no apparent
impact on economic growth.

Some might still object that only small, homogenous nations
can have a *big* government without hurting economic growth.
The story would be that a large, heterogeneous nation like
the United States may do just fine with a rise in government
spending of up to 35 percent of GDP, but beyond 35 percent
growth will slow down. It's conceivable that this is true, but the
story is based on assumption rather than evidence, so there is
reason for skepticism.

Let's extend the inquiry to the full set of twenty rich longstanding
democratic nations, concentrating, for reasons of data availability, on
the recent era. Given the shifts in the world and domestic economies
in the 1970s, I focus on the 1980s, 1990s, and 2000s.[24] Specifically,
I look at the period from 1979 to 2007 (both of these years were

business-cycle peaks). When comparing economic growth across nations, it's necessary to adjust for a process known as "catch-up," whereby countries that begin the period with lower per capita GDP grow more rapidly simply by virtue of starting behind.

Figure 4.7 shows the average level of government revenues (horizontal axis) and the average catch-up-adjusted economic growth rate (vertical axis) in these countries between 1979 and 2007. There is no association between the size of government and economic growth. More detailed cross-country studies have reached a similar conclusion.[25]

Can Our Economy Thrive with Less Institutional Coherence?

Though I favor significant changes to America's social programs, I see a need for only limited restructuring of other economic institutions, such as our financial system, corporate governance, labor relations, and so on. But might a shift toward more generous public social programs hurt the economy by disrupting the coherence of its current institutions and policies?

An influential perspective on differences among the world's rich nations, known as the *varieties of capitalism* approach, contends that economies perform better to the extent that their institutions and policies are coherent.[26] According to Peter Hall and David Soskice, those policies and institutions aren't drawn up in advance by a master planner, but because of selection pressures they end up fitting together. The result is a relatively coherent package—a gestalt, a whole that functions more effectively than the sum of its parts. So if we graft a set of social democratic government policies onto America's liberal market economy, will we upset the gestalt and thereby hurt the economy?

Hall and Soskice suggest that rich economies fall into one of two groups. Coordination is market-based in "liberal market economies," such as the United States and the United Kingdom.

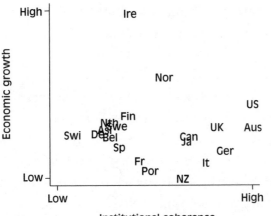

FIGURE 4.8 Institutional coherence and economic growth, 1979–2007
Economic growth: Average annual rate of change in GDP per capita, adjusted for
initial level (catch-up), 1979–2007. *Data source*: OECD, stats.oecd.org. Institutional
coherence: degree of coherence of institutions and policies within and across economic
spheres. *Data source*: Peter A. Hall and Daniel W. Gingerich, "Varieties of Capitalism and
Institutional Complementarities," *British Journal of Political Science*, 2009. The correlation is .01 (with Ireland and Norway excluded). "Asl" is Australia; "Aus" is Austria.

Coordination is based largely on nonmarket or extramarket institutions in "coordinated market economies" such as Germany and
Austria. Neither type, according to Hall and Soskice, is inherently
better at generating good economic performance. What matters
for successful economic growth is not the type of economic coordination, but the degree of institutional coherence. Countries with
coherent institutions—that is, with consistently market-oriented
or consistently non-market-oriented institutions and policies—
should grow more rapidly.[27]

Peter Hall and Daniel Gingerich have created a measure of institutional coherence for twenty rich nations, focusing on two economic spheres: labor relations and corporate governance. Nations
score higher to the extent that their institutions and policies are
coherent within each sphere and consistent across both spheres.[28]

Figure 4.8 shows countries' institutional coherence and their
rates of growth of GDP per capita from 1979 to 2007 (adjusted
for catch-up). There is no indication of the hypothesized positive
association between coherence and economic growth. All along the

coherence spectrum—at the high end, in the middle, and at the low end—there are some fast-growing nations and some slow-growing ones.[29]

The hypothesis that institutional coherence is good for economic growth makes sense. But the empirical record suggests it's wrong. Nations with hybrid institutions and policies, or with a mix that changes over time, have grown just as rapidly as those with more coherent arrangements.[30] Concern about a potential slowdown in economic growth resulting from inconsistent or shifting policies and institutions is therefore unjustified.

Does Innovation Require High Inequality and Minimal Cushions?

Daron Acemoglu, James Robinson, and Thierry Verdier also contend that there are two varieties of capitalism, but in their view one does tend to perform better than the other.[31] They hypothesize the following:

- Countries choose between two types of capitalism. "Cut-throat" capitalism provides large financial rewards to successful entrepreneurship. This yields high income inequality, but it stimulates entrepreneurial effort and hence is conducive to innovation. "Cuddly" capitalism features less financial payoff to entrepreneurs and more generous cushions against risk. This yields modest income inequality but less innovation.
- Because of the difference in innovation, economic growth is initially faster in cutthroat-capitalism nations. But technological advance spills over from cutthroat nations to cuddly ones, so growth rates then equalize. Over the long term, the level of GDP per capita is higher in cutthroat nations (due to the initial burst), while economic growth rates are similar for both types.

- Average well-being may be higher in cuddly countries because the more egalitarian distribution of economic output more than compensates for the lower level of output.
- Nevertheless, it would be bad for all countries if the cutthroat-capitalism nations switched to cuddly capitalism. That would reduce innovation in the (formerly) cutthroat nations, thus reducing economic growth in all nations.

Acemoglu, Robinson, and Verdier say their model might help us understand patterns of economic growth and well-being in the United States and the Nordic countries—Denmark, Finland, Norway, and Sweden. The United States has chosen cutthroat capitalism, whereas the Nordics have opted for cuddly capitalism. The United States grew faster for a short time, but since then, all five countries have grown at roughly the same pace. America's high inequality encourages innovation, so the Nordics can be cuddly and still grow rapidly because of technological spillover from the United States. If America were to decide to go cuddly, innovation would slow. Both sets of nations would then grow less rapidly.

How does this square with the data? To keep things simple, I'll compare the United States with just one of the Nordic nations: Sweden.

An indicator of financial incentives for entrepreneurs is the top 1 percent's share of household income. An indicator of the extent of cushions against risk is government expenditures' share of GDP. Both are shown in figure 4.9, going back to 1910. What we see in the data is a lot of similarity between the United States and Sweden until the second half of the twentieth century. Government spending begins to diverge in the 1960s, and income inequality diverges in the 1970s.

Sweden's top 1 percent get a smaller share of the total income than their American counterparts, but are incentives for entrepreneurs really much weaker in Sweden? Although Swedish CEOs and financial players don't pull in American-style paychecks and

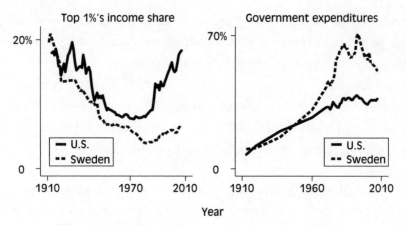

FIGURE 4.9 When did the United States go "cutthroat" and Sweden go "cuddly"? Top 1 percent's income share: share of pretax income, excluding capital gains. *Data source*: World Top Incomes Database, topincomes.g-mond.parisschoolofeconomics.eu. Government expenditures: government spending as a share of GDP. *Data sources*: Vito Tanzi, *Government versus Markets*, Cambridge University Press, 2011, table 1; OECD, stats.oecd.org.

bonuses in the tens of millions of dollars, there is little to prevent an entrepreneur from accumulating large sums of money. In the 1990s Sweden undertook a major tax reform, reducing marginal rates and eliminating loopholes and deductions. It lowered corporate income and capital gains tax rates to 30 percent and the personal income tax rate to 50 percent. Later, it did away with the wealth tax. In the early 2000s, a writer for *Forbes* magazine mused that Sweden had transformed itself from a "bloated welfare state" into a "people's republic of entrepreneurs."[32]

Suppose the incentives for entrepreneurs began to differ in the two countries around 1960 or 1970. The model predicts that innovation would diverge as well. Acemoglu, Robinson, and Verdier refer to a measure of patent applications per capita that shows the United States leading Sweden starting in the late 1990s. This timing is consistent with the model's prediction if we allow a substantial lag. But they also cite a measure that has the United States ahead of Sweden in 1980. This suggests that America's innovation advantage may have preceded the type-of-capitalism choice, rather than followed it.

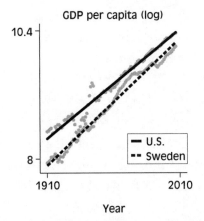

FIGURE 4.10 When did US and Swedish GDP per capita diverge?
Natural log of inflation-adjusted GDP per capita. A log scale is used to allow comparison
of rates of change. The lines are linear regression lines. *Data source*: Angus Maddison,
www.ggdc.net/maddison/historical_statistics/vertical-file_02-2010.xls.

The final outcome is GDP per capita. Here the model clearly
stumbles. As figure 4.10 shows, the gap between the two countries isn't recent; it started more than a century ago. Apart from
a few hiccups, each country has stayed on its long-run growth
path throughout the past one hundred years, with Sweden slowly
catching up to the United States.

The really interesting question posed by Acemoglu, Robinson,
and Verdier is whether innovation will slow in the United States
if we strengthen our safety net and/or reduce the relative financial payoff for entrepreneurial success. I doubt it will, for three
reasons.

The first is America's past experience. According to Acemoglu
and colleagues' logic, incentives for innovation in the United States
were weakest in the 1960s and 1970s. In 1960, the top 1 percent's
share of pretax income had been falling for several decades and
had nearly reached its low point. Government spending, meanwhile, had been rising steadily and was close to its peak level. Yet
there was plenty of innovation in the 1960s and 1970s, including
notable advances in computers, medical technology, and other
fields.

Second, the Nordic countries, with their low income inequality and generous safety nets, are now among the world's most innovative countries. The World Economic Forum's Global Competitiveness Index has consistently ranked them close to the United States in innovation. The most recent report, for 2012–13, rates Sweden as the world's most innovative nation, followed by Finland. The United States ranks sixth. The World Intellectual Property Organization (WIPO)-INSEAD Global Innovation Index 2012 ranks Sweden second and the United States tenth. This suggests reason to doubt that modest inequality and generous cushions are significant obstacles to innovation.

Third, if Acemoglu and colleagues are correct about the value of financial incentives in spurring innovation, we should see this reflected not only in the United States but also in other nations with relatively high income inequality and low-to-moderate government spending, such as Australia, Canada, Ireland, New Zealand, and the United Kingdom. But as figure 4.11 indicates, we don't.

There is one additional possibility worth considering. If financial incentives truly are critical for spurring innovation, it could be the opportunity for large gains that matters, not the absence of cushions. Suppose we increase government revenues in the United States by imposing higher taxes on everyone—steeper income taxes on the top 1 percent or 5 percent plus a new national consumption tax. Imagine we use those revenues to expand public insurance and services—fully universal health insurance, universal early education, a beefed-up EITC, a new wage insurance program, more individualized assistance with training and job placement. These changes wouldn't alter income inequality much, but they would enhance economic security and opportunity. Would innovation decline? I suspect not.

We may get a test of this moderate-to-high inequality with generous cushions scenario at some point. I suspect this is where America is heading, albeit slowly. Interestingly, the Nordic

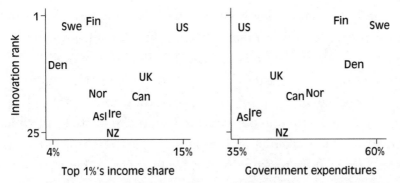

FIGURE 4.11 Is type of capitalism a good predictor of innovation when we include additional "cutthroat" nations?
"Cutthroat" nations: Australia, Canada, Ireland, New Zealand, United Kingdom, United States. "Cuddly" nations: Denmark, Finland, Norway, Sweden. Innovation rank: average ranking on the World Economic Forum's innovation index in 2008–09 and 2012–13.
Data source: World Economic Forum, *Global Competitiveness Report*, www.weforum.org/reports, pillar 12. Top 1 percent's income share: share of pretax income, excluding capital gains, 1989–2007. *Data source*: World Top Incomes Database, topincomes.g-mond.parisschoolofeconomics.eu. Government expenditures: government spending as a share of GDP, 1989–2007. *Data source*: OECD, stats.oecd.org.

countries, where the top 1 percent's income share has been trending upward, might get there first.[33]

Do We Know How to Grow Faster?

If healthy economic growth doesn't require small government, institutional coherence, or high income inequality, what *does* contribute to growth? Surprisingly, when it comes to rich nations, we don't really know.

Consider the United States since World War II. From the mid-1940s through the early 1970s, the American economy experienced healthy growth, low unemployment, and modest inflation. But then the economy sputtered for a decade—a deep downturn in 1973–75, followed by high unemployment and inflation, followed in turn by a double-dip recession in 1980 and 1981–82. Stagflation, manufacturing decline, and foreign competition had policy makers befuddled.

The changed context spurred a slew of recommendations on how to rejuvenate the economy. The right blamed government overreach. Taxes, regulations, Keynesian demand management, and welfare state generosity had all, in this view, gone too far.[34] The left proposed myriad solutions, including industrial policy, managed trade, a stakeholder-centered financial system, flexible specialization, lean production, corporatist partnerships between business, labor, and government, and collaboration between and within firms.[35]

In the mid-to-late 1990s, during the Clinton presidency, a Clinton-Reich-Rubin-Sperling variant of pro-growth progressivism emerged.[36] It embraced some of these ideas but emphasized education and skill development, free trade, and a (social democratic[37]) commitment to balance the government budget during economic upswings. Like the "Third Way" orientation championed by Anthony Giddens and Tony Blair in the United Kingdom,[38] the aim was to reconcile traditional justice and fairness concerns of the left with an emphasis on economic growth. The approach maintained a commitment to basic economic security but de-emphasized equality of outcomes in favor of enhancing opportunity, capabilities, and employment.

As it turned out, America's economic growth from 1979 to 2007 was pretty healthy.[39] It was slower than during the post–World War II "golden age." But that isn't surprising; growth was especially rapid in those years because it had been so slow in the 1930s and because so much of the industrial capacity in Western Europe and Japan was destroyed during the war. US GDP per capita grew at a rate of 1.9 percent per year between 1979 and 2007. That's right on the long-run trend; the American economy's average growth rate from 1890 to 2007 was 1.9 percent.[40] The United States also did well in 1979–2007 compared to nineteen other rich longstanding democracies. If we adjust for catch-up—nations that begin poorer grow more rapidly because they can borrow technology from the leaders—America's growth rate was third best.

Unfortunately, we know little about why. Was it due to the US economy's traditional strengths, such as its large domestic market and its array of large firms with established brands? To its strong universities and research and development (R&D), which keyed a successful transition to a high-tech service economy? To deregulation, tax cuts, and wage stagnation? To the adoption of some of the strategies proposed by the pro-growth progressives? To stimulative monetary policy (after the early 1980s)? To stock market and housing bubbles? To something else? We don't know.

Nor do social scientists have a compelling explanation for why some rich nations have grown more rapidly than others in recent decades. We know that catch-up matters. Limited product and labor market regulations and participation by business and labor in policy making ("corporatism") seem to help, but they account for only a small portion of the country differences in economic growth between 1979 and 2007.[41] Even education seems to have played little or no role. Growth hinges on technological progress, which should be boosted by education, particularly in the modern knowledge-driven economy. Yet across the rich countries, those with higher average years of schooling, larger shares of university graduates, or faster increase in educational attainment have not grown more rapidly than others since the 1970s.[42]

An interesting and perplexing piece of the growth puzzle is the tendency of countries to do well for a while and then falter. In the past half century, a number of national models have gone in and out of fashion, first surging to the front and then falling back: Sweden ("middle way") in the 1960s, Germany ("modell Deutschland") and Japan ("Japan Inc.") in the 1970s and 1980s, the United States ("great American jobs machine") in the 1980s and 1990s, the Netherlands ("Dutch miracle") in the 1990s, Denmark ("flexicurity") and Ireland ("Celtic tiger") in the 1990s and 2000s. Some later rebounded, such as Sweden in the 2000s and Germany in the 2010s.

Economic growth is valuable. Yet for affluent democratic countries, we know very little about what causes faster or slower growth. Should we throw up our hands in despair? Not necessarily. The upside is that policies and institutions aimed at other outcomes, such as security and fairness, seldom doom the economy to stagnation.

A Future of Slow Growth?

Will the economies of rich nations such as the United States continue to grow at a healthy clip? Some are pessimistic. A key reason for pessimism is the shift from manufacturing to services. In most manufacturing industries, there is significant room for improvement in efficiency. In many services, that is not true. Think of cleaning rooms in a hotel or waiting tables in a restaurant or performing basic nursing tasks in a hospital. Productivity improvement in these jobs is difficult, in part because they are hard to automate. William Baumol calls this the "cost disease" of services.[43] If a significant portion of our economy consists of such tasks, the thinking goes, we could be stuck with low growth.

I suspect this is wrong. While productivity improvement is difficult in low-end services, it is not impossible. Hotels, for instance, have made considerable strides in improving efficiency in room cleaning. Yes, improvement in services occurs at a slower pace than in manufacturing, but it happens. Think, too, of telephone operators, typists, bank tellers, and travel reservation agents. These positions have been largely automated via advances in technology.

Moreover, even if productivity growth is sluggish in low-end services, it may, as Baumol himself points out, be rapid in other parts of the economy.[44] Technological advance and improvements in work organization can yield leaps forward. The computer and communications revolutions already have generated considerable advance in manufacturing, finance, and an array of other services. They will soon do so in medicine, education, and elsewhere.

In recent years, several analysts, including Robert Gordon and Tyler Cowen, have expressed pessimism about the likelihood of further productivity-enhancing innovations.[45] The information technology revolution has largely run its course, they say, and in any case it never boosted productivity to the same degree as earlier innovations such as steam engines, railroads, electricity, the assembly line, indoor heating and air conditioning, running water, sewers, roads, and the internal combustion engine.

It's true that we don't see the benefits of the IT revolution in the productivity statistics. But that doesn't necessarily mean there has been a decline in innovation or in the payoff from innovation. For one thing, benefits may appear only after a nontrivial delay. The period of strongest productivity growth stemming from earlier innovation was the thirty years between the mid-1940s and the mid-1970s, but that was quite a while after the innovations occurred. The same may be true for the digital revolution.

For another, since the 1970s the impact of innovation on productivity has been partly masked by rising employment. Productivity is calculated as output per employed person or per hour worked. Since employment is the denominator, a significant increase in employment will reduce the measured amount of productivity growth. In the 1950s and 1960s, the share of American adults with a paying job held steady at about 56 percent. In the 1970s, 1980s, and 1990s that share increased steadily, reaching 64 percent at the end of the 1990s before leveling off in the 2000–2007 business cycle.[46] This is part of the reason measured productivity growth has been slower in recent decades.

Finally, as countries shift away from fossil fuels toward renewable sources of energy, the world's existing commercial and residential building space will need to be retrofitted or rebuilt from scratch. This promises to be a source of growth for quite some time.

Rapid economic growth is a relatively recent phenomenon, dating from the beginning of the Industrial Revolution around

1750. There is no reason to assume it will continue forever. But nor are there compelling grounds for thinking it will halt anytime soon. Innovation is a product of innate human creativity, education, and an institutional framework that provides financial reward to successful innovators.[47] As long as countries such as the United States ensure ample opportunity for learning and don't allow large firms or government regulations to stifle incentives for innovation, we should expect a relatively robust rate of economic advance.

Is Big Government Bad for Employment?

Working-age Belgians, French, and Germans spend, on average, about 1,000 hours a year in paid employment. In the United States, Switzerland, and New Zealand, by contrast, the average is about 1,300 hours. That's a big difference. Is it due to differences in the size of government?

These averages are determined by the share of people who have a paying job and by the number of hours they work over the course of a year. In the United States, for instance, the employment rate in 2007 was 72 percent, and the employed worked an average of 1,800 hours (.72 x 1,800 ≈ 1,300). In France, the employment rate was 64 percent, and the average number of hours worked was 1,550 (.64 x 1,550 ≈ 1,000).[48]

Because high taxes reduce the financial reward for paid work, they may reduce employment.[49] On the other hand, as I noted earlier, some people might work *more* when taxes are higher, in order to reach their desired after-tax income. And lots of other things affect people's calculations about whether and how much to work, including wage levels, employment and working-time regulations, paid vacation time and holidays, availability and generosity of government income transfers, access to health insurance and retirement benefits, the cost of services such as childcare, and preferences for work versus leisure.[50]

Figure 4.12 shows the association between government revenues as a share of GDP over the years 1979 to 2007 and employment hours per working-age person in 2007. The pattern looks broadly supportive of the notion that high taxes reduce work hours.

But knowledgeable comparativists will notice a familiar clustering of countries in figure 4.12.[51] One group, in the lower-right corner, includes Belgium, France, Germany, Italy, and the Netherlands. These countries, along with Austria, have several features that might contribute to low employment hours. One is strong unions. Organized labor has been the principal force pushing for a shorter work week, more holiday and vacation time, and earlier retirement. These nations are also characterized by a preference for traditional family roles—breadwinner husband, homemaker wife. This preference, often associated with Catholicism and Christian Democratic political parties, is likely to influence women's employment rates and work hours. It is manifested in lengthy paid maternity leaves, lack

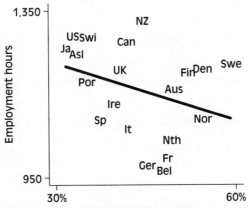

FIGURE 4.12 Government revenues in 1979–2007 and employment hours in 2007
The line is a linear regression line. Government revenues: Average level of government revenues as a share of GDP, 1979–2007. Includes all levels of government: central, regional, and local. *Data source*: OECD, stats.oecd.org. Employment hours: employment rate (employed persons as a share of the population age 15–64) multiplied by average yearly employment hours per employed person, 2007. *Data source*: OECD, stats.oecd.org. The correlation is –.34. "Asl" is Australia; "Aus" is Austria.

of government support for childcare, income tax structures that discourage second earners within households, and practices such as Germany's school day ending at lunch time and France's schools being closed on Wednesday afternoons. These countries also fund their social insurance programs through heavy payroll taxes, the kind most likely to discourage employment growth in low-end services.[52]

A second group consists of the four Nordic nations: Denmark, Sweden, Finland, and Norway. These countries also have strong unions. But they have had electorally successful social democratic parties that promote high employment.[53] Denmark and Sweden, in particular, have led the way in using active labor market programs to help get young or displaced persons into jobs, public employment to fill gaps in the private labor market, and government support for childcare and preschool to facilitate women's employment.

The third group of countries, in the upper-left corner, includes Australia, Canada, Japan, New Zealand, and the United States. These nations have relatively weak labor movements and limited influence of social democratic parties and Catholic traditional-family orientations.

The other five countries—Ireland, Portugal, Spain, Switzerland, and the United Kingdom—are a hodgepodge.[54]

Based on their institutional-political makeup, we would expect the weak-labor countries to have comparatively high employment hours, the social-democratic countries to be intermediate, and the traditional-family-roles countries to have low hours. As figure 4.13 indicates, that's exactly what we see.

If we adjust statistically for institutional-political group membership, the negative association between tax levels and work hours shown in figure 4.12 disappears. Differences in union strength and in preferences for traditional family roles are the likely source of differences in employment hours across the world's rich nations.[55]

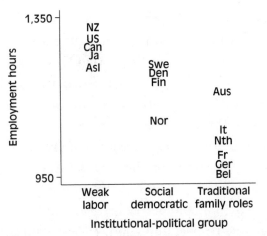

FIGURE 4.13 Institutional-political group and employment hours, 2007
Institutional-political group: See the text for description. Employment hours: employment
rate (employed persons as a share of the population aged 15–64) multiplied by average
yearly employment hours per employed person, 2007. *Data source*: OECD, stats.oecd.org.
The correlation is –.89. "Asl" is Australia; "Aus" is Austria.

Is Big Government Bad for Liberty?

Public provision of social services and transfers is paternalistic.
Government takes money from us and spends it to ensure economic security, expand opportunity, and enhance living standards. In doing so, it reduces individual freedom.[56]

That isn't especially objectionable. Only diehard libertarians
believe individual liberty should trump all other considerations.
Virtually everyone supports government paternalism in the form
of property protection, traffic lights, and food safety regulations,
to mention just a few examples. And many people support public
social programs. When our basic needs are met, we tend to want
greater security, broader opportunity, and confidence that living
standards will improve over time. We are willing to allocate some
of our present and future income to guarantee these things, and
we are willing to allow government to take on that task. That's
why public social programs tend to expand in size and scope as
nations grow richer.

Does a big safety net imply other limitations on economic liberty? No, it doesn't. In fact, a social democratic approach to government can feature a relatively light regulatory touch. In the best real-world examples of modern social democracy, the Nordic nations, government sets basic standards for employee and consumer protections, but it doesn't tell economic actors how to meet those standards. The aim is to maximize individuals' opportunities and to provide security for those who fail (consistent with the spirit of our limited liability and bankruptcy protections) while impinging as little as possible on competition and flexibility. It's big government in one respect and small government in another.

We can see this in some prominent measures of economic liberty. The Heritage Foundation, a conservative think tank, partners with the *Wall Street Journal* to score countries on ten dimensions of economic freedom: security of property rights, freedom from corruption, business freedom (the right to establish and run an enterprise without interference from the state), labor freedom (absence of hiring and firing restrictions and other limitations on work conditions), monetary freedom (a stable currency and market-determined prices), trade freedom (absence of regulatory barriers to imports and exports), investment freedom (absence of restrictions on the movement of capital), financial freedom (a transparent and unrestricted financial system), low taxes ("fiscal freedom"), and low government spending. The vertical axis in figure 4.14 shows the average scores for the United States and other rich nations on eight of these ten dimensions, with the taxes and government spending dimensions left out. Three of the four Nordic countries score higher than the United States.

A relatively similar picture emerges from the World Bank's scoring of the ease of doing business. Countries are ranked according to how easy it is to start a business, deal with construction permits, register property, get credit, protect investors, pay taxes, trade across borders, enforce contracts, resolve insolvency, and get electricity. The rankings on these aspects of doing business are then combined to establish an overall ranking. The rich countries'

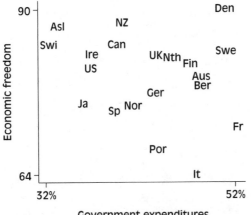

FIGURE 4.14 Government spending and economic freedom
Economic freedom is measured as the average score for eight items: business freedom, trade freedom, monetary freedom, investment freedom, financial freedom, property rights freedom, freedom from corruption, labor freedom. Each item is scored from 0 to 100. Data are for 2012. *Data source*: Heritage Foundation, www.heritage.org/index. Government spending: total government expenditures as a share of GDP, in 2007. *Data source*: OECD, stats.oecd.org. The correlation is –.14 (with Italy excluded). "Asl" is Australia; "Aus" is Austria.

positions in the rank-ordering of all countries is shown on the vertical axis in figure 4.15. Here the United States edges out the Nordic nations, but not by much. Two of the Nordic countries are among the top four, and the other two are among the top nine.

In other words, a nation can tax and spend quite heavily while still giving economic actors considerable freedom to start and operate a business, allocate capital, hire and fire employees, and engage in all manner of economic activities. This approach is sometimes called "flexicurity." Government allows individuals and firms substantial freedom, with one exception: they pay a significant share of their earnings to the collectivity. This revenue is used to enhance security and opportunity and to ensure that prosperity is widely shared across the society. Economic freedom is abridged in one important respect, but is kept at a high level in all others.

This approach is tailor-made for a country like the United States, where citizens and firms prize economic liberty and flexibility.

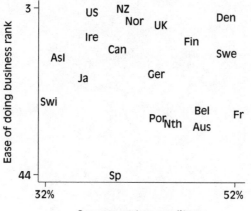

FIGURE 4.15 Government spending and ease of doing business
Ease of doing business: country rank in 2011. Italy's rank is 87; it is omitted here. *Data source*: World Bank, www.doingbusiness.org/rankings. Government spending: total government expenditures as a share of GDP, in 2007. *Data source*: OECD, stats.oecd.org. The correlation is .12 (with Italy excluded). "Asl" is Australia; "Aus" is Austria.

Does Big Government Reduce Competition?

Competition drives innovation and economic dynamism. Americans embrace competition as much or more than their counterparts in any other rich nation. Yet our economy is riddled with rules, regulations, and practices that inhibit competition or privilege particular firms and industries. Half-hearted antitrust enforcement allows corporate behemoths to maintain market share and profitability despite little innovation. Patents limit competition in pharmaceuticals, computer software, entertainment, and a slew of other product markets.[57] Licensing, credentialing, and certification requirements for occupations or particular types of businesses dampen competition in product markets ranging from medical care to legal services to education to taxi transportation to hairdressing and beyond.[58] Zoning restrictions and historic preservation designations limit the expansion of housing units in large cities by imposing building height restrictions and preventing new construction on much of the land.[59] The federal government's practice of treating large banks as "too big to fail" allows those banks to engage in riskier strategies, with potentially higher profit margins, and encourages investors to choose those banks over competitors. Both investors and management know that they are likely to be rescued by taxpayers if their bets go sour.[60] Our federal tax code is chock-full of exemptions, loopholes, and benefits for particular firms and sectors.

Does an increase in the size of government weaken competition? On one view, the answer is yes. Here is Luigi Zingales, channeling Milton Friedman:

> When government is small and relatively weak, the most effective way to make money is to start a successful private-sector business. But the larger the size and scope of government spending, the easier it is to make money by diverting public resources. After all, starting a business is difficult and involves a lot of risk. Getting a government favor or contract is easier, at least if you have connections, and is a much safer bet.[61]

This sounds sensible. But figure 4.16 shows that across the rich nations there is no association between the magnitude of government expenditures and the degree of competition in product markets. Competition is measured here as the degree of intensity of local competition, the degree to which corporate activity is spread across many firms rather than dominated by a few, the degree to which anti-monopoly policy effectively promotes competition, and the absence of barriers to imports. The scoring for each of these elements is based on a survey of executives conducted by the World Economic Forum. Though not a foolproof measure of competition, this is likely to be a reasonably accurate one. The data suggest that nations with big governments are just as likely as those with small governments to have competitive product markets.

Why is that? First, the hypothesis that big government results in less competition fails to consider the types of programs that make government big. Public insurance programs mainly transfer

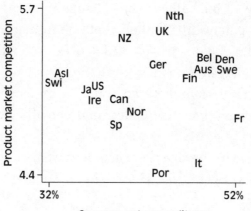

FIGURE 4.16 Government expenditures and product market competition
Product market competition: average responses by executives in each country in 2011–2012 to four questions: (1) How would you assess the intensity of competition in the local markets in your country? 1 = limited in most industries; 7 = intense in most industries. (2) How would you characterize corporate activity in your country? 1 = dominated by a few business groups; 7 = spread among many firms. (3) To what extent does anti-monopoly policy promote competition in your country? 1 = does not promote competition; 7 = effectively promotes competition. (4) In your country, to what extent do tariff and nontariff barriers limit the ability of imported goods to compete in the domestic market? 1 = strongly limit; 7 = do not limit. *Data source*: World Economic Forum, *The Global Competitiveness Report 2012–13*, www.weforum.org/reports. For survey details, see pp. 69–78 of the report. Government expenditures are measured as a share of GDP, in 2007. *Data source*: OECD, stats.oecd.org. The correlation is .04. "Asl" is Australia; "Aus" is Austria.

money to individuals; they offer little opportunity for firms or interest groups to grab a piece of the pie. This is largely true for government provision of services as well. Opportunity for large-scale diversion of public resources is present mainly in government service programs that rely on private provision, such as the US military or Medicare's prescription drug benefit.

Zingales discusses a number of instances of American firms seeking and obtaining government favors. But most are efforts to avoid regulations or to shape regulations to their benefit; relatively few are attempts to gobble up government spending. A more generous set of social policies implies higher government expenditures as a share of GDP, but it need not imply greater regulation. Zingales has in mind countries like Italy, which has a government that both spends a great deal and regulates heavily. But as the measures of economic liberty shown in the previous section reveal, there are other possibilities. The Nordic nations have comparatively high expenditure levels but modest regulations on business activity.

Second, much of firms' political activity involves lobbying for tax favors. If they devote a great deal of effort to this and succeed, the result will be a smaller state—in terms of expenditures as a share of GDP—rather than a larger one. American business is surely a world leader at lobbying for preferential tax treatment, and the loopholes, deductions, and exemptions in our tax system leave our government with less revenue, not more.

The hypothesis that higher government spending will lessen competition in product markets seems compelling. But in practice that's not what we observe. An expansion of America's public social programs is likely to have little or no impact on competition.

Does Big Government Mean Bad Government?

A related argument, made by Alberto Alesina and George-Marios Angeletos, is that "a large government increases corruption and rent-seeking."[62] The more a government taxes and spends, in this view, the more it invites lobbying by interest groups for favors, and the more opportunity and incentive it creates for policy makers and other public officials to dispense such favors.

Do big governments perform worse than small ones? There are various ways to measure the quality of government.[63] A common indicator is the World Bank's government effectiveness measure, which attempts to gauge public and expert perceptions of the quality of public services, the quality of the civil service and the degree of its independence from political pressures, the quality of policy formulation and implementation, and the credibility of the government's commitment to such policies. Figure 4.17 shows the relationship between countries' scores on this measure and their

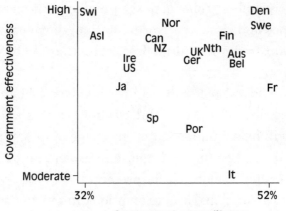

FIGURE 4.17 Government expenditures and government quality
Government effectiveness attempts to capture perceptions of the quality of public services, the civil service and the degree of its independence from political pressures, policy
formulation and implementation, and of the credibility of the government's commitment
to such policies. Measured in 2007. The data set includes most of the world's countries,
so "moderate" or "high" government effectiveness is relative to this larger group. *Data
source*: Jan Teorell, Nicholas Charron, Marcus Samanni, Sören Holmberg, and Bo
Rothstein, The Quality of Government Dataset, version April 6, 2011, University of
Gothenburg: The Quality of Government Institute, www.qog.pol.gu.se, variable WBGI_
GEE, using data from the World Bank. Government expenditures are measured as a
share of GDP, in 2007. *Data source*: OECD, stats.oecd.org. The correlation is −.12. "Asl"
is Australia; "Aus" is Austria.

level of government spending as of 2007. There is no association.
Countries with bigger governments don't tend to have less effective ones.[64]

Does Big Government Produce Excessively
Complex Policy?

The United States has some complicated government programs with an array of overlapping rules, benefits, and exemptions.[65] We have, for instance, an assortment of programs and
regulations that facilitate access to medical care: Medicare,
Medicaid, the Children's Health Insurance Program (CHIP),
the Veteran's Administration, tax breaks for employer contributions to employee health insurance, healthcare exchanges

run by federal and state governments in which private insurers compete for customers, a requirement that private insurance plans don't exclude people with preexisting conditions, a requirement that private plans allow parents to include their children up through age 25, and much more. Our tax system, with its multitude of deductions and exemptions, is equally complex.

This complexity can be costly. The IRS Taxpayer Advocate Service estimates that the direct and indirect costs of complying with the US tax code total more than $150 billion a year, or 1 percent of GDP.[66] Inefficiencies caused by overlapping regulations and jurisdictions in healthcare are likely considerable, though I'm not aware of concrete cost estimates. The chief beneficiaries are those who lobby for and are best able to take advantage of the multitude of specific provisions and exemptions—industries, firms, and affluent individuals.

Simpler would be less costly. The tax overhaul in 1986 removed a number of exemptions and deductions and was able to raise the same revenue with lower tax rates. Similarly, a Medicare for All healthcare system would likely be less expensive. In both cases, a simpler system also would reduce ordinary Americans' confusion and frustration.

Is policy complexity caused by government's size? No. Social Security is one of our biggest government programs, but it also is very simple. Medicare for All would increase government expenditures' share of GDP, but it would be much less complex than the system we have now. The size of government and the complexity of government policy are distinct issues.

Policy complexity in the United States is a result not of government's size but of its structure. Our policy-making process is ridden with veto points that allow legislative opponents and interest groups to insert loopholes and special benefits in exchange for allowing proposed policies to go forward. The fact that we have multiple levels of government—federal, state, local—often adds an additional layer of complexity.

Does Big Government Turn Us into Moochers?

A frequent concern about big government is that it breeds dependency. Republican presidential candidate Mitt Romney famously quipped that there are

> 47 percent of Americans...who are dependent upon government, who believe that they are victims, who believe that government has a responsibility to care for them, who believe that they are entitled to health care, to food, to housing, to you name it—that that's an entitlement and the government should give it to them.[67]

Nicholas Eberstadt makes a more detailed case for this sentiment in his book *A Nation of Takers*.[68] Eberstadt notes that over the past half century, the share of Americans who receive a government cash transfer and/or public health insurance—Social Security, Medicare, Medicaid, unemployment compensation, and so on—has grown steadily. The United States, he concludes, is now "on the verge of a symbolic threshold: the point at which more than half of all American households receive, and accept, transfer benefits from the government." According to Eberstadt, growing reliance on government for help is undermining Americans' "fierce and principled independence," our "proud self-reliance."

Is this really reason for concern? Eberstadt's alarm stems from his deployment of a misleading dichotomy. In his view, people are either givers or takers—taxpayers or benefit recipients. But this is mistaken. Each of us is both a giver and a taker. Every American who doesn't live entirely off the grid pays some taxes. Anyone who is an employee pays payroll taxes, and anyone who purchases things at a store pays sales taxes. Likewise, every American receives benefits from government—if you or your children have attended a public school, if you've driven on a road, if you've had a drink of tap water or taken a shower in your dwelling, if you've deducted mortgage interest payments or a business expense from your federal income taxes, if you haven't been stricken by polio, if you've never had a band of thugs remove you from your home at gunpoint, if you've visited a park or lounged on a beach or hiked a mountain trail, if you've used the Internet, and on and on.

Eberstadt's emphasis on receipt of cash from government also is puzzling. He thinks receiving a government cash transfer or health insurance somehow renders people less self-reliant than receiving the myriad public goods, services, and tax breaks that government provides. But why?

Once upon a time, individuals and privately organized militias ensured the public safety. Then we shifted to government police forces and armies. At one point humans got their own water and disposed of their own waste. Then we created public water and sewage systems. The education of children was once a family responsibility. Then we created public schools. There's a good reason for these shifts: government provision offers economies of scale and scope, which reduces the cost of a good or service and thereby makes it available to many people who can't or won't get it on their own. Did Americans' character or spirit diminish when these changes occurred? Is there something different about the more recent shift from individual to government responsibility in how we deal with retirement saving, healthcare, unemployment, and other risks? Here Eberstadt is silent.

Government does more now than it used to. All of us, not just some, are dependent on it. And life is better because of it.

Revitalize Families?

In 1950s and 1960s America, many large employers offered their employees health insurance and a generous pension. Most children grew up in a stable family with both of their biological parents. Churches, parent-teacher associations (PTAs), Kiwanis Clubs, sports teams, and other community organizations helped to foster a cooperative spirit, aid struggling adults and children, and check government abuse of authority. Labor unions helped to ensure rising wages and improvements in working conditions and product safety.[69]

Some elements of American life during that era, particularly the racism and sexism and other forms of intolerance, have deservedly been relegated to history's dustbin. But what of families and voluntary associations? Could families, community groups, and labor unions achieve economic security, equal opportunity, and shared prosperity as well or better than the government programs I highlighted in chapter 3?

Let's begin with families. (The next section looks at communities, and I'll come to unions later in the chapter.) Historically, the family has played a central role in providing economic security, promoting opportunity, and enhancing living standards for its members. But in the past half century marriage has decreased among Americans, and so too has the share of children growing up in intact families.[70]

Our principal concern should be the children. As figure 4.18 shows, the share of American kids living with both biological parents decreased by nearly twenty percentage points over the past half century.[71] We have substantial evidence, first marshaled by Sara McLanahan and Gary Sandefur in the mid-1990s and steadily buttressed since then, that children who grow up with both biological parents tend to fare better on a range of outcomes, from school completion and performance to crime to earnings and income to maintaining lasting relationships.[72] This advantage holds compared to children whose parents never married, who married and then divorced, or who married, divorced, and remarried.[73]

But it's not just the kids who are affected. In the past generation median income has increased only for households and families with two earners. For those with a single earner it has been flat.[74] And the risk that unemployment, sickness, or disability will result in significant income decline is much greater among households with only a single adult. As Ross Douthat and Reihan Salam point out, "For the working-class American, who inhabits a more

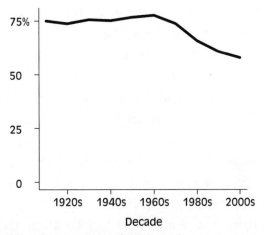

FIGURE 4.18 Children living with both biological parents at age 16
Data source: General Social Survey, sda.berkeley.edu/archive.htm, series family16.

precarious world than the rich or the upper-middle class, family stability is a prerequisite for financial stability."[75]

Three shifts have combined to delay marriage and reduce its prevalence among American women.[76] The first is their financial autonomy. Since the 1950s, women have become better educated and more likely to be employed and to earn enough to live independently. Plus, government benefits allow those with limited labor market prospects to survive without depending on a husband. For many women, marriage is no longer a financial necessity. Second, along with this change, and in part because of it, the stigma attached to divorce, nonmarital cohabitation, and out-of-wedlock childbearing has dissipated. Third, women's expectations of partnership and fulfillment have increased. Women are now much less likely to marry, or stay married to, a man who isn't a good partner.

What hasn't changed is women's desire to have children. This helps us understand a key feature of the decline of marriage and of both-biological-parent child rearing in America: it is much more pronounced among those with less education.[77] Better-educated adults are now a little less likely to stay together to raise children, while less-educated adults are *much* less likely to do so.

Better-educated women now place considerable emphasis on a career, so they delay not only marriage but also pregnancy and childbearing. This gives them more time to get established and to find the right partner. Among less-educated women, in contrast, age at first pregnancy and first childbirth hasn't changed. Because they take less time to mature personally and to find a partner with whom they are compatible, because their partners' financial prospects tend to be weaker, because their partners more often have a preference for traditional gender roles, and because the presence of a child can heighten financial and interpersonal tensions, women with less education are less likely than their better-educated counterparts to stay with their child's biological father. For these reasons, the decline in marriage, in happiness among those who are married, in sustained cohabitation, and in both-biological-parent child rearing is much sharper among the less educated. This is true across racial and ethnic groups.

In fact, among Americans with a college degree or better the decline in family is minimal. They are less likely to marry or stay married than their counterparts of half a century ago and less likely, whether married or not, to remain together throughout their kids' childhood. But the change has been minor. The collapse of the two-biological-parent family has occurred mainly among those without a college degree, and particularly among those who haven't completed high school.

If marriage were being replaced by long-term cohabitation, we might have little reason for worry. In principle, cohabitation can confer the same advantages as marriage. Look at Sweden. Relatively few Swedish children have parents who are married, yet many live with both biological parents throughout childhood. In effect, cohabitation is a substitute for marriage. The United States is different. More Americans are cohabiting, but most cohabiting partners split up. As of the early 1990s (the most recent data I'm aware of), a Swedish child born to cohabiting parents had about a 60 percent chance that her parents would still be together fifteen years later. Her American counterpart had about a 20 percent chance.[78]

Proposals for revitalizing family in America usually aim to increase marriage.[79] One recommendation is to restructure government taxes and benefits to more strongly favor marriage, with a special focus on rewarding marriage among couples with low incomes. A second is to mount an advertising and messaging campaign aimed at shifting the culture, perhaps coupled with enhanced dissemination of information. A third is to provide intensive marital counseling sessions and support services for vulnerable couples.

Unfortunately, none of these recommendations is likely to have much success in revitalizing marriage.[80] More important, the focus on marriage is misplaced.[81] Getting more low-income couples in their teens or early twenties who find themselves pregnant to decide to marry is unlikely to produce many lasting relationships. The shotgun wedding approach worked a half century ago because marriage was a financial necessity for many women and because they tended to have limited expectation of emotional fulfillment or shared decision making in a relationship. This has changed.[82] If more couples in that position were to get married these days, many of them might end up divorced.

The key is for more women with limited education to delay childbirth until their mid-to-late twenties, when they are in a better position financially or at least are more likely to have found a genuinely suitable partner.[83] Greater availability of stable jobs along with higher wages probably would help, particularly if supplemented by a more generous EITC for those without children. This would make less-educated men more attractive as long-term partners or husbands.[84] And it would heighten the influence of employment in women's calculations about when to have a child. At the moment, many women with little education consider their work prospects to be so dim that they are eager to move quickly to what they perceive as the other key source of fulfillment in life: having a child.[85]

When a trend is moving in the wrong direction, our first incli-
nation is to try to reverse it. But this isn't always the most useful
approach. Sometimes the wisest course of action is to offset the
adverse impacts. I believe that's our best bet with respect to family
decline. We should look for institutions and policies that can help
struggling families, particularly families with a single adult or
limited labor-market capability. Denmark and Sweden have effective programs: one-year paid parental leave and high-quality
affordable early education. I discussed both in chapter 3.

Opponents of these programs come from various camps. Some
oppose the expansion of government because they believe it
constricts liberty or harms the economy. I suggested earlier
in the chapter that these arguments aren't compelling. Others
worry that a government early education program will weaken
the family as an institution. Of course, some might have had
the same fear when public elementary and secondary schools
were introduced, but no evidence suggests that universal public
K-12 schooling is a key cause of family decline. There is the
further awkward fact that fewer American children grow up in
homes with both biological parents than do their counterparts
in Sweden, a nation with extensive public early education. As
I noted above, Swedish parents don't marry as frequently as
American parents, but they are more likely to stay together,
often as cohabiting couples.

Other opponents support helping families but favor a strategy
that is neutral with respect to parental employment. Some suggest a cash grant or tax benefit that would allow a family to *either*
pay for good-quality childcare and preschool *or* keep one parent
at home.[86] This is what Finland and Norway do. Since 2008, some
municipalities in Sweden also have offered a small home-care
allowance. This approach offers parents more choice, but it has
two drawbacks. First, it leads mothers to stay out of the labor
market longer, which hurts their long-run employment, promotion, and earnings prospects, a problem that could be particularly pronounced in the American context.[87] Based on an in-depth

study of 160 women with limited education, Kathryn Edin and Maria Kefalas conclude that, because they see their labor-market prospects as poor, these women view children as the key source of meaning and fulfillment in their lives.[88] Offering this group a subsidy to stay home might further weaken their labor-market attachment.[89] Second, this approach may be suboptimal for children in less advantaged households. Income is only one of many disadvantages in such households.[90] Early education is likely to be more effective than additional household income in offsetting these barriers to opportunity.[91]

To summarize: Families play a vital role in ensuring economic security, enhancing opportunity, and raising living standards. Yet the American family has weakened considerably, mainly among those with less education. Gone are the days when a couple who gets pregnant and has a child in their late teens or early twenties stays together through thick and thin. Expectations of satisfaction from a partnership are higher, the stigma attached to out-of-wedlock birth and divorce has faded, and economic necessity no longer exerts the same influence on women. Women with college degrees are delaying having children until they find a partner with whom they have a decent shot at long-term harmony and happiness. When they have kids, they are now only a little less likely to stay together than their grandparents were. In contrast, many women with less education still get pregnant and have a child before their mid-twenties. Whether they marry the father or not, the relationships seldom last. Many of these children do not grow up in a household with both of their original parents.

We can alter this trend, through a combination of increased women's education, improved financial prospects for those at the low end of the labor market, and a shift in attitudes among less-educated women in favor of later childbearing. But it may take a while, and in the meantime we could do a lot of good for children and parents by providing year-long paid parental leave and high-quality, affordable early education.

Revitalize Communities?

Communities, like families, are considered a mainstay of well-being in the United States. Churches, PTAs, civic clubs, sports leagues, YMCAs, and other community organizations underpin America's success, according to some, because they enable us to address social and economic needs without a big government. These organizations foster norms conducive to employment and civic participation, facilitate trust and thereby enhance economic cooperation, sponsor activities that keep adolescents and young men occupied and out of trouble, assist the less fortunate, and monitor and participate in political decision making.

Alexis de Tocqueville, Robert Putnam, Theda Skocpol, and Charles Murray, all keen observers of American society, have linked the health of the country to the health of its communities and voluntary organizations.[92] Putnam, for example, finds civic participation to be associated with government quality across regions in Italy, economic success across nations, and a host of social, economic, and political outcomes across America's states.[93]

Can community organizations address America's current deficits in economic security, opportunity, and shared prosperity?

The problem is twofold. First, like families, community organizations are weakening, and this trend is unlikely to reverse. After calculating average membership in thirty-two national chapter-based associations, Putnam finds a steady drop between 1970 and 2000 (the last year in his analysis).[94] Using time diary data to calculate the extent of participation in civic associations, Robert Anderson and colleagues also find a decline beginning in the 1970s.[95] Theda Skocpol points out that as the older organizations studied by Putnam have decayed, they have been replaced by newer ones. But the new organizations, according to Skocpol, tend to be professionally managed mass-membership groups. "Participation" often consists simply of writing a check once a year.[96]

Second, even if we could restore community organizations to the level of participation and vibrancy they had half a century ago, it still wouldn't be sufficient. Voluntary organizations can do a lot of good. But very few are designed to provide comprehensive coverage. They help who they can, but some who need assistance fall through the cracks, and some types of assistance that should be offered aren't. That is one reason government programs have steadily expanded—to fill in those cracks, to ensure no one gets left out.

Would Social Democracy Require Too Big a Leap?

In 1990, Gøsta Esping-Andersen published a book titled *The Three Worlds of Welfare Capitalism*.[97] In it, and in subsequent work,[98] Esping-Andersen argues that the social-policy package in most rich countries falls into one of three categorically different groups, or "worlds." The "social democratic" world includes the Nordic countries—Denmark, Finland, Norway, and Sweden—along with the Netherlands. The "conservative" world consists of most of the continental European nations, including Austria, Belgium, France, Germany, and Italy. The "liberal" world features a number of English-speaking countries, including the United States, Australia, Canada, and New Zealand.[99] A few nations, such as the United Kingdom, don't fit neatly into a single group.

As I outline in chapter 3, we could improve economic security, expand opportunity, and ensure rising living standards for all by moving toward a social democratic policy approach. But if Esping-Andersen is correct, that requires shifting to a fundamentally different type of safety net, which might be a very tall order.

Esping-Andersen's classification is based on three dimensions of social programs:

- Social democratic dimension: How universal are public social insurance programs and how uniform is the benefit level?

- Liberal dimension: To what degree is means testing used in determining eligibility for benefits and to what degree is provision of health insurance and old-age pensions private rather than public?
- Conservative dimension: To what degree does the generosity of public social insurance programs vary depending on a person's occupation and on whether she or he is employed in the public sector or the private sector?

Esping-Andersen scored countries on each of these three dimensions. He discovered that the highest-scoring countries were different for each dimension: the countries that scored highest on the social democratic dimension were not among the highest scoring on the liberal or conservative dimension, and so on. He defined the social democratic world of welfare capitalism as comprising the countries that scored highest on the social democratic dimension, the liberal world as comprising those that scored highest on the liberal dimension, and the conservative world as comprising those that scored highest on the conservative dimension.

This seems sensible. But a more formal statistical analysis yields a different picture. Rather than three worlds, there are two.[100]

One of the two, also called "social democratic," combines Esping-Andersen's social democratic and liberal worlds. Those two worlds are actually the opposite ends of a single continuum, with the Nordic countries at one end and the United States at the other. This isn't just the product of fancy number crunching; it also makes intuitive sense. Nations that provide universal (rather than targeted) benefits are, almost by definition, less likely to make extensive use of means testing as an eligibility criterion. And nations with egalitarian, universalistic benefits tend to be strongly oriented toward government, as opposed to private, provision of healthcare and pensions.

The second of the two worlds of welfare capitalism corresponds to Esping-Andersen's "conservative" world. Its top-scoring nations are Italy, Austria, Belgium, France, and Germany.

This tells us that the difference between Nordic and American policies is one of degree, not of kind. For America to get its social policies to where Denmark, Finland, Norway, and Sweden are now involves a continuation of the advance that has occurred over the past century, not a radical break. That doesn't mean the politics of moving forward are easy, but it does mean we can stick to our historical path.

A Smaller, More Targeted Public Safety Net?

Compared to other rich countries, particularly other English-speaking ones, Australia has done well in recent decades on a variety of outcomes, combining healthy economic growth with modest poverty and income inequality. Australia has done this with a lower level of government taxing and spending than most other nations.

One key to Australia's success may be that its government transfers are highly targeted. As the two charts in figure 4.19 show, they are directed toward lower-income households to a greater degree than in any other affluent country. On the horizontal axis of both charts in the figure is a measure of the degree to which government transfers are targeted to the poor. Countries with greater targeting are to the right; countries with a more universalistic public safety net, with transfers spread more evenly up and down the income ladder, are to the left. In the first chart, the vertical axis shows public transfers as a share of total household income; here we see that Australia's transfers are highly targeted and that the country spends comparatively little on them. In the second chart, the vertical axis shows the degree to which transfers reduce income inequality; given its low spending, Australia's public transfer system is effective at redistributing income.[101]

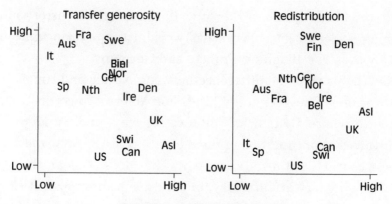

FIGURE 4.19 Australia's government transfers: heavily targeted, inexpensive, and redistributive

Australia is "Asl." Targeting: concentration coefficient for government transfers; "high" indicates more targeted, "low" more universal. Transfer generosity: government transfers as a share of household income. Redistribution: percentage reduction in inequality of household income (Gini coefficient) when government transfers are added. *Data source*: Ive Marx, Lina Salanauskaite, and Gerlinde Verbist, "The Paradox of Redistribution Revisited," unpublished paper, 2012, using Luxembourg Income Study data.

Is the Australian model an attractive one? Yes, in some respects. Is it a feasible alternative for the United States? Probably not.

A key concern is the durability of a public safety net that relies on heavy targeting. Universal transfer programs are likely to have broader political support, because everyone (or nearly everyone) is a recipient. Targeted programs, in contrast, will be seen as benefiting only a few and will therefore be more vulnerable to cutbacks.[102] While Australia's targeted system has managed to confound this expectation, the country has an exceptionally egalitarian culture. With their deep-seated commitment to a "fair go," Australians willingly support transfer programs that are disproportionately directed to those with low incomes. By way of contrast, think of America's public pension program. If Social Security were restructured so that few upper-middle class or affluent Americans received any benefits, its political support might plummet.

This isn't to say that all social transfer programs need to be universal. In the United States, some targeted programs such as Medicaid and the EITC have been expanded rather than retrenched. And Denmark, which has one of the world's most expansive public safety nets, has moved toward greater targeting.[103] It *is* to say that it may be difficult for us to duplicate the Australian model.

Finally, it's important not to overstate Australia's success. Figure 4.20 shows the rate of material deprivation plotted by the share of GDP going to public social programs, including both transfers and services. Australia, like the United States, is above the prediction line; in other words, it does worse than expected given its level of public social expenditures. This is partly due to its limited public provision of services. Services enhance access to medical care, childcare, and housing, and they allow poor households to spend their limited income on other necessities.

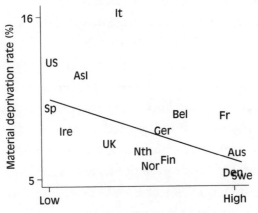

FIGURE 4.20 Social policy generosity and material deprivation, mid-2000s
Australia is "Asl." The line is a linear regression line, calculated with Italy omitted.
Material deprivation: share of households experiencing one or more of the following:
inability to adequately heat home, constrained food choices, overcrowding, poor environmental conditions (e.g., noise, pollution), arrears in payment of utility bills, arrears
in mortgage or rent payment, difficulty in making ends meet. Measured in 2005. *Data
source*: OECD, *Growing Unequal?*, 2008, pp. 186–188, using data from the Survey on
Income and Living Conditions (EU-SILC) for European countries, the Household Income
and Labour Dynamics in Australia (HILDA) survey for Australia, and the Survey of
Income and Program Participation (SIPP) for the United States. Social policy generosity: public social transfers and services as a share of GDP, adjusted for the share of
the population age 65 and over and for the unemployment rate (see Lane Kenworthy,
Progress for the Poor, Oxford University Press, 2011, pp. 116–117), measured as an average over 2000–2005. *Data source*: OECD, Social Expenditure Database, stats.oecd.org.

Expand Our Private Safety Net?

The total quantity of "social" expenditures is larger in the United States than in social democratic archetypes Denmark and Sweden. A key reason is that in the United States there is a lot of private spending on transfers and social services, mainly by employers.[104] Could we address America's problems of economic insecurity, inadequate opportunity, and slow income growth by expanding our private safety net?

There are two drawbacks to this approach. First, it tends to be of less help to the poor than a public safety net.[105] Second, it is ill-suited to a modern economy that relies on flexibility and mobility.

Let me back up. How can it be that social expenditures are larger in America than in Denmark and Sweden? The standard measure is gross public social expenditures as a share of GDP. The first row in figure 4.21 shows that on this measure Denmark and Sweden are much higher than the United States. But this leaves out some important things. Private social expenditures, such as those on employment-based health insurance and pensions, are greater in the United States. Also, the US government distributes more social benefits in the form of tax reductions than do Denmark and Sweden, those two countries tax back a larger portion of public transfers than the United States does, and America's per capita GDP is larger than Denmark's or Sweden's.

If we shift to net (rather than gross) public and private (rather than public alone) expenditures per person (rather than as a percentage of GDP), we get a different picture. According to the calculations of OECD researchers Willem Adema and Maxime Ladaique, by this measure the United States is the biggest spender of the three.[106] These numbers are in the second row in figure 4.21.

This seems like good news for America's poor. Unfortunately, it isn't. Private social spending accounts for roughly two-fifths of the US social expenditure total shown in row 2 of figure 4.21. It consists mainly of employer contributions to health insurance and employment-based pension benefits. These expenditures are

	Denmark	Sweden	U.S.
Gross public social expenditures as a share of GDP	27%	29%	16%
Net public and private social expenditures per person	$7,400	$9,100	$10,000
Average posttransfer-posttax income of households in the bottom income decile	$9,600	$8,200	$5,900
Average net government transfers received by households in the bottom income decile	$6,800	$5,300	$2,900
Average share of the population reporting deprivation in seven areas	5%	5%	13%

FIGURE 4.21 Social expenditures and living standards of the least well-off in Denmark, Sweden, and the United States, mid-2000s
Row 1: From OECD, Social Expenditure Database, stats.oecd.org. Row 2: 2000 US dollars. From Willem Adema and Maxime Ladaique, "How Expensive Is the Welfare State? Gross and Net Indicators in the OECD Social Expenditure Database (SOCX)," OECD Social, Employment, and Migration Working Paper 92, 2009, table 5.5. Rows 3 and 4: 2000 US dollars per equivalent person. The numbers refer to a household with a single adult; for a family of four, multiply by two. Danish and Swedish kroner are converted into US dollars using purchasing power parities (PPPs). Luxembourg Income Study data. Row 5: From OECD, *Growing Unequal?*, 2008, pp. 186–188.

encouraged by government tax advantages.[107] But they do little to help people at the bottom of the ladder, who often work for employers that don't provide retirement or health benefits. Another version of the private safety net approach is tax-advantaged individual accounts, such as individual retirement accounts (IRAs) and health savings accounts (HSAs). These rely heavily on individual capacity and initiative to contribute, so the poor end up with inadequate protection.[108]

What about tax "clawbacks"? Public transfer programs in Denmark and Sweden tend to be "universal" in design: a large share of the population is eligible for the benefit. While this boosts public support, it makes the programs very expensive. To make them more affordable, the government claws back some of the benefit by taxing it as though it were regular income. All countries do this, including the United States, but the Nordic countries do it more extensively. Does that hurt their poor? Not much. The tax rates increase with household income, so much of the tax clawback hits middle- and upper-income households.

So how well-off are the poor in the United States, with its private welfare state, relative to their counterparts in social democratic Denmark and Sweden? One measure is average posttransfer-posttax income among households in the bottom income decile. The third row in figure 4.21 shows my calculations using the best available comparative data, from the Luxembourg Income Study (LIS).[109] There is a sizable difference, not in America's favor.[110]

This cross-country difference in the incomes of low-end households is a function of government transfers. I've calculated averages among households in the bottom income decile for the three chief sources of household income: earnings, net government transfers (transfers received minus taxes paid), and "other" income (money from family or friends, alimony, etc.). Average earnings are virtually identical across the three countries, at about $2,500. The same is true for "other" income, which averages around $500 in each of the three. Where bottom-decile Danish and Swedish households fare much better than their American counterparts is in net government transfers, as shown in the fourth row of figure 4.21.

Not only are incomes in the bottom decile higher in Denmark and Sweden; they also have increased more rapidly over the past generation. That's because in those two countries net government transfers have risen more or less in line with economic growth. Not so in the United States.[111]

Another difference is that public services such as schooling, childcare, medical care, housing, and transportation are more plentiful and of better quality for the poor in the Nordic countries. Public services reduce deprivation and free up income to be spent on other needs. It's difficult to measure the impact of services on living standards, but one indirect way is to look at indicators of material deprivation, such as the OECD measure I described in chapter 3. The material deprivation rates for Denmark, Sweden, and the United States are shown in the fifth row of figure 4.21.[112] The gap between the countries in material deprivation is larger than the gap in low-end incomes, which is what we would expect to see if public services help the poor more in the Nordic countries than in the United States.

So while we spend more money on social protection than is often thought, that spending doesn't do nearly as much to help America's poor as we might like. The private-safety-net model has another important weakness: it fits poorly with employers' need for flexibility and workers' need for mobility. Tying a person's health insurance and pension to a job doesn't make much sense in a modern economy.[113] Either is fine as a supplement, but people's main health insurance and retirement pension should be independent of their employer.

Private Provision of Services?

Not so long ago, many political parties on the left believed government should be the producer of key manufactured goods, such as steel, cars, and chemicals. But it's now widely agreed that private ownership and market competition are more effective at delivering innovation, good quality, and low cost in manufacturing.

Services are different in that we often want not just innovation, quality, and low cost but also universal access. It isn't necessary that all citizens have a car. But everyone should have physical safety, schooling, healthcare, basic transportation (roads, buses, subways, trains), clean water, sewage, electricity, mail delivery (yes, still), and Internet access.

That doesn't mean government must be the provider, however. We could rely on private providers, regulating them to ensure that they extend service to all. Broadly speaking, we have three options: monopoly public provision, a mix of public and private provision, and fully private provision with regulation. Which should we choose when universal access to a service is critical? That will depend on particularities of the service and national or local circumstances.[114] The world's rich nations vary widely in provision of education, healthcare, transportation, policing, mail delivery, utilities, and other services. There is no reason to presume that fully public or fully private provision will always be the best option. The choice should be dictated by the goals—universal access, quality of provision, cost control, and innovation.

Service provision tends to be a blind spot for the political left. The public sector is a source of stable, decent-paying jobs, and for some that becomes the goal rather than a side benefit. Where public employees are unionized, concerns about the quality of service provision are often interpreted by the left as veiled attacks on unions.

This is the wrong approach. Our focus should be on the users of services, not the producers. A society isn't fairer when some people enjoy better job protection or working conditions or pay simply because they happen to be employed by government. Here Tony Blair got it right: "The end is quality services irrespective of wealth.... The end is utterly progressive in its values. But the only progressive means are those that deliver the progressive ends."[115] Or, as Ezekiel Emanuel has said about medical care: "Health care is about keeping people healthy or fixing them up. It is not a jobs program."[116] We should expect public services to perform as well as private-sector counterparts. They ought to be responsive, accountable to consumers, and innovative.

In many instances, this requires embracing competition from private providers. Service users should be allowed to choose among providers, including private ones. That doesn't mean taxpayers must bear the full cost of a private provider if it exceeds that of a public one. What it means, in most cases, is allowing users to choose between public and private providers.

There are two potential drawbacks. The first is that if enough users switch to private providers, the public provider may no longer be able to offer high quality at low cost. If enough students in an area choose to attend a private school (or a public school in another area), the local public school may not be able to effectively serve its remaining students. But this shouldn't cause us to shy away from allowing private alternatives. It simply requires extra effort, including providing extra resources, to ensure that public provision to the remaining students in the local school is as good as possible or to help those students move to other schools.

The second (related) problem is social division. When people with greater means choose private service providers and those with less use public providers, inequality of income and assets spills over into other realms of life. Economic inequality becomes social inequality. Arguably, societies function better—they achieve a greater sense of common purpose—when there are elements of life in which the rich, middle, and poor share the same space or experience.[117]

But forced togetherness is not an optimal solution here. We don't limit the number of grocery stores in a town in order to force people to shop together. By the same token, we shouldn't try to mandate togetherness by limiting the choice of schools. A better path is to strive for excellence in public service provision so that middle-income and wealthy users—a sizable share of them, at any rate—voluntarily select the public option. In addition, we might consider requiring a year of national service after high school as an alternative mechanism for achieving social mixing.[118]

At the same time, we shouldn't go overboard in embracing choice. Education and medical care are much more complicated and consequential than toothpaste. Most of us have little expertise, and even the most knowledgeable among us can make poor selections.[119] Allowing choice in elementary and secondary schooling doesn't mean we should offer parents a menu of "education plans" with various combinations of subject coverage or different options for sequencing math classes. We should simply allow parents to choose which school their child will attend. In healthcare, the most sensible approach is similar. It doesn't ask citizens to choose among dozens of healthcare plans. Government pays and offers a small number of plans, perhaps even just one, and citizens choose their providers.[120]

Put the Brakes on Globalization?

Imports, outsourcing, and immigration have contributed to job loss and wage stagnation for Americans in the middle and below. Should we reduce them?

No. This shouldn't be even a minor part of a strategy for improving economic security, opportunity, and income growth, much less its chief focus. Trade, investment abroad, and immigration tend to benefit people in developing nations, most of whom are much poorer than even the poorest Americans.[121] It's true that globalization enriches some rapacious corporations and despotic rulers and that vulnerable workers are exploited. But access to the American market and to employment by US-based transnational firms has improved the lives of hundreds of millions of Chinese, Indians, and others in recent decades. And moving to the United States almost invariably enhances the living standards of immigrants from poor nations. It would be a bitter irony if American progressives succeeded in making a real dent in the country's wage and jobs problems at the expense of the world's poorest and most needy. We should look elsewhere for solutions.[122]

That doesn't mean we should sit idly by and let globalization have its way with Americans who lose their jobs or suffer falling wages. We should cushion the fall and enhance their ability to adapt via policies such as wage insurance, better unemployment compensation, portable health insurance and pensions, support for retraining, and assistance with job placement. Indeed, these types of policies are attractive not just because they blunt the adverse consequences of globalization, but because they do so for economic change in general, whether it's a product of technological progress or geographic shifts of industries and firms within the United States.

Arguing for limits on globalization directs our attention away from these policies, making their adoption less likely. Paradoxically, we then end up with the worst of both worlds: marginal trade limits, half-hearted steps to curtail investment abroad, confused and ineffective immigration policy, and too little support and cushioning for successful adjustment.[123]

Reindustrialize?

For persons with limited education, a job in manufacturing is one of the few paths to decent and rising pay. Protecting existing manufacturing jobs, bringing back lost ones, and creating new ones is a perennial aim of the left. Is this a viable strategy?

No, it isn't. As figure 4.22 shows, since the 1970s, manufacturing employment has been shrinking steadily in all rich nations. As in agriculture, this employment decline is due partly to automation. It owes also to the availability of low-cost production in poorer nations. Neither is likely to abate. Two decades from now, manufacturing jobs will have shrunk to less than 10 percent of employment in most affluent countries. Here in the United States, they may well be less than 5 percent.

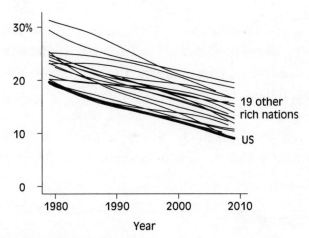

FIGURE 4.22 Manufacturing employment
Manufacturing employment as a share of total employment. The lines are loess curves.
Data source: OECD, stats.oecd.org.

Revitalize Unions?

Labor unions ensure that employers pass some of their profits on to workers in the form of pay raises. They improve economic security by negotiating for employer contributions to health insurance and pensions. And they enhance opportunity for the less advantaged by tying pay raises and promotion partly to seniority instead of solely to performance.[124]

In principle, a revitalization of unions could reduce the need for government intervention in the United States, especially with respect to income growth. For US workers at the median and below, inflation-adjusted wages have barely risen since the 1970s. If unions were strong enough to help change that, as they were in the 1950s and 1960s, there would be less need for government to step in.

But it is extremely unlikely that US unions will return to their previous size or strength. Among private-sector employees, the unionized share is down to just 7 percent.[125] Indeed, union membership has been falling in most affluent nations. Figure 4.23 shows unionization rates since the 1970s in the United States and nineteen other rich democracies. Only five now have rates above 40 percent, and in four of those (Belgium, Denmark, Finland, and Sweden), access to unemployment insurance is tied to union membership.

Many on the American left see unions as a critical part of a solution to wage stagnation, slow income growth, inadequate economic security, and unequal opportunity. But unions are too weak now to have much impact, and there is little reason to expect that their decline can be reversed. To the extent unions play a significant role going forward, it is likely to be an indirect one—as proponents of government programs and supporters of the Democratic Party.

Profit Sharing?

If we can't count on steady wage increases from manufacturing jobs or unions, would profit sharing be a useful alternative? In

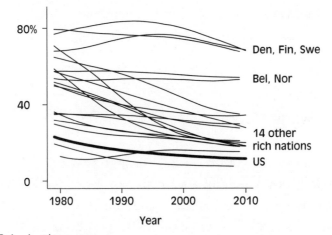

FIGURE 4.23 Unionization rates
Union members as a share of all employees. The lines are loess curves. *Data source*: Jelle Visser, "ICTWSS: Database on Institutional Characteristics of Trade Unions, Wage Setting, State Intervention, and Social Pacts," version 3, 2011, Amsterdam Institute for Advanced Labour Studies.

profit-sharing plans, employees receive part of their compensation in the form of a portion of the firm's profit rather than as a guaranteed wage or salary. This has an upside for both owners and workers. For owners, the advantage is that when the firm is struggling, for example during a recession, its labor costs will fall, because workers will absorb part of the reduction in profits in the form of lower take-home pay. For workers, the advantage is that if profits rise, their pay will automatically rise. Over time, their pay will be higher than it would have without profit sharing.[126]

The chief disadvantage for employees is that they will bear part of the cost of falling profits during bad economic times. That heightens insecurity. Then again, the enhanced flexibility in labor costs makes it less likely that firms will need to fire employees during rough times.[127] In this respect workers' security is increased.

Despite its attractiveness, profit sharing is likely to be only a partial solution going forward. The idea has been around for quite some time, yet it has made limited headway in rich nations. That could change, but the historical record suggests little reason for optimism.

A High Wage Floor?

Social democratic countries have a high wage floor—a high minimum wage that employers must pay, even for low-end service jobs. In Denmark, for instance, the hourly wage for a hotel room cleaner as of 2006 was about $16 per hour, making annual full-time earnings around $32,000. In the United States, by contrast, a comparable job would have yielded earnings of about $11,000. In fact, according to calculations by Peter Edelman, half of the jobs in the United States pay less than $34,000 a year, and nearly a quarter pay less than $22,000.[128]

There is no prospect of low-end service employees in the United States achieving Danish-level wages via collective bargaining. American unions are too weak. But suppose we raised the statutory minimum wage from its current level of $7.25 per hour to $15. Would that be a good thing to do?

Maybe not. We should care more about posttransfer-posttax household income than about individual wages, and there are ways to get to a decent income floor that don't require a high wage floor.[129]

The Denmark–United States comparison illustrates this. The first chart in figure 4.24 shows the massive gap in annual earnings just mentioned for a hotel cleaner in Denmark and the United States. The second chart compares their income after government transfers are added and tax payments are subtracted. There is much less difference.

In Denmark, a significant portion of the earnings are taxed away; our hotel cleaner would pay about $10,000 in income tax, $5,000 in consumption tax, and $1,000 into an unemployment insurance

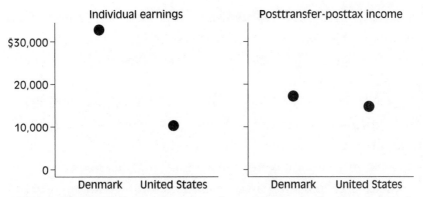

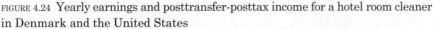

FIGURE 4.24 Yearly earnings and posttransfer-posttax income for a hotel room cleaner in Denmark and the United States

As of 2006. Assumes two children. Currency conversion: 5.5 Danish kroner = 1 US dollar. *Data sources*: Center on Budget and Policy Priorities, www.cbpp.org; Niels Westergaard-Nielsen, personal communication.

fund. In the United States, our cleaner has no federal income tax payments and modest state income tax and consumption tax payments. And earnings are supplemented by government transfers. For a person with this amount of earnings and two children, the EITC adds nearly $5,000. Food Stamps add another $2,500.

So a high wage floor isn't the only way to get to a particular income floor. Is it nevertheless the *best* way to do so?

Reasons to Favor a High Wage Floor

There are six main objections to a low or modest wage floor coupled with an EITC-style supplement. Let's consider each in turn.

1. *Low wages are demeaning.* Some feel a low wage conveys lack of respect for the work a person does. This surely is true to an extent. But if there is a tradeoff between the level of the wage floor and the number of jobs available, then the real question is whether people would rather work for a low wage or not be employed at all. The fact that millions of Americans currently choose to work in low-paying positions suggests that the former is true for many.

2. *Relying on a wage supplement forces taxpayers, rather than employers, to pick up the tab.* Mandating moderate-to-high wages for low-end service jobs forces employers (shareholders, entrepreneurs, heirs, and others) to bear the cost of assuring decent incomes for low-end households. To some that seems more desirable, on fairness grounds, than having taxpayers foot the bill.

Compare this, however, to how we think about health insurance, pensions, unemployment insurance, and sickness/disability insurance. Like income, these contribute to economic security and material well-being. In all affluent nations, they are financed at least partly by taxpayers, and few object to the fact that firms are not the sole funders. Why, then, is it objectionable for taxpayers to provide part of the funding for what amounts to insurance compensation for low earnings? In addition, if firms bear the full cost, via mandatory moderate-to-high wages, they will pass some of it on to consumers. But if taxpayers bear part of the cost, prices for eating out, clothes cleaning, home cleaning, and similar services will be lower. This is akin to provision of public services.

3. *A generous wage supplement allows employers to keep wages low.* An EITC-style employment-conditional earnings subsidy may lead to reductions in low-end wage levels, offsetting the improvement in income.[130] This can happen in two ways. First, if the subsidy pulls more people into work, the increased competition for jobs will put downward pressure on wages. Second, regardless of labor supply, employers will be tempted to incorporate the value of the subsidy into the wages they offer.

The solution is a decent wage floor—perhaps higher than the current US minimum, though not as high as in Denmark. As long as the minimum wage is high enough, these problems will be minor or irrelevant.

4. *Low wages reduce employers' incentive to improve productivity.* This argument has some appeal, but I'm not convinced it matters much for long-run productivity trends. Even in the United States, which has a comparatively low wage floor, employers regularly

seek out ways to increase productivity, via new technology or by making changes in the work process.[131] They have had limited success for tasks such as cleaning offices and hotel rooms, waiting tables, and stocking shelves in supermarkets. But it is not for lack of trying.

5. *Low-wage jobs are less likely to come with employer-provided benefits.* In the United States, employees in low-wage jobs seldom get employer benefits such as health insurance and a private pension plan. But that doesn't mean increasing the wage floor would result in more workers receiving such benefits. If anything, it might have the opposite impact. If employers' wage costs go up, some will respond by cutting costs in other areas, such as benefits.

6. *A low wage floor would disrupt the social democratic gestalt.* As I've suggested throughout this book, the Nordic countries come as close as any nation in history to having a set of institutions and policies conducive to a good society. On one view, those policies and institutions work well precisely because they reinforce one another. They are complementary—a coherent mix, a gestalt. The whole, in this view, is greater than the sum of the parts.[132]

Jonas Pontusson identifies six core features of the Nordic social democratic model: (1) universalism in the design of social insurance schemes, (2) direct public provision of social services, (3) solidaristic wage bargaining (including a high wage floor), (4) active labor market policies, (5) policies that promote female employment and gender equality in the labor market, and (6) high levels of investment in public education and policies to equalize educational opportunity.[133]

How might a lower wage floor with household incomes boosted by an employment-conditional earnings subsidy threaten the Nordic gestalt? I see three possibilities. First, reliance on an EITC-type benefit means greater targeting in government transfers, and that could weaken the solidarity that underpins policy generosity.[134] Second, allowing a low-wage segment of the labor market to emerge might reduce social equality, a mainstay of the social democratic model.[135] Third, unions would be weakened, and in the absence of strong unions, these countries might be less likely to continue their high levels of government services and transfers.

Each of these worries is plausible. Yet history suggests grounds for optimism about the robustness of the social democratic model. In Sweden, the past half century has witnessed a continuous stream of alterations and adaptations: family-friendly programs were created and steadily expanded beginning in the 1960s and 1970s; centralized wage bargaining collapsed in the early 1980s; financial markets were deregulated in the 1980s and 1990s; the 1990s and 2000s have featured growing use of private competition in services (schools, childcare); an employment-conditional earnings subsidy was introduced in 2007. Any one of these changes might have been predicted to trigger the demise of the model. And yet it persists, as successfully as ever.

Moreover, the social democratic model varies across the Nordic countries. Large-scale active labor market policy was confined to Sweden until Denmark began in the 1990s, and Finland and Norway make limited use of it even today. Finland and Norway also have a different childcare arrangement: a home-care allowance to parents during the first three years of the child's life. And these four nations differ in the degree of universalism of their transfer programs.[136]

It is difficult to know beforehand whether a particular element of an institutional configuration truly is or is not a lynchpin. What seems vital may turn out not to be. I suspect the United States can emulate much of what works well in the social democratic countries—in particular, generous public provision of goods, services, and transfers—without needing to also have a high wage floor.

Reasons to Accept a Low or Modest Wage Floor

Is there any reason to *prefer* a modest wage floor? I think there are two.

1. *A high wage floor may reduce employment*. The degree to which high wages are bad for employment often is overstated. Yet there *is* a tipping point; no one disputes that. The question is where the tipping point lies and how large the effect is once that point is crossed.

For low-end service positions, the wage level in Denmark is high enough to discourage employment. In fact, in private-sector low-end service jobs, the Nordic countries have both lower employment rates and less employment growth than countries with lower wage floors.[137] The reason is straightforward: productivity in such jobs tends to be relatively low and difficult to increase.[138]

Some feel that if low productivity prevents decent wages in low-end service jobs, a good society ought to reduce the prevalence of such jobs. This position is related to the core notion behind the Swedish Rehn-Meidner model, which aimed to raise wages in order to force inefficient employers out of business, thus creating both healthy wages and a highly-productive economy—the best of both worlds. But there is a difference between forcing out the least efficient employers in a particular industry, as in the Rehn-Meidner model, and discouraging particular types of jobs.

The argument in favor of allowing low-end service jobs that pay low wages is that there is both a demand and a supply. As we get richer, we are more willing to outsource childcare, food preparation, cleaning, repair work, and related activities. And there are people willing to do such jobs. This is especially relevant for the young and immigrants, two groups who already struggle in the labor market.

But then why impose any wage floor at all? If there is someone willing to work for a very low wage, why not let an employer hire at that wage? The answer is that most of the time there are more people seeking jobs than employers seeking workers. The resulting power asymmetry tends to force wages down to a very low level. Legislation (a statutory minimum wage) or collective bargaining can impose a wage floor with no employment-reducing impact, and so it is a good idea to do so. The trick is to figure out the tipping point—the level above which employment is impeded—and set the wage floor at or near that point.

The optimal wage floor will differ across regions. In the United States the federal government sets a minimum wage, but many states and some cities establish a higher minimum. That's a sensible arrangement. The optimal floor also will differ across industries. This is something collective bargaining is ideally suited to address, but America's unions are so weak that at some point government may have to play a more active role.

2. *As a practical matter, in the United States efforts to supplement low wages are likely to get farther than efforts to impose a high wage floor.* Earlier I asked you to imagine a rise in the US minimum wage to $15 per hour. In reality, this is extremely unlikely to happen. Figure 4.25 shows the evolution of America's minimum wage and EITC, expressed in annual (rather than hourly) values. The minimum wage increased steadily until the 1970s, but it then fell and has been flat since. As of 2013 the federal minimum is $7.25 per hour, less than half the Danish (collectively bargained) minimum. We certainly can afford a higher minimum wage, yet recent history offers no reason to believe it will get close to the Danish level.

More likely is a moderate increase in the minimum wage coupled with an increase in the EITC. In 1993 the EITC was indexed to the inflation rate, so it, unlike the minimum wage, always keeps up with price increases. In the past several decades it has risen faster than prices, due to legislated increases in the late 1980s, the early 1990s, and 2009.

Past is not always prologue, of course. Extrapolating from developments in recent decades doesn't necessarily tell us what will happen in the future. But it does suggest that a big jump in the minimum wage is unlikely. We're much more likely to get a modest rise in the minimum wage and an expansion of the EITC.

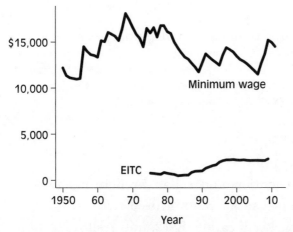

FIGURE 4.25 The minimum wage and the Earned Income Tax Credit (EITC) Federal minimum hourly wage multiplied by 2,000. Average yearly EITC benefit per recipient household. Federal minimum wage and EITC only; many states have a higher minimum wage and/or an additional EITC. 2011 dollars; inflation adjustment is via the CPI-U-RS. *Data sources*: Bureau of Labor Statistics; Tax Policy Center.

Beyond Earnings and Income

Despite getting paid a much higher wage, a typical low-end service worker in Denmark ends up with a posttransfer-posttax income that is only a little higher than that of her American counterpart. This doesn't, however, mean their living standards are similar. Denmark does a better job than the United States at three things that boost material well-being but don't show up in income statistics.

Public goods and services. Governments in affluent nations provide or subsidize a host of services and public goods. Here is a partial list:

- Physical safety: policing, the military
- Assurance of basic liberties: freedom of thought, speech, political participation, and religious practice
- Money
- Enforcement of property rights and contracts
- Financial safeguards: limited liability for passive investors, bankruptcy, bank deposit insurance, protection against unauthorized use of credit cards

- Clean air and water
- Street cleaning, removal and disposal of sewage and garbage
- Housing
- Healthcare
- Disability services
- Elderly services
- Workplace safety
- Consumer safety
- Disaster prevention and relief: firefighting, levee building, cleanup, compensation to uninsured victims
- Schooling: early education, K-12, university
- Childcare
- Job training
- Job search and placement assistance
- Antidiscrimination enforcement
- Public transportation
- Facilitation of private transportation: roads, bridges, stoplights, enforcement of speed limits, air traffic control
- Public spaces: roads, sidewalks, museums, parks, sports fields, forests, campgrounds, beaches, oceans, lakes, swimming pools, zoos
- Communication, information, and entertainment: support for phone lines, broadband, the Internet, public television and radio programming, subsidization of free private television and radio networks, libraries, festivals
- Free time: work-hours regulations, paid holidays, paid vacation days, paid parental or family leave, paid sick leave

When governments provide or subsidize public services and goods, they expand the sphere of consumption for which the cost to households is zero or minimal. This lifts the living standards of those on the low rungs of the income ladder, and it frees up their limited income to purchase other goods and services.[139]

Work conditions. Many low-end jobs offer limited mental stimulation or opportunity to participate in decision making, and many are stressful.[140] There is a limit to the amount of stimulation that some low-end jobs will ever be able to provide, but most could do better, and efforts to figure out how and to push firms in that direction are well worth undertaking. Indeed, we should aim to improve working conditions in *all* jobs, rather than assuming that higher-skilled, better-paying positions automatically have decent work quality.[141]

There is evidence that efforts by government, unions, and employers to improve working conditions and to increase employee participation in decision making can make a difference. Denmark and Sweden have made concerted efforts in this direction, and survey evidence suggests that they stand out among European nations as the ones in which job quality and employee participation are highest.[142]

Duncan Gallie recommends an auditing procedure whereby government sets outcome standards for work conditions, leaves it up to firms to decide how to meet the standards, and monitors their efforts to do so. He describes it as

> a system of periodic "health audits" in organizations, which will provide for an external evaluation of an organization's strategy in relationship to both physical and psychological health, of the internal system for monitoring working conditions, and of the internal procedures for acting upon issues that are likely to be detrimental to the health (in the broad sense of the term) of employees. Such audits would require organizations to develop systematic risk assessments, which would clearly need to take account of employees' reports of their jobs and working conditions, as part of the evidence collected. As well as providing a strong incentive to organizations to improve their practices, such audits would provide a means for the diffusion of best practice information to individual work organizations. Such a system would require the development of specialized health-audit organizations that would be licensed to assess and approve company policies.[143]

Work schedules are important too. According to Harriett Presser, about two-fifths of the American labor force works at nonstandard times—during the evening or at night, on a rotating shift, or on the weekend.[144] This calls for an increase in the availability of high-quality affordable childcare, so that those with children have more options.[145]

Mobility out of low-wage jobs. Whether the wage floor is low, high, or in between, we should aim to help people exit from low-end jobs into better ones. Government services can help by enhancing human capital, assisting with job search and placement, and facilitating work-family balance. Here we tend to think mainly of the K-12 school system, but there is far more, including health-care, early education, lifelong learning opportunities, retraining, job placement assistance, special services for the mentally or physically disabled, language assistance for immigrants, targeted programs for the young and the elderly, assistance with transportation, and help in organizing formal job ladders.[146]

A Basic Income Grant?

Like the EITC, a basic income grant would give American adults a lump sum of money every year. But unlike the EITC, a basic income grant would be unconditional; it wouldn't depend on need or employment status. In most proposals, it also would provide a larger amount than the EITC. The idea originated with Milton Friedman, and Congress gave a version of it serious consideration in the early 1970s.[147] Today, it is supported by some on the left, most prominently Philippe Van Parijs, and some on the right, such as Charles Murray.[148]

On the left, the argument in favor focuses on the potential enhancement of freedom—specifically, freedom from work. In the words of Van Parijs:

A basic income would serve as a powerful instrument of social justice: it would promote freedom for all by providing the material resources that people need to pursue their aims....A UBI [universal basic income] makes it easier to take a break between two jobs, reduce working time, make room for more training, take up self-employment, or join a cooperative. And with a UBI, workers will only take a job if they find it suitably attractive....If the motive in combating unemployment is not some sort of work fetishism—an obsession with keeping everyone busy—but rather a concern to give every person the possibility of taking up gainful employment in which she can find recognition and accomplishment, then the UBI is to be preferred.[149]

For proponents on the right, the chief advantage is reduction in the deadweight costs of public social programs. If the government simply cuts a check to each adult, there is no need for caseworkers or bureaucratic oversight.

Proponents also point to the universality of a basic income grant. If everyone receives the grant, and in the same amount, recipients of government assistance face no stigma.

Despite these considerations, I don't think a basic income grant is a good idea for the United States, for two reasons. First, a grant that is large enough to allow adults to live without earnings would reduce employment.[150] We need high employment to ensure that we have a tax base large enough to pay for generous social programs and government's other functions.[151] Moreover, the notion of reciprocity is strong among Americans,[152] so a program that reduces employment might weaken support for public social protections, including the basic income grant itself.

Second, while letting people choose what to do with the help they receive from government has a certain attractiveness, a key purpose of government is to do things that individuals should do but don't. Government builds roads, ensures clean air and water, and protects us from physical harm. It educates us, provides access to medical care, and forces us to save for retirement. These types of services and public goods ought to take precedence over maximization of individual choice.[153] Giving people cash is consistent with a libertarian approach to the good society. The idea has some merit. But in my view, the case for a paternalistic orientation is stronger.

Asset Building?

The final alternative strategy I consider in this chapter is promotion of asset accumulation by middle and low-income households. There are various proposals for how to do this. Some recommend a government match for saving by the poor, others a government grant at birth (a "baby bond") that can grow in a tax-exempt savings account throughout the childhood years, and still others a "stakeholder grant" of, say, $20,000 to be given to each American on reaching adulthood.[154]

Assets can help to reduce economic insecurity and expand opportunity. But the lessons of recent decades suggest that asset building is not the best strategy for achieving these goals. If the assets are liquid—in a savings account, for example, or a retirement account that can be accessed early—those with low incomes will be tempted to spend them. We see this most clearly in the tendency of Americans with a defined-contribution pension, such as a 401(k), to cash it out when switching jobs. Another problem is the vulnerability of money invested in stocks or housing to market swings. Since 2000, the US stock market has had two sharp declines, leaving those who invested at or near the peak with a severely depleted net worth. The crash in home prices beginning in 2006 was just as devastating, and unlike stock values, the housing market's recovery is likely to be very slow.

For these reasons, I see asset building as a potentially useful supplement to the types of social programs I emphasize in chapter 3. But we shouldn't allocate funds to it at the expense of those programs.

It's important to distinguish asset building from banking. Recent estimates suggest that one in four low-income Americans don't have a bank account, compared to just one in fifty in Sweden and the United Kingdom.[155] As a result, many use check-cashing outlets and payday lenders, which charge very high fees and interest rates. Getting more of America's poor banked, via a checking account or even simply prepaid spending cards, would be helpful.[156]

Are the Nordic Countries Exceptional?

Throughout this book I have drawn lessons for America from the experience of the Nordic countries. Have I gone too far?

According to some, those nations' small size, homogeneity, and tradition of good government allows them to have strong economies despite their generous public social programs and high taxes, so it's best not to draw any inferences for the United States.[157] The problem with this argument is that when we examine the full set of rich nations, there is no apparent advantage to small size, homogeneity, or government quality for national economic success.[158]

Actually, the economic success of the Nordic nations is not puzzling. Orthodox economic theory suggests that markets encourage innovation and allocate resources effectively but don't adequately provide infrastructure, education, safety, protection against risks, or other valuable goods and services. The most efficient way to address these failings is with public programs rather than through regulation of private behavior. This is essentially what the Nordic countries do: they let markets work, and government fills in the gaps. It isn't *in spite of* their policies and institutions that the Nordic nations achieve economic security, equal opportunity, and shared prosperity together with strong economic performance. It's *because of* them.[159]

America's Path

Growth of government spending is not, for the most part, a consequence of rent-seeking special interests or narrow-minded bureaucrats expanding their turf. It's a product of affluence. As people and nations get richer, they are willing to allocate more money for insurance (protection against risks) and for fairness (extension of opportunity and security to those who are less fortunate). There are quite a few proposed private-sector remedies for economic insecurity, inadequate opportunity, and slow income growth. But none is likely to work as thoroughly and effectively as the government programs I outline in chapter 3.

We don't only want security and fairness, however. We also want freedom, flexibility, and a vibrant economy. It's perfectly reasonable to worry about the impact of big government on the economy and on freedom. Happily, the available evidence suggests that rich nations can generate the tax revenues needed to pay for generous social programs, couple big government with an innovative and growing economy, and do so without excessively restricting liberty.

The evidence also suggests we can reap the benefits of generous social programs without importing the full Nordic gestalt. We have much to learn from those nations' policies and institutions, but that doesn't mean we need to adopt all of them.

5

Can It Happen?

I EXPECT THE size and scope of American social policy will expand significantly in coming decades. My reasoning can be stated simply:

- The United States has deficiencies in economic security, opportunity, and shared prosperity.
- The economic and social trends at fault will continue and perhaps get worse.
- Experience here and abroad suggests that government social programs can help.
- Policy makers try to solve problems. Reason and evidence will lead some of them to propose new government programs and the expansion of existing ones.
- On occasion, they will succeed. (The hypothesis doesn't specify when or why. It's probabilistic.)
- Those successes will tend to stick.

This is how social policy in the United States has evolved over the past century. It has expanded in fits and starts, bursts and lulls. Movement has been largely forward; backsliding has been rare. Simple extrapolation suggests that this is what we should expect for the future. Further advance won't necessarily happen soon, and progress almost certainly won't be steady or regular.

But if we think in terms of decades or, better yet, a half century, the most reasonable projection is for a significant expansion of public social programs along the lines of those suggested in chapter 3.

Is it sensible to extrapolate? In this chapter, I consider five reasons for skepticism. First, Americans don't want big government. Second, opponents of big government have become very effective at deploying the rhetoric of reaction. Third, the left will increasingly struggle to get elected. Fourth, the balance of organized power in the United States has shifted to the right. Fifth, the structure of our political system impedes progressive policy change.

Each of these is a potentially powerful obstacle to progress. Yet none is likely to derail America's slow but steady movement toward an expanded government role in improving economic security, enhancing opportunity, and ensuring rising living standards for all.

Obstacle 1: Americans Don't Want Big Government

Compared to other rich nations, the United States has a relatively small government—particularly with respect to programs that provide economic security, enhance opportunity, and facilitate rising living standards. Many say this is because it's what Americans want. More than our counterparts in other rich nations, we tend to believe that individual effort, rather than luck, determines success in life. We therefore see a need for only minimal government assistance.

This view has a long history. One of its best expositions is by Seymour Martin Lipset, who helped to popularize the notion of American exceptionalism. Lipset argues that Americans' belief in individualism and liberty and their hostility to government are the source of many differences between the United States and other rich countries.[1]

In the early 2000s, John Micklethwait and Adrian Woolridge, a British editor and writer for the *Economist* magazine, took a close look at the peculiarities of American politics and political culture. In their book *The Right Nation*, they conclude that "the United States has always been a conservative country, marinated in religion, in love with business, and hostile to the state....Americans are exceptionally keen on limiting the size of the state and the scope of what it does."[2]

A more recent statement of this view comes from Alberto Alesina and Edward Glaeser, who argue that differences in the generosity of government social programs across the world's rich nations stem from differing popular views of the causes of poverty. Alesina and Glaeser find that in countries in which a larger share of the population believes people's effort is the key determinant of their income, government spending on social programs tends to be lower. In nations where people deem luck more important, social program expenditures tend to be higher.[3] The United States is among the former. Only about 35 percent of Americans in the survey feel luck is more important than effort, compared to 60 percent of Danes.

Ideologically Conservative but Programmatically Progressive

Public opinion data support the notion that Americans don't like big government. Surveys conducted since the mid-1970s have asked representative samples of American adults, "If you had to choose, would you rather have a smaller government providing fewer services or a bigger government providing more services?" In only a few years did the the share choosing "bigger government providing more services" reach 50 percent; in most years, it has hovered between 30 percent and 45 percent.[4] Gallup periodically asks, "In your opinion, which of the following will be the biggest threat to the country in the future—big business, big labor, or big government?" Since the early 1980s, 50–70 percent of Americans have said "big government" is the largest threat.[5] For more than twenty years, the Pew Research Center has asked Americans whether they agree or disagree that "when something is run by the government, it is usually inefficient and wasteful." In each year 55–75 percent have said they completely agree or mostly agree.[6] The National Election Study (NES) regularly asks, "Do you think that people in government waste a lot of the money we pay in taxes, waste some of it, or don't waste very much of it?" In most years 60–75 percent have said "a lot."[7] Finally, since the early 1970s, the General Social Survey (GSS) has asked Americans if they have "a great deal of confidence, only some confidence, or hardly any confidence at all" in various organizations and institutions. For Congress and the president, the share responding "a great deal of confidence" has been below 30 percent in every year.[8]

Public opinion data like these buttress the impression that Americans are averse to activist government. But they hide a deeper truth: although Americans are ideologically conservative when it comes to the size and scope of government, we're programmatically progressive. We're averse to big government in the abstract, but we like a lot of the things government actually does.

The GSS regularly asks a set of questions prefaced by the following statement: "We are faced with many problems in this country, none of which can be solved easily or inexpensively. I'm going to name some of these problems, and for each one I'd like you to tell me whether you think we're spending too much money on it, too little money, or about the right amount." Since the late 1970s, a large majority, always over 80 percent and often more than 90 percent, has said current spending is too little or about right on "assistance to the poor," on "improving the nation's education system," on "improving and protecting the nation's health," and on "Social Security."[9] An irregular series of polls between 1980 and 2007 asked, "Do you favor or oppose national health insurance, which would be financed by tax money, paying for most forms of healthcare?" In almost every instance 50–65 percent have said they are in favor, while 25–40 percent are opposed.[10] In 2011, the Pew Research Center found 61 percent of Americans saying "people on Medicare already pay enough of the cost of their health care" versus 31 percent saying "people on Medicare need to be more responsible for the cost of their healthcare in order to keep the program financially secure."[11] In 2007, Benjamin Page and Lawrence Jacobs asked a representative sample of Americans, "Would you be willing to pay more taxes in order to provide health coverage for everyone?" Nearly 60 percent were willing versus just 40 percent who were unwilling.[12] They asked the same question about paying more in taxes for "early childhood education in kindergarten and nursery school." Here, 64 percent were willing versus 33 percent unwilling.[13] Finally, Page and Jacobs asked whether the EITC should be increased, decreased, or kept about the same. More than 90 percent wanted it increased or kept the same.[14]

There is only one significant exception to the popularity of existing social programs in America: welfare. In the GSS surveys, between 40 percent and 60 percent of Americans say we spend too much on welfare.[15] Though the question doesn't specify the particular program, it's likely that most respondents have in mind AFDC, which was replaced in the mid-1990s by TANF. As Martin Gilens has documented, AFDC was uniquely unpopular with the American public.[16] This owes to a variety of factors, according to Gilens, prominent among them race and media portrayals of the recipients. The perception is deeply ingrained. Despite the pronounced changes introduced by the 1996 welfare reform—strict time limits on benefit receipt, reduced benefit levels, stronger employment requirements—the GSS responses suggest little, if any, shift in public opinion about "welfare" since then.

Conventional wisdom holds that Americans have become more conservative in recent decades—the so-called age of Reagan.[17] Have our views about government's role or specific programs shifted? For the most part, no. The share of Americans identifying as conservative and/or Republican increased a bit in the 1970s and 1980s. But views about government effectiveness and how much we should be spending on particular policies have remained fairly constant.[18]

Many Americans dislike the idea of big government. But when we think about it in terms of specific programs, we're not at all averse to a government that is medium-sized or even large.

Is Public Support Necessary to Get Social Programs Adopted?

When the American public favors a proposed policy change, it is more likely to be adopted. When the public opposes a change, it is less likely to be adopted. That's the finding of a study titled "Effects of Public Opinion on Policy" by Benjamin Page and Robert Y. Shapiro, published in 1983.[19] Page and Shapiro find considerable congruence in public opinion and policy changes in the United States from 1935 to 1979. They also find that public opinion influences policy changes rather than the other way around.

In a book published thirty years later, Martin Gilens looks at patterns between the mid-1960s and the mid-2000s.[20] His findings echo those of Page and Shapiro. When only 5 percent of Americans favored a proposed policy change, as gauged by public opinion surveys, the change was adopted just 10 percent of the time. When 45–55 percent favored the change, it was adopted 25–30 percent of the time. When 95 percent were in favor, the proposed change was adopted 60 percent of the time.

Robert Erikson, Michael MacKuen, and James Stimson conducted a similar test but in a slightly different way.[21] Rather than examine the relationship between public opinion and policy change for each specific issue, they constructed an index of public opinion liberalism and an index of policy liberalism and looked at how these indexes correlate over time. They too find strong indication of an association between public opinion and policy, and they too conclude that the relationship is causal.

What these types of studies can tell us is constrained by the limits of available survey data. Public opinion data don't exist for some issues, and for others the questions don't effectively tap the issue at stake. Still, these findings suggest a basic harmony between what Americans want and what their policy makers give them.

From the perspective of democracy, that's a reassuring conclusion. But it raises a question about my expectation that government social policy will expand in coming decades: do we need strong public support beforehand in order to get new programs adopted or existing ones expanded?

No, we don't. Consider Martin Gilens's recent findings. In his data, if public support for a proposed policy change is in the neighborhood of 45–55 percent, the likelihood that the change will be adopted is 25–30 percent. In other words, even if public opinion is split, the change has a one in four chance of getting passed. Public support helps, but it isn't necessary.

Additional evidence comes from a study by Katherine Newman and Elisabeth Jacobs.[22] Examining public opinion on the major social policy innovations of the 1930s and the 1960s, they find evidence of considerable ambivalence and/or opposition among ordinary Americans to the proposed programs. The public, according to Newman and Jacobs, had "mixed and contentious attitudes about activist government."[23] Policy advances owed mainly to the efforts of political leaders, particularly Franklin Roosevelt and Lyndon Johnson, presidents who "moved boldly into a policy vacuum or forged on against growing antagonism. They pushed and pulled legislators into creating and then sustaining the progressive history of the 1930s and 1960s that we now—mistakenly—see as a sea change in popular political culture."[24] Here, too, the message is that while public support increases the likelihood of policy advance, it isn't a necessary condition. Policy makers can overcome ambivalence among the citizenry.

Public Opinion Impedes Policy Reversal

Often, ordinary Americans aren't sure what they think about a social program until it has been around for a while. That's hardly surprising; it's difficult to know ahead of time how, and how well, a program will function. Once people see a program in action, they are better able to form an opinion. If a program works well, and there don't appear to be any major adverse side effects, they tend to like it.

Since public views about programs tend to be stronger after they have been put in place, we might expect public opinion to have more influence on proposed changes to existing programs than on proposals for new programs. And since the public tends to like existing social programs, we might expect public opinion to act as a brake on proposals to cut back or remove them. This is exactly what Paul Pierson finds through his examination of changes in social policy in the United Kingdom during the Thatcher years and in the United States during the Reagan years.[25] Both administrations were committed to reducing the size and scope of government, including social programs. Both put forward multiple proposals for cutbacks. Both were in power for a fairly lengthy period. Yet neither Thatcher nor Reagan had much success.

Popularity doesn't make a program invulnerable to retrenchment or removal. But it reduces the likelihood of that happening. This is a key reason why the trajectory of American social policy has been forward, and why we might reasonably expect that to continue.

Obstacle 2: The Rhetoric of Reaction

Proponents of small government are adept at deploying what Albert Hirschman terms the "rhetoric of reaction"—arguments suggesting that efforts to enhance justice and fairness are misguided.[26] Hirschman identifies three types: futility arguments, perversity arguments, and jeopardy arguments. Futility arguments hold that government programs fail to have any impact. For instance, public schools fail to educate because they face little or no competition. Perversity arguments contend that government programs worsen the problem they aim to address. An example is the contention that generous government benefits discourage work and thereby increase poverty instead of reducing it. Jeopardy arguments claim that government programs threaten some other desirable outcome. For instance, if we increase government spending, we'll get less economic growth.

Will these types of arguments block future progress in American social policy? I suspect not. Futility, perversity, and jeopardy arguments seem compelling. That's why they are effective. Sometimes they are empirically true, but often they aren't. Hirschman points out that in centuries past these types of claims were made to oppose the introduction of democracy. It was suggested, for instance, that if voting rights were extended to the "ignorant masses," they would elect a tyrant, who would subsequently abolish democracy (futility). Or democracy would result in the expropriation and redistribution of property, thereby wrecking the economy and making everyone poorer (jeopardy).

In principle, such claims are testable. But prior to the introduction of democracy, there was no evidence.

Until recently, that's been the case for many claims about the futility, perversity, or jeopardy of generous social programs. Social scientists have lacked sufficient data to subject those claims to empirical scrutiny. But this is changing. We're now in a much better position to evaluate these hypotheses, and our ability to do so will continue to improve going forward. Empirical assessment won't end the influence of such claims in policy debate, but it will reduce that influence enough to open up some political space.

Climate change may prove to be a turning point. As I write, in 2013, climate experts are in near-unanimous agreement that human-generated carbon dioxide emissions are causing the planet to warm. There is uncertainty about the impact this will have on the planet if left unchecked, and there is considerable debate about the appropriate policy response. But we are now past the point at which it is reasonable to deny that climate change is occurring and that humans are causing it. Yet a number of Republicans in

Congress still espouse this view, hampering the US government's ability to take action to reduce carbon emissions.[27] Their antiscientific orientation is reminiscent of cigarette manufacturers' denial that smoking causes lung cancer long after medical researchers had reached near-consensus on the facts.

This may usher in a shift in the standards to which the American public and media hold policy makers. Going forward, it is likely to become increasingly difficult for policy makers to rely on claims that are at odds with the preponderance of evidence.

Not every claim made in opposition to a large government role in protecting economic security, expanding opportunity, and ensuring shared prosperity can be assessed empirically. But some can, such as the notion that higher taxes will hurt the economy. As I explained in chapter 4, there is some level of taxation at which this is true, but available data suggest the United States is below that level. As evidence mounts, this claim will be heard less frequently. Hardly anyone today argues that nations should avoid democracy on the grounds that it leads to tyranny. The argument doesn't square with the facts. For the same reason, half a century from now few will claim that government taxing and spending at 45 percent of GDP is bad for the American economy.

Obstacle 3: The Left Can't Get Elected

Relative to its counterparts in other affluent nations, the Democratic Party in the United States has always been a centrist party, rather than a left party. Even so, most of the major advances in American social policy have occurred when Democrats held the presidency and one or both bodies of Congress. That's likely to continue.

As figure 5.1 shows, Democrats dominated the House of Representatives and the Senate from 1930 to 1980, though the presidency swung back and forth. Since 1980, control of the presidency and both chambers of Congress has been split fairly evenly

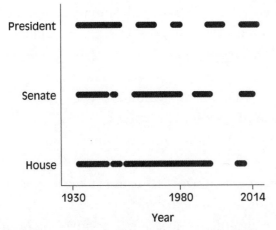

FIGURE 5.1 Democratic control of the presidency, the Senate, and the House of
Representatives
Lines indicate years of Democratic president, Democratic majority in the Senate,
Democratic majority in the House. The end point is 2016 for the president and 2014 for
the Senate and House. *Data source*: Wikipedia.

between the two parties. To achieve social policy advances in
coming decades, the Democrats need to avoid a lengthy period of
sustained minority status of the kind suffered by the Republicans
during the New Deal era.

Two hypotheses predict that this worst-case scenario may well
come to pass. The first says Democrats will struggle because
working-class whites, the party's traditional base, are now guided
in their party preference by social and cultural issues rather than
economic ones, which leads them to favor the Republicans. The
second says we are entering a period when enormous quantities of
private money will flow into election campaigns, with Republicans
the chief beneficiaries.

Do the Democrats Lack an Electoral Base?

Working-class whites have moved away from the Democrats.
In the mid-1970s, about 60 percent of white Americans
who self-identified as working class said they preferred the
Democratic Party. That number fell steadily from the late
1970s, bottoming out at 40 percent in the early 1990s, where it

has remained since.[28] The same trend is evident among whites with less than a high school degree and among whites on the lower third of the income ladder.[29] In the 2004, 2008, and 2012 presidential elections, whites with less than a four-year college degree favored the Republican candidate over the Democratic one by roughly twenty percentage points.[30]

Why has this happened? Ronald Inglehart's "postmaterialist" hypothesis suggests that as a society gets wealthy, issues other than those connected to material self-interest become more important to people.[31] There is no clear working-class interest in being either pro-choice or pro-life on abortion or in favoring or opposing equal rights for homosexuals. Hence, as material issues lose their centrality, working-class identification with the party that better serves its material interests is likely to decline. In his book *What's the Matter with Kansas?*, Thomas Frank suggests that working-class Americans' conservative inclinations on social and cultural issues have led many of them, particularly in rural parts of the South and the Midwest, to side with the Republicans at the expense of their economic interests.

Will this consign the Democrats to regular electoral defeat? That seems unlikely. As Ruy Teixeira and John Judis pointed out a decade ago in *The Emerging Democratic Majority*, the Democratic Party has a new electoral base centered on urban professionals, women, African Americans, and Latinos.[32] These groups are large, and most are growing. In addition, geographic trends will help the Democrats to remain competitive in national elections for the foreseeable future. The Northeast, the West Coast, and Illinois are now solidly Democratic, and most of the upper Midwest leans in that direction. None of this guarantees presidential victories or congressional majorities. But it does suggest that forecasts of impending electoral disaster for the Democrats probably are wrong.

Equally important, the health of the economy is the chief determinant of the outcome of national elections. Douglas Hibbs and Larry Bartels point out that presidential election outcomes can be predicted fairly well using just a single measure of economic performance—per capita income growth.[33] This is displayed in figure 5.2. On the vertical axis is the incumbent-party candidate's vote margin. On the horizontal axis is the growth rate of per capita real disposable personal income in the middle two quarters (April to September) of the election year, adjusted for how long the incumbent party has been in office. This simple model does a good job of predicting the vote outcome. Other models can predict even more accurately by including additional factors; but in all of them, measures of economic performance play a central role.[34]

What about Congress? House and Senate elections are, not surprisingly, more idiosyncratic than presidential elections. Yet the condition of the national economy has consistently been a good predictor of the outcome.[35]

The implication is clear: if the Democrats do reasonably well (or Republicans fare poorly) at managing the economy, they'll remain competitive in elections.

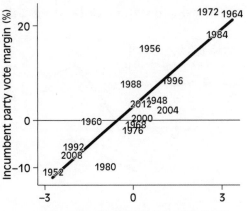

FIGURE 5.2 Income growth and presidential election outcomes
Vertical axis is the incumbent-party candidate's vote margin. Horizontal axis is the growth rate of per capita real disposable income in the second and third quarters of the election year, adjusted for incumbency (–1.29 for each consecutive term, beyond the first, that the incumbent party has held the White House). The correlation is .89. This replicates Larry Bartels's chart in "Obama Toes the Line," *The Monkey Cage*, January 8, 2013.

Does Citizens United Spell Electoral Doom for the Left?

The second hypothesis predicting electoral struggles for the American left suggests that the Supreme Court's 2010 *Citizens United* decision will allow private money to flood into Republican campaign coffers. That ruling prohibited restrictions on political campaign spending by organizations, such as firms and unions, opening the door to unlimited expenditures by outside groups on behalf of their preferred candidate or party.

It's too soon to be able to render an informed judgment on the impact of the *Citizens United* decision, but the degree to which it altered the legal landscape is sometimes overstated.[36] Before the super PACs (political action committees) and 501(c)(4)s that sprang up after *Citizens United*, individuals and corporations already could make unlimited donations to 527s. The only difference is that the new organizations are less constrained in naming the candidates they favor or oppose in advertisements running during the two months prior to the election.

Figure 5.3 shows campaign expenditures for Democrats and Republicans in presidential-year elections and off-year elections since 1998 (the earliest year for which data are available). In the

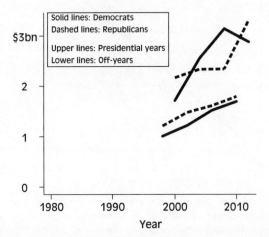

FIGURE 5.3 Campaign expenditures by and for Democrats and Republicans
Billions of inflation-adjusted dollars. Includes expenditures by candidates, parties, and outside groups. *Data source*: Center for Responsive Politics, "Total Cost of US Elections, 1998–2012," www.opensecrets.org, accessed January 18, 2013.

2012 election cycle, outside money favored Republican candidates, just as pessimists had predicted.[37] But that isn't surprising, given that the Republicans were the opposition party (the Democrats held the presidency and the Senate). As Matt Bai wrote during the 2012 election campaign,

> Rich conservatives weren't inspired to invest their fortunes in 2004, when Bush ran for the second time while waging an unpopular war, or in 2008, when they were forced to endure the nomination of McCain. But now there's a president and a legislative agenda they bitterly despise..., so it's not surprising that outside spending by Republicans in 2010 and 2012 would dwarf everything that came before. What we are seeing—what we almost certainly would have seen even without the court's ruling in Citizens United—is the full force of conservative wealth in America, mobilized by a common enemy for the first time since the fall of party monopolies.[38]

Even if money totals continue to favor Republicans, it's unclear how much that will matter. There are diminishing returns to money in influencing election outcomes: when a lot is already being spent, additional amounts have limited impact. The Democrats had less money in 2012, yet they were competitive in the presidential, House, and Senate elections.

The history of campaign finance in national elections in the past four decades is one of each party and its backers seeking new ways to raise and spend large amounts of money in spite of existing regulations. In the 1970s, the Democrats had the advantage. By the end of the 1980s, the Republicans had the upper hand. Toward the end of the 2000s, it shifted back to the Democrats. We may now be in the midst of another Republican surge. Even if that happens, however, past experience suggests that Democrats and their supporters will figure out ways to offset the advantage Republicans gain from *Citizens United*, or at least to mitigate its impact.[39] I'm not suggesting that money doesn't matter in American elections.

It does.[40] The point is simply that future developments in campaign financing are unlikely to doom the Democrats.

A variant of this second hypothesis says that the flood of private money won't kill Democrats' electoral fortunes, but it will push them to the right, reducing their support for social policy advance.[41] This is possible. However, we've already experienced a flood of private money into politics over the past three decades. According to the standard measure of policy makers' voting, it hasn't produced a shift to the center among Democratic legislators. Figure 5.4 shows voting trends on economic issues by House and Senate Democrats. Democrats did not move toward the center during this period. This is partly because the number of Democratic senators and representatives from the conservative South has been declining. But even among nonsouthern Democratic lawmakers, there is no sign of a move to the center.[42]

Focusing on voting might be misleading. After all, much of the important decision making by policy makers occurs before proposals come to a final vote. If we could measure this, we might find there has in fact been a move toward the center by Democrats in

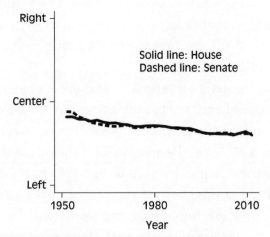

FIGURE 5.4 Voting by Democrats in the House and Senate
Average "dimension 1 DW-nominate" scores for Democratic legislators. The range shown here is –1 to +1 (left to right). *Data source*: Keith Poole and Christopher Hare, "An Update on Political Polarization through the 112th Congress," *Voteview*, January 16, 2013.

response to the growing influence of campaign contributors. But if that shift has happened, it has yet to be documented.

The Left Can Continue to Get Elected

Since Ronald Reagan was elected president in 1980, a significant portion of the American left has been in a near-constant state of despair about the electoral future of the Democratic Party. The party had drifted too far to the left, according to some. It had moved too far to the right, said others. It was incapable of nominating effective candidates. It couldn't keep up with the Republicans' fundraising. It lost touch with ordinary Americans. It was disorganized. It was too liberal on social issues. It was too dependent on big finance for campaign funding.

Each of these concerns is understandable. But the Democratic Party and its major candidates have, at least to this point, proven more resilient than pessimists expected. The Democrats have won four of the last six presidential elections, and in the past six congresses they've held a majority in the House twice and in the Senate four times. The recent past isn't necessarily a useful guide to the future. It's possible that American politics is on the verge of a sea change, with the Democrats' electoral fortunes dwindling. But that does not seem especially likely.

Obstacle 4: The Balance of Organized Power Has Shifted to the Right

According to a distinguished line of political analysis, from E. E. Schattschneider to William Domhoff to Thomas Ferguson and Joel Rogers to Jacob Hacker and Paul Pierson, the scope and generosity of government social policy in the United States is determined less by election outcomes than by the relative strength of organized interest groups.[43] Since the mid-1970s, American businesses and America's rich have mobilized, while

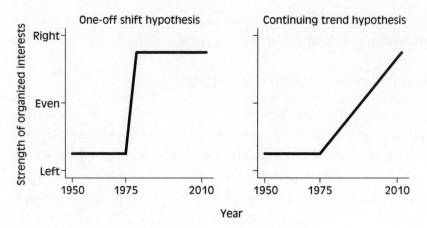

FIGURE 5.5 "One-off shift" and "continuing trend" hypotheses about the relative strength of organized interest groups
The vertical scale indicates the relative strength of organized interest groups. Higher on the axis indicates the right is stronger; lower indicates the left is stronger.

the left has fragmented and weakened.[44] Will this altered balance of power inhibit further progress in social policy?

There are two versions of this line of thinking. Figure 5.5 displays a stylized depiction of each. According to the first, the change was a one-off shift in the level of organizational strength. It happened in the late 1970s and/or the early 1980s, and there has been no change since. According to the second, the shift is a trend. It began in the late 1970s, has been ongoing since then, and will continue into the future.

If the change in the balance of interest group organization was a one-off shift, its impact on social policy advance should already be apparent, given that the shift occurred quite a while ago. Has progress in social policy stopped?

No. It has slowed, but it hasn't ceased.[45] There have been quite a few advances since the 1970s, including:

- Increases in the EITC and expansion of access (in 1986, 1990, 1993, 2009)
- Expansion of unemployment insurance (2009)
- Increases in Medicaid benefits and expansion of access (1984–88, 1998, 2010)

- Free immunization for kids in low-income families (Vaccines for Children, 1993)
- Expansion of Medicare to include prescription drugs (2004)
- Subsidy to low-income families' for childcare expenses (Child Care and Development Fund, 1990, 2009)
- Expansions of Head Start (1984, 1990, 1995, 2009)
- Expansion of public kindergarten to full days in most states and establishment of age-three and age-four prekindergarten programs in some states
- Reduction of funding inequality across elementary and secondary schools in most states
- Public funding of after-school activities in schools in low-income communities (21st Century Community Learning Centers program, 1998)
- Increases in college student loan funding (Pell Grant, Lifetime Learning Credit, Hope Credit)
- Expansions of retraining, job placement assistance, access to healthcare, and income support for people who lose a job due to international trade (1997, 2002, 2009)
- Antidiscrimination protection for people with disabilities (1990)
- Increase in disability benefits and expansion of access
- Creation and expansion of the Child Tax Credit (1997, 2003)
- Guaranteed right to unpaid family leave (1993) and introduction of paid leave in a few states (since 2004)
- Increase in housing assistance (1987)
- Establishment of and increases in energy assistance (Low-Income Energy Assistance, 1981, 2009)

The one notable move in the opposite direction took place with AFDC. From the 1970s on, benefit levels have decreased in inflation-adjusted terms, and the 1996 welfare reform put time limits on benefit receipt. But AFDC was a uniquely unpopular social program. In fact, welfare is the lone public social program consistently disliked by a majority of Americans.[46] In any event, its weakening is the exception, not the rule.

Some consider the 1983 Social Security amendments another exception. To shore up the program's funding, these reforms raised the retirement age, increased the payroll tax, and increased the taxation of Social Security benefits. The increase in the retirement age was a benefit cut, but it was merited, arguably, by rising life expectancy.

Additional evidence that social policy became more generous is found in CBO data. Figure 5.6 shows the CBO's estimates of the amount by which transfers and taxes boosted household incomes at the twentieth percentile of income from 1979 to 2007. The amount increased steadily. A good bit of this owed to increases in the value of Medicare and Medicaid benefits, but even so, these data suggest overall improvement in the size and scope of American social policy.[47]

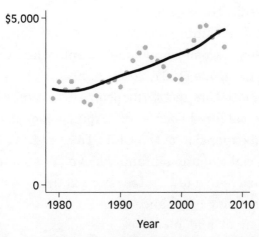

FIGURE 5.6 Difference between household market income and posttransfer-posttax income at the twentieth percentile of the income ladder

Incomes are adjusted for household size. The market income measure includes earnings, employer-paid health insurance premiums, the employer share of payroll taxes, business income, capital income, and capital gains. The posttransfer-posttax income measure subtracts federal tax payments and adds cash and in-kind government transfers, including Social Security, unemployment insurance, SSI, AFDC-TANF, veterans' benefits, workers' compensation, state and local cash assistance programs, food stamps, school lunches and breakfasts, housing assistance, energy assistance, Medicare, Medicaid, and S-CHIP. The health benefits are measured as the fungible value to the recipient. The incomes are in 2007 dollars; inflation adjustment is via the CPI-U-RS. The line is a loess curve. *Data source*: Congressional Budget Office, "Trends in the Distribution of Household Income Between 1979 and 2007," 2011, appendix tables A-1 and A-3.

If the shift in organized power was a one-off, the fact that public social policy has continued to advance despite the shift implies that we are likely to see further advance in the future.

The second version of the shift-in-the-balance-of-organized-power hypothesis, depicted in the second chart in figure 5.5, posits that the shift is a trend. It began in the late 1970s and has been on-going since then, with the strength of the right relative to the left steadily increasing. This paints a worrisome picture, suggesting we have not yet reached the point of maximum strength in the organized power of the right.

If this hypothesis is correct, what might the impact on advances in social policy be? We can glean some information by comparing policy change in the 1980s and the 2000s. If the continuing-trend hypothesis is correct, there should have been less social policy advance in the 2000s than in the 1980s. That isn't the case, according to the list of increases in the size and scope of social programs shown earlier and the information in figure 5.6. If we don't include the changes in the 2009 economic stimulus or the 2010 healthcare reform, the rate of advance in the two decades is similar. If we include those 2009–10 policy advances, the 2000s come out ahead by a good bit.

Here, too, the most reasonable conclusion is that the pattern of progress in social policy over the past century will continue.

Obstacle 5: The Structure of the US Political System Impedes Policy Change

Even if the obstacles I've considered so far can be overcome, progress toward more expansive and generous social policy might be impeded by our political system's abundance of "veto points"—a legislature and executive each elected directly by the people, two coequal legislative bodies, and the filibuster in the Senate.[48] These offer a determined minority multiple ways to block proposed policy changes.

On the one hand, these features of America's political system have been in place for some time, and while they surely have slowed the pace of social policy advance in the United States, they haven't prevented it. On the other hand, recent years have seen an increase in the cohesiveness, discipline, and confrontational posture of Republicans in Congress, making it very difficult for Democrats to get legislation passed unless they hold the presidency, a majority in the House, and sixty seats in the Senate. Does this spell the end of social policy advance?

Cohesive Parties in a Veto-Point-Heavy Political System

The extensiveness of veto points has taken on new importance in American politics because the Democratic and Republican parties have become much more cohesive. Until recently, both were loose collections of individuals with varying orientations and policy preferences. This was largely a legacy of the Civil War and the New Deal. In the South, many viewed the Civil War as a military invasion engineered by the Republican Party. For the better part of the following century, political competition in the South occurred entirely within the Democratic Party rather than between Democrats and Republicans. With the New Deal legislation in the 1930s, the Democrats became the party in favor of government intervention to enhance security and opportunity. Although this conflicted with the conservative orientation of many southern Democrats, they remained in the party until the Civil Rights Act of 1964 aligned the national Democratic Party with equal rights for African Americans.

While conservative southerners have been moving to the Republican Party, liberals in the rest of the country have been switching to the Democrats.[49] The ideological purification of the two parties is now complete: in both the House of Representatives and the Senate, the leftmost Republican is to the right of the rightmost Democrat.[50]

2

In prior eras, proponents of policy change often succeeded by fashioning a coalition across party lines. While this was seldom an easy task, it is now an extremely difficult one.[51]

From the perspective of democracy, there is a benefit to party cohesiveness: it provides voters with clear information about how a candidate will behave in office. But in a political system with multiple veto points, party cohesiveness increases the likelihood of gridlock. As long as the minority party controls one of the three lawmaking bodies—the presidency, the House, or the Senate—it can veto virtually any proposed policy change. Indeed, given the filibuster practice in the Senate, the minority doesn't actually need to control any of the three; it simply needs forty-one of the hundred seats in the Senate. The majority can circumvent the filibuster via a procedure known as "reconciliation," but this can be used only for a narrow range of bills.

The New Obstructionists

The polarization of America's two political parties has been asymmetrical: the Republicans have moved farther to the right than the Democrats have moved to the left. Figure 5.7 shows the average voting position on economic issues (broadly defined) among members of each party in the House of Representatives and the Senate. Both parties have shifted away from the center as they've become more cohesive. But Republicans in the House, and recently those in the Senate too, have moved farther from the center than have Democrats in either chamber.

Thomas Mann and Norman Ornstein point to another indicator of the rightward shift among Republican legislators:

the size of the House GOP's right-wing caucus, the Republican Study Committee, or RSC. Paul Weyrich and other conservative activists created the committee in 1973 as an informal group to pull the center-right party much further to the right. It had only 10 to 20 percent of Republican representatives as

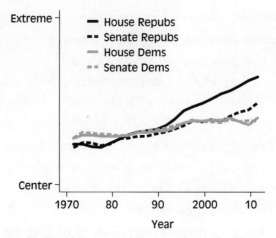

FIGURE 5.7 Voting by Republicans and Democrats in the House and Senate
Average "dimension 1 DW-nominate" scores for Republican legislators and Democratic
legislators in the House of Representatives and the Senate. The range shown here is
0 (center) to –1 or +1 (extreme left or right). *Data source*: Keith Poole and Christopher
Hare, "An Update on Political Polarization through the 112th Congress," *Voteview*,
January 16, 2013.

members as recently as the 1980s, a small fringe group. In
the 112th Congress [2011–12], the RSC had 166 members, or
nearly seven-tenths of the caucus.[52]

Republicans have become more unified in voting as well. Keith
Poole has measured the share of party members who follow their
party on votes in which a majority in one party votes opposite to
a majority in the other party (in other words, leaving out votes
on which there is significant bipartisan support). The share has
risen from 75 percent in 1970 to 90–95 percent in recent years.[53]
The Republicans' unity and their oppositional temperament were
on display during the debate on President Obama's proposed economic stimulus package in early 2009. Not a single Republican in
the House voted in favor of the package, even though many had
voted for a stimulus measure a year earlier when the economy was
in far less dire shape.[54]

In the Senate, both parties have made more frequent use of
the filibuster to block legislative proposals when they've been in

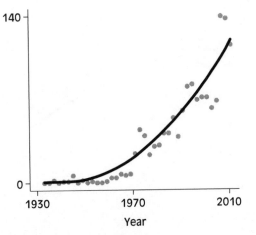

FIGURE 5.8 Use of the filibuster in the Senate
Number of cloture filings. The line is a loess curve. *Data source*: www.senate.gov, "Senate Action on Cloture Motions."

the minority. The best indicator of filibuster use is the number of cloture motions—motions to cut off filibuster attempts—that are filed. As figure 5.8 shows, the rise in filibustering began in the 1970s. Large jumps occurred in 1971, 1991, and 2007, with the latter being especially pronounced. In each case, Republicans initiated the rise.

Have these developments made it more difficult to pass legislation? Figure 5.9 shows the number of laws passed by Congress in each term since the early 1930s. Although there has been a decline, it began before the 1970s. And there was no acceleration in the 1970s when the polarization of the parties and increased use of the filibuster began, or in the 1990s when Republicans in the House began their sharp turn to the right and filibuster use jumped, or in the past few years as Republicans became especially obstructionist.

Even if we don't see a clear impact of the new Republican obstructionism, it could have an effect in the future. Will it? I suspect the Republican leadership in Congress will sooner or later turn away from the staunch antigovernment orientation that has dominated its approach of late. I see three potential triggers. One is a bad loss in an otherwise winnable election. This nearly happened in 2012,

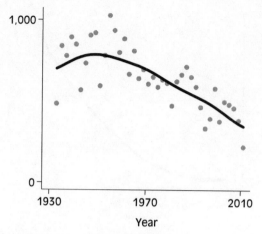

FIGURE 5.9 Number of laws passed by Congress
The line is a loess curve. *Data source*: Tobin Grant, personal communication.

as Republican voters in the presidential primaries flirted with a series of unelectable conservative candidates—Rick Perry, Newt Gingrich, Herman Cain, and Rick Santorum—before settling on Mitt Romney as the party's nominee. If it eventually does happen, it will prompt a move back toward the center, some key defections from the party, or a more frequent occurrence of Democrats holding the presidency, the House, and a filibuster-proof majority in the Senate.

Another push toward Republican moderation could come from the growing importance of working-class whites as a constituency for the party. Some thoughtful and prominent voices on America's right—David Brooks, Ross Douthat, David Frum, Charles Murray, Ramesh Ponnuru, Reihan Salam—have noted that this group is struggling economically and could benefit from government help.[55]

Finally, clear thinkers on the right will eventually realize that the key question isn't how *much* government should intervene but *how* it should do so. As I pointed out in chapter 4, an expansion of public social programs doesn't necessarily mean more government interference in markets and weaker competition. If Americans want protection and support and the choice is between social insurance and regulation, the former usually is preferable.

The Tea Party could forestall the Republican leadership's shift back to the center. It is an important force in elections to the House of Representatives in several dozen districts. If the Tea Party remains vibrant, it will continue to push Republicans toward the extreme.[56] The same is true of Grover Norquist and his "taxpayer protection" pledge, which most congressional Republicans have felt obliged to sign. But if history is any guide, these barriers to moderation eventually will be eclipsed or disappear. In the long run, the center of gravity in the Republican Party probably will be similar to that of center-right parties in Western Europe, most of which accept a generous welfare state and relatively high taxes.

Veto Points Impede Backsliding

In the race to the good society, America is a tortoise.[57] We advance slowly, but we do advance. While our veto-point-heavy political system impedes progressive change, it also makes it difficult for opponents of government social programs to dilute or do away with them once they are in place. Consequently, social policy advances tend to endure. The long-run trend in American social policy has been one of slow but steady ratcheting upward, and the most likely scenario going forward is a continuation of this trend.

Progress Is Probable

The notion of a social democratic America will strike some observers of US politics as a pipe dream. But consider this: in the realm of public social policy, the distance between the United States today and Denmark or Sweden today is smaller than the distance between the United States a century ago and the United States today. In the past one hundred years we've put in place a host of public programs that contribute to economic security, opportunity, and shared prosperity. Getting closer to the good society doesn't require a radical break from our historical path. It simply requires continuing along that path. In all likelihood, that is exactly what we will do.

This doesn't mean the future is predetermined. The trajectory I've laid out here is the most likely one, in my view, but it is by no means the only possibility. Moreover, even if we do move toward expanded government social programs, there will be plenty of space for actors to shape the timing, scope, and nature of future policy. My aim in writing this book is, above all else, to help inform those who seek to do so.

6

America's Social Democratic Future

AMERICA CAN DO better at ensuring economic security, opportunity, and shared prosperity by expanding some of our existing public social programs and adding some new ones, and I expect we will. What will the country look like half a century from now?

A larger share of adults will be in paid employment, though for many the workweek will be shorter and there will be more vacation days and holidays. Nearly all jobs will be in services; only 5 percent or so will be in manufacturing or agriculture. Many more Americans will work in helping-caring services—teaching, advising, instructing, aiding, nursing, curing, monitoring, assisting—and more of these services will be personalized. Quite a few of these jobs will be relatively low paying. Most of us will shift between jobs and even occupations more frequently than today.

Our economy will be more globalized. More of the goods and services we purchase will be produced or performed abroad. More of us will work for firms based in other countries. More US companies will employ workers in other nations or outsource tasks to firms located abroad. We will continue to attract lots of immigrants.[1]

Access to health insurance, old-age income security, and other types of insurance will no longer be tied to one's employer. The taxes that fund particular programs will still be levied partly on payroll, as the Social Security and Medicare taxes currently are. And companies will continue to offer particular types of benefits, such as contributions to a private pension plan, in order to attract better employees and keep existing ones. But these will supplement the public insurance programs.

A larger share of our GDP will go to taxes and government expenditures. Yet in another respect, government will be smaller: there will be fewer regulations on firms and individuals. We'll always need some restrictions to prevent financial excesses, protect worker and consumer safety, safeguard the environment, and more. But we will rely less on specifying what businesses can and can't do and more on competition coupled with cushions. If we do better at enforcing antitrust rules and scrap or reduce regulations that create barriers to entry, competition will help to align business behavior with the preferences of consumers. Insurance—both compensatory and proactive, both cash payments and services—will cushion those who are victimized by market processes or the vagaries of life.

Government also will be more efficient and effective in its administration. Those who favor expanding public insurance ought to be at the forefront of efforts to improve government's performance. This is the approach modern social democrats in the Nordic countries tend to take. As a Danish Social Democratic prime minister has put it, "If you have a large public sector, you have an obligation to wake up every morning searching for ways to make it work better."[2] The Clinton administration's Reinventing Government initiative, headed by Vice President Al Gore, contributed to this process in the United States. The Obama administration has attempted to streamline and improve regulation.[3] It also has encouraged stronger accountability standards for public schools and teachers. And the 2010 healthcare reform included steps to increase use of evidence-based treatment in Medicare. Though not always a priority for America's left, movement in the direction of better government is likely to continue.

Will outcomes improve? Here too I am optimistic, albeit cautiously so. A universal system of good-quality affordable early education beginning at age one will boost opportunity for American kids who grow up in disadvantaged homes and neighborhoods. Other policy shifts will help too: an increase in the Child Tax Credit, less incarceration of young men who commit minor offenses, and affirmative action targeted at the economically disadvantaged.

Shifts in markets and institutions will continue in the direction of less economic security. More of us will work in jobs with low pay, lose a job once or more during our work career, and reach retirement age with insufficient savings and an inadequate 401(k). Families, community organizations, and labor unions may be even weaker than they are now. But if we fill in the gaps in our public safety net—with universal health insurance, less-porous unemployment insurance, wage insurance, a new public defined-contribution pension program with automatic enrollment, sickness insurance, paid parental leave, a minimum wage indexed to prices, better support for making work pay, more robust social assistance, and individualized advising and support throughout the life course—most Americans will be more secure in spite of these shifts.

What of shared prosperity? It's quite possible that inequality of market incomes will continue to rise in coming decades. More to the point, there is a good chance that wages for Americans in the middle and below will be stagnant, as they have since the 1970s. But if we increase provision of public goods, services, spaces, and free time, living standards will rise even if incomes don't. And if we restructure the Earned Income Tax Credit in the way I suggest in chapter 3—expand eligibility, boost the benefit level for persons with no children, and index it to average compensation or GDP per capita—we can ensure that the incomes of lower-half households more closely track growth of the economy even in the absence of rising wages.

This America will be a society with greater security and fairness. The economy will be flexible, dynamic, innovative. Employment will be high. Liberty will be abundant. Balancing work and family will be easier. Though we'll need to pay higher taxes, this sacrifice will be a small one, because we will receive a lot in return.

We've come a long way on the road to the good society, but we have many miles yet to travel. Happily, our history and the experiences of other rich nations show us the way forward. The United States is a much better country today than it was a century ago, and a key part of the reason is that government does more to ensure security, opportunity, and shared prosperity now than it did then. In the future it will do more still, and we'll be the better for it.

Acknowledgments

I'VE PRESENTED PARTS of this book at an array of venues over the past few years and have had numerous discussions about its ideas in less formal settings. I thank the many participants, discussants, critics, colleagues, and friends who've offered valuable comments and suggestions. The venues include the American Sociological Association annual meeting, Chung-Ang University (Seoul), the 14th International Conference of the Giordano Dell'Amore Observatory (Milan), the Harvard Kennedy School, the Korea Labor Institute, the Next Centre-Left Century conference (Oxford, UK), the Paris School of Economics, the Resolution Foundation (London), the Roosevelt Institute (New York and Washington, DC), the University of Arizona, the University of California-Berkeley, the University of California-Los Angeles, the University of Kansas, the University of Kentucky, the University of Pennsylvania, the University of Toronto, Washington University (St. Louis), and Yale University. I'm particularly grateful to Corey Abramson, Bruno Amable, Jon Bakija, Jared Bernstein, Irene Bloemraad, Jerome Bourdieu, Ron Breiger, John Bullock, Kathryn Edin, Neil Fligstein, Martin Gilens, Jacob Hacker, Alex Hicks, Michael Hout, Christopher Jencks, Frank Lechner, Peter Lindert, Julia Lynch, Jeff Madrick, Ive Marx, Leslie McCall, Karen Myers, John Myles, Paul Pierson, Charles Ragin, Joel Rogers, Tim Smeeding, Joe Soss, Robin Stryker, Jeff Weintraub, Bruce Western, and Scott Winship. Apologies to anyone I've inadvertently failed to include in this list.

Thanks also to David McBride and the production and marketing teams at Oxford University Press, and to Elizabeth Thompson and Ginny Faber for editing.

As always, I'm thankful most of all for my family: Kim, Mia, Hannah, Noah, and Josh.

Notes

CHAPTER 1

1. Kessler 2011; Yglesias 2011.
2. Reich 2007, p. 50.
3. See chapter 2.
4. See chapter 4.
5. Ibid.
6. Graetz and Mashaw 1999; Chetty and Finkelstein 2013.
7. Graetz and Mashaw 1999; Barr 2001; Moss 2002; Quiggin 2007.
8. See chapter 3.
9. I made this title up, assuming there was no such thing as a "Progressives' Handbook." It turns out there is.
10. Gangl 2006.
11. Duncan, Huston, and Weisner 2007.
12. Polanyi 1944.
13. Yglesias 2013.
14. See chapter 4.
15. Atkinson 1999; Lindert 2004.
16. Przeworski 1985; Esping-Andersen 1990; Berman 2006; Sejersted 2011.
17. Esping-Andersen 1990.
18. Esping-Andersen et al. 2002; Huo, Nelson, and Stephens 2008; Kenworthy 2008a, 2010b; Kristensen and Lilja 2011; Pontusson 2011; Hemerijck 2012; Morel, Palier, and Palme 2012.
19. Baumol, Litan, and Schramm 2007.
20. See chapter 4.
21. See Kenworthy 2011c, ch. 5.
22. Due to the coming retirement of the baby boom generation and projected increases in healthcare costs, Medicare and Social Security costs are likely to rise by 2–4 percent of GDP.

23. See chapter 4.
24. See chapter 4.
25. Kenworthy 2011c, ch. 8.
26. This conclusion is similar to that of Wilensky 1975, 2002.
27. Prominent exceptions include expansion of Social Security in the 1950s and indexation of its benefits to inflation in the early 1970s, creation of the EITC in 1975 and its expansion in the 1980s, designation of food stamps as a federal entitlement in the mid-1970s and expansion of food stamp eligibility in the early 2000s, increases in Medicaid coverage and benefits in the 1980s, and the extension of Medicare coverage to prescription drugs in 2004.
28. See Heclo 1974.

Chapter 2

1. Lebergott 1976; Cox and Alm 1999; DeLong 2009; Fischer 2010, ch. 2.
2. Moss 2002; Castles et al. 2010. These laws and programs offered, in Franklin Roosevelt's words, a "safeguard against misfortunes which cannot be wholly eliminated" (speech to Congress, June 1934).
3. For a contrary view, see Winship 2012.
4. Osterman 1999.
5. Uchitelle 2006.
6. Hacker 2006. See also Hacker 2011.
7. Gosselin 2008.
8. Hacker, Rehm, and Schlesinger 2010, figure 4.
9. Osterman 1999; Baumol, Blinder, and Wolff 2003; Fligstein and Shin 2003; Uchitelle 2006; Blinder 2009a; Farber 2010; Kalleberg 2011.
10. Western, Bloome, Sosnaud, and Tach 2012.
11. Congressional Budget Office 2010. The standard indicator of low income is the poverty rate, which tells us the share of people in households with incomes below a particular level—the poverty line. But there is little agreement about where the line should be drawn, so skeptics rightly worry that if the line is a little bit lower or higher, the estimate of how many are poor will change significantly. I prefer to instead look directly at the incomes of the least well-off. See Kenworthy 2011b, 2011c; also Burtless and Smeeding 2001.
12. Rector 2007; Eberstadt 2008.
13. Edin and Lein 1997; Ehrenreich 2001; DeParle 2004.
14. Caner and Wolff 2004.
15. Mayer and Jencks 1993; Edin and Lein 1997.
16. Rank 2004, table 4.2, using Panel Study of Income Dynamics (PSID) data.
17. Ibid.
18. Boushey, Brocht, Gundersen, and Bernstein 2001. See also Gould, Wething, Sabadish, and Finio 2013.
19. Wider Opportunities for Women 2011.
20. Census Bureau 2011, table B-2.

21. Wolff 2011, table 4.1.
22. Center for Retirement Security 2009, using data from the Survey of Consumer Finances. The numbers sum to more than 100 percent because some people are enrolled in both types of plan.
23. Another potential advantage is that a defined-contribution plan isn't vulnerable to a firm going out of business or declaring bankruptcy. Such an occurrence can leave those in a traditional company pension plan out in the cold, though most such pensions are guaranteed by the federal government-backed Pension Guarantee Benefit Corporation.
24. *Economist* 2008; Ghilarducci 2008; Wolff 2011; Fletcher 2013.
25. My calculations using OECD data.
26. Layard 2005.
27. Rose and Winship 2009, figure 6.
28. Rose and Winship 2009, figure 2. For additional estimates based on the PSID data, see Gosselin and Zimmerman 2008; Hacker and Jacobs 2008; Jensen and Shore 2008; Dynan 2010; Dynan, Elmendorf, and Sichel 2012.
29. Winship 2012, figure 1. For additional estimates based on the SIPP data, see Acs, Loprest, and Nichols 2009.
30. Congressional Budget Office 2008, figure 5, p. 10.
31. See economicsecurityindex.org. Accessed January 15, 2013. These numbers are for people who lost one-fourth of their income, not including out-of-pocket medical costs or repayment of debt.
32. Mark Rank and Thomas Hirschl have done a related calculation, also using PSID data. They ask what share of Americans experience five or more total years of income below the poverty line, of welfare receipt, or of unemployment between the ages of 25 and 60. The answer is 35 percent. See Rank and Hirschl, forthcoming.
33. See also Dynan, Elmendorf, and Sichel 2012.
34. Elizabeth Jacobs, personal communication.
35. Families USA 2009.
36. Mendes 2012, using Gallup data.
37. Jacoby 2012.
38. Pew Research Center. For more, see Page and Jacobs 2009; McCall 2013.
39. Sen 1999; Nussbaum 2011.
40. Noah 2012.
41. The share of women aged 25 to 29 who have completed four or more years of college has risen steadily over the past half century. In fact, by the early 1990s women had caught up with men in college graduation, and in the ensuing decades they raced ahead. By 2010, 36 percent of women aged 25 to 29 had completed college, compared to just 28 percent of men. This gap in favor of women was as large as the gap favoring men was in 1960. (Census Bureau, "Educational Attainment: CPS Historical Time Series Tables," table A-2, using Current Population Survey data.)

Women have made significant strides in employment as well. According to OECD data, in 1960 just 41 percent of prime-working-age (25 to 54) women were employed. By 2010 that had jumped to 73 percent. Among men in this age group, the employment rate fell from 92 percent to 87 percent.

Median earnings among women employed full-time and year round likewise have risen steadily, from (in 2010 dollars) $21,000 in 1960 to $28,000 in 1979 to $38,000 in 2010 (Census Bureau, "Historical Income Tables," table P-21.). This is an advance in an absolute sense and also relative to men. In the 1960s and 1970s, women's median earnings were about 60 percent of men's. In the 1980s women began gaining ground, and by 2010 the ratio was 77 percent. In fact, if we narrow the comparison to those aged 25 to 34, the ratio is 91 percent. (Bureau of Labor Statistics 2011. The female-to-male earnings ratio then decreases for older age groups, partly because women are much more likely to leave work temporarily for family reasons. Part of the gap is accounted for by work hours (men are more likely to work overtime) and employee benefits (women are more likely to hold jobs with better benefits but lower pay). See CONSAD Research Corp 2009.)

As of 2012 women held 52 percent of managerial, professional, and related positions (Bureau of Labor Statistics 2011). At the top of the corporate hierarchy there is still a large gender gap; yet here, too, progress has been significant. Women represent only 18 percent of senior officers (vice president or higher) in Fortune 500 firms, but that's up from 9 percent in 1995. Women hold only 3 percent of Fortune 500 CEO slots, yet that's up from 1 percent in 2000. At the very top, on the boards of directors of Fortune 500 companies, women hold 16 percent of the seats, up from 1 percent in 1988. (These data are from Catalyst, catalyst.org.)

All told, women's capabilities have expanded markedly. Noteworthy gaps with men persist in various aspects of labor market success, but progress has been substantial.

42. In 1960, only 40 percent of African Americans aged 25 to 29 had completed high school. By the end of the 1970s, the share had increased to 77 percent, and in 2010 it reached 89 percent (this includes those with a GED). The advance was not only absolute, but also relative to whites. White high school completion in this age group was 67 percent in 1960, nearly double the black share. In 2010 the white high school completion rate was 95 percent, just 6 percentage points higher than among blacks. (Census Bureau, "Educational Attainment: CPS Historical Time Series Tables," table A-2, using Current Population Survey data.)

College graduation among African Americans has risen substantially. In the early 1960s, only 5 percent of 25-to-29-year-old blacks had a four-year college degree. By 2010, 20 percent did. On the other hand, we might have hoped for a larger increase. College completion among whites jumped from 15 percent to nearly 40 percent during that half century, and college completion among women rose from 10 percent to 35 percent.

Reliable employment data for African Americans date from the early 1970s (Bureau of Labor Statistics, "Labor Force Statistics (CPS): Household Data," using Current Population Survey data). Between 1973 and 2007 (business-cycle peak years), the employment rate among blacks rose by about 5 percentage points. The same was true for whites. For both groups the 2008–09 recession brought a significant decline.

In earnings, African Americans have experienced less advance (Census Bureau, "Historical Income Tables," table P-38, using Current Population Survey data). Among those employed full-time and year-round, median earnings rose steadily in the 1960s and 1970s. But then the improvement ceased, apart from a few years in the late 1990s. Whites experienced a similar fate, though, which suggests the barrier was changes in the economy rather than obstacles specific to African Americans.

The same is true for household income (Census Bureau, "Historical Income Tables," table H-5 and Census Bureau 2011, using CPS data). The late 1990s is the only period in the past several decades in which we observe improvement in either median household income or the share of African Americans with above-poverty-level income. Again, though, the same holds for whites.

In the past generation, incarceration has become a relatively common feature in the life course of African American men. Spending time in prison and having a prison record significantly diminishes the likelihood of employment during young adulthood, and it reduces the earnings of those who do find employment (Western 2006). We don't yet know the degree to which this effect continues through people's working career, but it seems likely to act as a permanent brake on labor market opportunity for a considerable number of black men.

Overall, opportunity for many African Americans has improved, though in some important areas both absolute and relative progress has been limited.

43. The following discussion draws on Wilson 1978, 1987, 1996, 2009; Jencks and Mayer 1990; Fischer et al. 1996; Duncan and Brooks-Gunn 1999; Mayer 1999; Lareau 2003; MacLeod 2009; Currie 2011; Duncan and Murnane 2011; Kenworthy 2012b.

44. Economic Mobility Project 2012.

There is additional evidence of unequal opportunity by family background. Begin with educational attainment. Caroline Ratcliff and Signe-Mary McKernan (2010, figure 5, using PISD data) examined American children who grew up in the 1970s and 1980s and found those with low-income parents less likely to graduate from high school. Among those whose household never was poor during their childhood (never had an income below the official poverty line), 96 percent got a high school diploma. Among those whose household was poor for half or more of their childhood years, only 77 percent did.

As adults, children of low-income parents are less likely to be employed and more likely to have low earnings and incomes. Ratcliff and McKernan found that among males whose family was poor in half or more of their childhood years, only 34 percent were employed consistently as young adults (from ages 25 to 30). Among those never poor during childhood, 76 percent were consistently employed.

Markus Jäntti and colleagues (2006, using National Longitudinal Survey of Youth data) examined the adult earnings of boys who grew up in the 1960s and 1970s. Of those whose father was in the lowest fifth of earnings, 42 percent were themselves in the lowest fifth as adults, compared to just 10 percent of those whose father was in the top fifth.

A similar pattern holds for household income. David Harding, Christopher Jencks, Leonard Lopoo, and Susan Mayer (2005, table 3.4) examined the adult incomes of various generations of American children. Of those whose parents' income was in the bottom quarter, 40–45 percent were themselves in the bottom quarter as adults. Of those whose parents' income was in the top quarter, only 10 percent were in the bottom quarter as adults. Ratcliff and McKernan found that among people whose household income was below the poverty line in more than half of their childhood years, 32 percent ended up themselves poor as young adults. The share among those who grew up in a never-poor home was just 1 percent. ("Nonpoor" as a young adult is defined as having a household income above the official poverty line in two or fewer of the six years from ages 25 to 30.)

45. Hauser et al. 2000.
46. McLanahan and Sandefur 1994; McLanahan 2001.
47. Ellwood and Jencks 2004; Murray 2012a; Parlapiano 2012.
48. Lareau 2003; Duncan and Murnane 2011.
49. Reardon 2011.
50. Jencks 2009; Bailey and Dynarski 2011.
51. Western 2006.
52. Wilson 1987, 1996; Wright and Dwyer 2003; Autor 2010; Western and Rosenfeld 2011; Blinder 2009a.
53. Schwartz and Mare 2005.
54. Some recent studies find no indication of an increase in inequality of opportunity. See Harding, Jencks, Lopoo, and Mayer 2005, using data from the General Social Survey (GSS) and the PSID; Lee and Solon 2009, using data from the PSID; Winship 2013, using data from the National Longitudinal Survey of Young Men and the National Longitudinal Survey of Youth. Others conclude that there likely has been an increase. See Aaronson and Mazumder 2008, using estimates from Census data; Bloome and Western 2011, using data from the National Longitudinal Survey of Young Men and the National Longitudinal Survey of Youth.

55. Rawls 1971; Friedman 2005; Kenworthy 2011c.
56. These data are created by merging information from the Current Population Survey of households with tax records from the IRS. Each of these two sources has a strength and a weakness. Household surveys provide good information for the bulk of the population, but not for those at the top. Tax records give us much better information on those at the top, but are not very good for those at the bottom. By merging the two, the CBO has created the most accurate and complete data series available. Unfortunately, it only goes back to 1979.
57. See, for instance, Samuelson 1995; Cox and Alm 1999; Easterbrook 2003; Rose 2010; Burkhauser, Larrimore, and Simon 2011; Meyer and Sullivan 2011.
58. Kenworthy 2012a.
59. Actually, it's worse than the trend for all families. That's because median income among the retired has been growing at a slightly faster pace than median income among prime-working-age families, due to rising Social Security benefit levels. The data are at Census Bureau, "Historical Income Tables," table F-11.
60. Census Bureau, "Foreign Born."
61. The data are at Census Bureau, "Historical Income Tables," table F-5.
62. Johnson 2004; Meyer and Sullivan 2011. See also Attanasio, Hurst, and Pistaferri 2012.
63. See Wolff 2012.
64. Isaacson 2011.
65. The data in the following paragraphs come from a variety of sources, including Lebergott 1976; Cox and Alm 1999; Easterbrook 2003; Fischer 2010.
66. For an argument that the pace of innovation has been *less* rapid since the mid-1970s, see Cowen 2011.
67. See in particular Warren and Tyagi 2003; Lesmerises 2007; Blank 2010.
68. Census Bureau, "Historical Income Tables," table F-12.
69. Census Bureau, "Historical Income Tables," table P-38.
70. Census Bureau, "Historical Income Tables," table F-12.
71. Jacobs and Gerson 2004.
72. Presser 2003.
73. McKenzie and Rapino 2011.
74. Some suggest that the cost of goods and services consumed by low-income households has risen less rapidly than that of the bundle used to adjust for inflation. See Broda and Romalis 2008. Others argue that this is wrong. See Meyer and Sullivan 2011.
75. Lesmerises 2007, figure 12, using data from Warren and Tyagi 2003. See also DeLong 2012.
76. College Board, "Trends in College Pricing 2006," table 4a.
77. Allegretto 2011, table 10, using Survey of Consumer Finances data.
78. Warren and Tyagi 2003; Weller 2012.

CHAPTER 3

1. Census Bureau 2011, table 8.
2. The 2010 Affordable Care Act may accelerate this shift. See Hacker 2011.
3. Seidman 2013.
4. For additional cost-reduction ideas, see Emanuel et al. 2012; Gawande 2011, 2012; Soltas 2012; Aaron 2013.
5. Klein 2007; Reid 2009; Davis, Schoen, and Stremekis 2010; OECD 2011.
6. Heymann et al. 2009.
7. Bureau of Labor Statistics 2012b, using data from the March 2012 National Compensation Survey.
8. Waldfogel 2006, ch. 2. See also Kenworthy 2009c.
9. Ferrarini and Duvander 2010.
10. Anrig 2006.
11. House Ways and Means Committee, Green Book, various editions.
12. Kletzer and Litan 2001; LaLonde 2007; Kling 2008.
13. Kenworthy 2009b.
14. Murray 1984; Ellwood 1988; Marmor, Mashaw, and Harvey 1990; Jencks 1992; Skocpol 1992; Blank 1997; Gilens 1999; Haskins and Sawhill 2009; Thiebaud 2012.
15. This logic could also be applied to existing disability policy. See Autor and Duggan 2010; Burkhauser and Daly 2012; Reno and Ekman 2012.
16. Hays 2003; DeParle 2004, ch. 14; Morgen, Acker, and Weigt 2010.
17. Edin and Lein 1997; Newman 1999, 2006; DeParle 2004; Edin and Kefalas 2005; England and Edin 2009; Nelson and Edin 2013.
18. Ben-Galim and Dal 2009.
19. Gottschalk 1998.
20. DeParle 2012; Shaefer and Ybarra 2012.
21. Diamond and Orszag 2004; Ruffing 2011; Aaron 2013.
22. Graetz and Mashaw 1999; Munnel 2012; US Senate Committee on Health, Education, Labor, and Pensions 2012.
23. Currie 2006; OECD 2008, ch. 9; Esping-Andersen and Myles 2009; Garfinkel, Rainwater, and Smeeding 2010; Kenworthy 2011c, ch. 7.
24. OECD 2008, ch. 7.
25. Heckman 2008; Ermisch, Jäntti, and Smeeding 2012, p. 465; Duncan and Murnane 2011, p. 9.
26. Downey, von Hippel, and Broh 2004; Alexander, Entwisle, and Olson 2007.
27. See Bowen, Chingos, and McPherson 2009; Hout 2009; Jencks 2009; Arum and Roksa 2011; Dynarski and Scott-Clayton 2013; National Commission on Higher Education Attainment 2013.
28. Jencks 2009, p. A7.
29. OECD 2010, table B5.1; OECD 2012.
30. Murray 2009; Vedder et al. 2010.

31. This excludes those who get a certificate of high school equivalency by passing the General Educational Development tests (GED). Heckman and LaFontaine 2007.
32. Kozol 1991.
33. Hoxby 2003.
34. Gleason et al. 2010; Center for Research on Education Outcomes 2013.
35. DeLuca and Rosenblatt 2010.
36. Hanushek 2010; Chetty, Friedman, and Rockoff 2011.
37. Gordon, Kane, and Staiger 2008; Auguste, Kihn, and Miller 2010; Kristof 2012; Wilson and Laurent 2012.
38. Esping-Andersen 2004, 2011; Smeeding, Erickson, and Jäntti 2011; Ermisch, Jäntti, and Smeeding 2011; Esping-Andersen and Wagner 2012.
39. Heckman 2008; Ruhm and Waldfogel 2011.
40. Gornick and Meyers 2003; OECD 2006; Esping-Andersen 2009.
41. Vandell and Wolfe 2000; Waldfogel 2006. Among three- and four-year-olds, approximately 28 percent are enrolled in public prekindergarten and 52 percent in any type of prekindergarten school. See Barnett et al. 2011, table 4; National Center for Education Statistics 2012, table A-1-1.
42. Heckman 2008; Barnett 2013.
43. Kenworthy 2012b.
44. Duncan, Ziol-Guest, and Kalil 2010.
45. Waldfogel 2009, p. 52.
46. Western 2006.
47. Western 2012.
48. Bowen and Bok 1998; Reskin 1998.
49. Kahlenberg 1995; Murray 2012b.
50. For more detail, see Kenworthy 2011c.
51. For a more detailed discussion, see Kenworthy 2011i.
52. Mishel and Shierholz 2013.
53. Bernstein and Baker 2003.
54. Kenworthy 2008a, 2013a.
55. Kenworthy 2008a.
56. For more discussion, see Kenworthy 2011g.
57. Rising employment is particularly important for those at the low end of the labor market. Here, too, the 2000s upturn was a disappointment. In working-age households in the bottom quarter of income, average employment hours failed to rise at all. See Kenworthy 2011c, ch. 3.
58. Gordon 2010.
59. Blinder 2009a; Pierce and Schott 2012.
60. Brynjolfsson and McAfee 2011; Jaimovich and Siu 2012.
61. With the ebbing of the outsourcing and offshoring craze, some manufacturing and service jobs have begun to move back to the United States. But the number is, and will be, relatively small. See Fishman 2012; Economist 2013b.

62. Ben-Galim and Dal 2009.
63. Katz 1998; Gottschalk 1998. A good candidate here is green jobs; see Apollo Alliance 2008; Block 2011.
64. The Bureau of Labor Statistics projects that in 2020 approximately one third of US jobs will be in occupations with a median wage of $25,000 or less. See Bureau of Labor Statistics 2012a.
65. For similar sentiment, see Gans 2011.
66. Baumol 2012; Carlin 2012.
67. My suggestion is similar in spirit to the idea of "inequality insurance" proposed by Robert Shiller; see Shiller 2003, ch. 11. See also Reich 2010.
68. Average compensation tends to rise in sync with GDP per capita. See Pessoa and Van Reenen 2012.
69. Note that to be effective, a rising earnings subsidy will need to be coupled with a rising minimum wage. Otherwise, the subsidy may lead to reductions in low-end wage levels, which will offset the improvement in income achieved by the subsidy. This can happen in two ways. First, if the subsidy succeeds in pulling more people into work, the increase in competition for jobs will put downward pressure on wages. Second, regardless of labor supply, employers will be tempted to incorporate the value of the subsidy into the wages they offer. For more discussion see Kenworthy 2011c, ch. 5.

CHAPTER 4

1. Kenworthy 2008a, ch. 8; 2011, ch. 8.
2. Kenworthy 2009a.
3. OECD 2008, ch. 4; Kenworthy 2011c, ch. 8.
4. Mahler and Jesuit 2006; Kenworthy 2011c, ch. 8; Wang and Caminada 2011.
5. This means households with incomes below approximately $250,000.
6. Kenworthy 2011a.
7. Our GDP in 2007 was $14 trillion. Ten percent of that is $1.4 trillion. That year the top 5 percent of Americans, 5.9 million households, had an average pretax income of $611,200, according to the Congressional Budget Office (CBO), making their total pretax income $3.6 trillion (Congressional Budget Office 2010). The $1.4 trillion needed to boost tax revenues by 10 percent of GDP amounts to 38.8 percent of that $3.6 trillion. Thus, the effective tax rate on the incomes of the top 5 percent of households would need to be increased by 38.8 percentage points.
8. Kenworthy 2008a, figure 8.12.
9. This estimate is based on information in Krueger 2009; Toder and Rosenberg 2010; Barro 2011; Campbell 2011.
10. In fact, a consumption tax can be made progressive. See Frank 2008.
11. Bartlett 2012b.
12. Kenworthy 2011c, ch. 8.
13. Kenworthy 2011h.

14. Surowiecki 2010.
15. Carasso, Reynolds, and Steurle 2008; Toder et al. 2010.
16. Irons 2010.
17. The total payroll (Social Security and Medicare) tax rate is about 15 percent, and since the mid-1980s it has consistently collected 6.6 percent to 7.0 percent of GDP.
18. I use the shares of pretax income going to each quintile as of 2007. See Congressional Budget Office 2010.
19. Huang 2012; Bartlett 2012a; Saez, Slemrod, and Giertz 2012.
20. The list of relevant citations is lengthy. A good start is Polanyi 1944; Stiglitz 1989; Gough 1996; Lindert 2004; Madrick 2009.
21. Jones 1995.
22. This line of reasoning follows Stokey and Rebelo 1995; Myles 2000.
23. Tanzi 2011.
24. For more discussion, see Kenworthy 2008a, ch. 4.
25. Slemrod and Bakija 2008; Myles 2009; Bakija 2012. As with almost any phenomenon, it's possible, with enough tweaking, to find an association that conforms to one's prior beliefs. For instance, some studies find a negative association between taxation and economic growth by adding a group of moderate-tax high-growth countries or a particular set of control variables. See Fölster and Henrekson 2001; Bergh and Karlsson 2010; Bergh and Henrekson 2011.

    When comparing across countries, our best bet, from an analytical perspective, is to compare changes over time rather than levels. (This is a strategy known as "differences in differences"; see Kenworthy 2011d.) This means looking at the cross-country association between changes in the size of government and changes in economic growth. But this requires a good bit of variation among the countries in the degree of change in the hypothesized cause, and we don't have that here, unfortunately. During this period, government revenues rose by a few percentage points of GDP in nearly all countries. See Kenworthy 2011d, figure 2.
26. Hall and Soskice 2001.
27. Coherence applies both within and across economic spheres. A country's institutional mix is deemed more coherent to the extent that its institutions within each sphere are closer to one or the other of the two poles (liberal market or coordinated market) rather than in between and its institutions are consistent across spheres. Incoherence can be a product of being in the middle within each sphere or having liberal market institutions in some spheres and coordinated market institutions in others.
28. There have been other attempts to measure institutional coherence: Amable 2003; Hall and Gingerich 2004; Kenworthy 2006; Schneider and Paunescu 2012.
29. Hall and Gingerich have several control variables in their regressions, including inflation, change in the country's terms of trade (export prices

divided by import prices) weighted by its degree of trade openness, and the share of the population younger than age 15 or older than age 64. However, none of these is related to economic growth in their analyses. A fourth is the average growth rate among the group of countries as a whole weighted by the degree of trade openness in each nation. In an analysis with yearly data, this is useful to control for business cycle effects, but it is unnecessary in an analysis that covers one or more complete business cycles. I estimated a series of regressions with various combinations of three other controls: education (average years of schooling completed), real interest rates, tax revenues (as a share of GDP). This did not yield a positive association between institutional coherence and economic growth.

30. See also Campbell and Pedersen 2007; Kristensen and Lilja 2011.
31. Acemoglu, Robinson, and Verdier 2012.
32. Heller 2001.
33. Atkinson, Piketty, and Saez 2011, figure 10.
34. Schultze 1977; Anderson 1978; Simon 1978; Wanniski 1978; Friedman and Friedman 1979; Weidenbaum et al. 1980; Gilder 1981; Murray 1984.
35. Magaziner and Reich 1982; Reich 1983; Zysman 1983; Piore and Sabel 1984; Thurow 1984; Osborne 1987; Dertouzos et al. 1989; Kuttner 1989; Florida and Kenney 1990; Womack, Jones, and Roos 1990; Harrison and Kelley 1991; Tyson 1992.
36. Reich 1991, 1999; Clinton 1995; Sperling 2005.
37. Boix 2000.
38. Giddens 1998, 2000.
39. Both years were business-cycle peaks.
40. These historical GDP per capita data are from Angus Maddison, www.ggdc.net/maddison/historical_statistics/vertical-file_02-2010.xls.
41. Kenworthy 2010a.
42. Kenworthy 2012c.
43. Baumol 1967.
44. Mandel 2000, 2012; Baumol 2012.
45. Cowen 2011; Gordon 2012. Part of Gordon and Cowen's pessimism owes to the fact that the benefits of innovation no longer reach all households in the form of income growth. This is an important problem, as I emphasized in chapter 2. But it's a problem of distribution, not production. See Kenworthy 2011f.
46. St. Louis FRED, employment-population ratio (LNU02300000), using Bureau of Labor Statistics data.
47. North 1990.
48. These employment rates are for persons age 16–64.
49. Prescott 2004; Ohanian, Raffo, and Rogerson 2007.
50. Blanchard 2004; Alesina, Glaeser, and Sacerdote 2005; Immervoll and Barber 2006; Ray and Schmitt 2007; Boeri and Cahuc 2008; Causa 2008; Kenworthy 2008a.

51. Burgoon and Baxandall 2004.
52. Scharpf 2000; Kemmerling 2009; OECD 2007; Kenworthy 2008a, 2011.
53. Gornick and Meyers 2003; Huo, Nelson, and Stephens 2008; Kenworthy 2010b.
54. Some include Ireland and the UK in the "weak labor" group and Spain and Portugal in the "traditional family roles" group, but doing so doesn't alter the conclusion.
55. Nor are tax levels associated with *change* in employment hours from the 1980s to the 2000s. See Kenworthy 2011e.
56. A good discussion is Tanzi 2011, ch. 1.
57. Baker 2011, ch. 10.
58. Weeden 2002; Carpenter et al. 2012.
59. Avent 2011; Glaeser 2011; Yglesias 2012.
60. Baker and Moss 2009; Stiglitz 2009; Baker 2011, ch. 9; Zingales 2012.
61. Zingales 2012, p. 6. See Friedman 1962; Friedman and Friedman 1979.
62. Alesina and Angeletos 2005, p. 1241.
63. Rothstein 2011.
64. Using other measures of the quality of government, such as Transparency International's corruption perceptions index, does not change the story.
65. Teles 2012.
66. IRS Taxpayer Advocate Service, *2010 Annual Report to Congress*, vol. 1, cited in Teles 2012.
67. "Full Transcript of the Romney Secret Video," *Mother Jones*, September 2012.
68. Eberstadt 2012. See also Murray 1984, 2012a.
69. Though they represented just one in three employees, gains from collective bargaining spilled over to other firms whose management was keen to preempt unionization efforts.
70. Some worry about these developments because they believe stable couple families engender better behavior, thereby improving communities and individual happiness. See, for instance, Murray 2012a. For my purposes, family decline is a source of concern insofar as it has contributed to rising economic insecurity, to inadequate opportunity, and to the slow growth of living standards for America's lower half.
71. This updates figure 1.1 in Ellwood and Jencks 2004.
72. McLanahan and Sandefur 1994; McLanahan 2001.
73. Ellwood and Jencks 2004, p. 9. According to Charles Murray (2012a, p. 158): "No matter what the outcome being examined—the quality of the mother-infant relationship, externalizing behavior in childhood (aggression, delinquency, and hyperactivity), delinquency in adolescence/criminality as adults, illness and injury in childhood, early mortality, sexual decision making in adolescence, school problems and dropping out, emotional health, or any other measure of how well or poorly children do in life—the family structure that produces the best outcomes for children, on average, are two biological parents who remain

married. Divorced parents produce the next-best outcomes. Whether the parents remarry or remain single while the children are growing up makes little difference. Never-married women produce the worst outcomes. All of these statements apply after controlling for the family's socioeconomic status."

74. Census Bureau, "Historical Income Tables," www.census.gov/hhes/www/income/data/historical, tables F-12 and H-12.
75. Douthat and Salam 2008, p. 53.
76. Edin and Kefalas 2005; Cherlin 2009, ch. 7; England and Edin 2009.
77. Ellwood and Jencks 2004; Edin and Kefalas 2005; Cherlin 2009, ch. 7; England and Edin 2009; Haskins and Sawhill 2009, ch. 10; Wilson 2009, ch. 4; Conger, Conger, and Martin 2010; Isen and Stevenson 2010; England, McClintock, and Shafer 2012; England, Wu, and Shafer 2012; Murray 2012a, ch. 8; Nelson and Edin 2013.
78. Ellwood and Jencks 2004, figure 1.13. See also England and Edin 2009.
79. Douthat and Salam 2008, ch. 7; Haskins and Sawhill 2009, ch. 10.
80. Improving the financial incentive for marriage was a key aim of the mid-1990s welfare reform. See DeParle 2004. But it hasn't worked. AFDC-TANF benefit levels have been falling steadily and substantially since the 1970s, with no impact on the trend in family dissolution among less-educated Americans. See Aber et al. 1994; Moffitt and Scholz 2009.

An advertising and messaging campaign might help a bit, but I doubt it will yield much progress. Yes, similar campaigns helped reduce smoking and teen births. But marriage is different. We have strong evidence that smoking and teen parenthood are bad for the decision maker. The evidence is less overwhelming that avoiding or exiting marriage is bad for the person doing so. It tends to be bad for children, but it may or may not be bad for the adults. Also, smoking is an (addictive) activity, whereas marriage is a relationship. A partner or spouse who treats you poorly or cheats on you may be less tolerable than a daily routine without cigarettes.

The Healthy Marriages Initiative, which ran from 2005 to 2010, provided marital counseling and support for vulnerable couples. A thorough review found no noteworthy beneficial impact. See Wood et al. 2012; also Furstenberg 2008.
81. Cherlin 2009.
82. Ibid.; England and Edin 2009, chs. 1, 3, 6; Wilson 2009, ch. 4.
83. Sawhill 2002.
84. Wilson 1987, 1996, 2009.
85. Edin and Kefalas 2005.
86. Douthat and Salam 2008.
87. OECD 2001; Rønsen 2001; Rønsen and Sundstrom 2002; Morgan and Zippel 2003; Gangl and Ziefle 2012.
88. Edin and Kefalas 2005.

89. In Sweden the home-care allowance is used much more frequently by immigrant mothers, who because of language and education deficits have weaker labor market prospects than native-born women. See Earles 2011.
90. See chapter 2.
91. Mayer 1999.
92. Tocqueville 1840; Putnam 2000; Skocpol 2003; Brooks 2012b; Murray 2012a.
93. Putnam 1993a, 1993b, 2000.
94. Putnam 2000, figure 8.
95. Anderson et al. 2006.
96. Skocpol 2003.
97. Esping-Andersen 1990.
98. E.g., Esping-Andersen 1999.
99. The social democratic world is sometimes called "socialist" or "universalist." The conservative world is sometimes called "corporatist" or "social insurance." The liberal world is sometimes called "residual."
100. Hicks and Kenworthy 2003. See also Esping-Andersen 2003. These findings hold if the elements fed into the statistical analysis are expanded beyond traditional social insurance programs to include labor market policies and work-family policies.
101. Pension payments are a significant portion of government transfers in all rich countries. In one interpretation, counting public pensions in a measure of targeting-universalism or redistribution is misleading, because pension programs are best conceptualized as forced saving. The government requires employed citizens to put money away during their working years and then returns it to them (with interest) in their retirement years. In retirement, many people have no income from employment, so the pension they receive appears in the calculations as though it is going to a very poor household. According to this view, the measures therefore overstate the degree of targeting and the degree of redistribution achieved by transfers. Peter Whiteford (2008, 2009) has attempted to address this concern by calculating targeting-universalism and redistribution using households' position in the income distribution *after* transfers are added and taxes subtracted, rather than before. If a retired couple's income consists solely of a public pension payment, they will be at the very bottom of the distribution according to the calculations in figure 4.19. In Whiteford's calculations they instead might be at the twentieth percentile or even higher, depending on the size of their pension. In these calculations, Australia remains the most targeting-heavy of the rich nations, but it ranks higher on redistribution than in figure 4.19.
102. Korpi and Palme 1998; Kim 2000; Pontusson 2005.
103. Kenworthy 2011c, ch. 6; Marx et al. 2012.

104. Adema 2001; Adema and Ladaique; 2009; Fishback 2010. See also Adema 1997; Howard 1997, 2007; Hacker 2002; Garfinkel, Rainwater, and Smeeding 2010; Gilbert 2010; Mettler 2011.

105. Kenworthy 2011c, ch. 9; Morgan 2013.

106. Adema and Ladaique 2009, table 5.5; Fishback 2010, table 5.

107. One important tax benefit for low-income households is the EITC, but it is already included in the standard OECD data on government social expenditures. Another is the Child Tax Credit, but it is only partially refundable and thus of limited value to low-income households, many of whom don't owe any federal income tax.

108. They also tend to cost more, due to higher administrative costs and management fees. Graetz and Mashaw 1999; Attewell 2012.

109. LIS 2012.

110. Consumption tax rates are higher in the Nordic countries than in the United States. But these are incorporated in the purchasing power parities (PPPs) used to convert incomes to a common currency, so the income numbers in the third row of figure 4.21 are adjusted for differences in consumption taxes.

111. Kenworthy 2011c, ch. 2.

112. See also Kenworthy 2011c, ch. 4.

113. Graetz and Mashaw 1999; Kim et al. 2007.

114. For more discussion, see Hacker 2002; Hills 2011; Morgan and Campbell 2011; Konczal 2012.

115. Blair 2010, p. 569.

116. Emanuel 2013.

117. Judt 2010.

118. Kaus 1992.

119. Gosselin 2008, ch. 10; Kahneman 2011; Kliff 2012.

120. And those who would like additional coverage are free to purchase it.

121. Milanovic 2011.

122. Sen 1999, ch. 4; Sperling 2005; Stiglitz 2006, ch. 3; Collier 2007, ch. 10; Galbraith 2007; Krugman 2007; Rodrick 2007, ch. 9; Blinder 2009b; DeLong 2008; Kristof 2009.

123. Kenworthy 2008b.

124. Freeman and Medoff 1984.

125. In the public sector the unionization rate is 37 percent.

126. Kruse, Freeman, and Blasi 2008.

127. Weitzman 1984.

128. Edelman 2012, p. 32.

129. Household income tends to be shared (even if not necessarily equally), so it, much more than individual earnings, determines consumption and living standards. Moreover, household income appears to have a stronger effect on happiness than personal earnings; see Firebaugh and Schroeder 2009.

130. Immervoll and Pearson 2009.

131. Herzenberg, Alic, and Wial 1998.

132. E.g., Hall and Soskice 2001; Hall and Gingerich 2004; Barth and Moene 2009.
133. Pontusson 2011.
134. Rothstein 1998.
135. Goodin et al. 1999.
136. Kenworthy 2008a, ch. 6.
137. Kenworthy 2008a.
138. Baumol 1967.
139. OECD 2008, ch. 9; Esping-Andersen and Myles 2009; Paulus, Sutherland, and Tsakloglou 2009; Garfinkel, Rainwater, and Smeeding 2010; Kenworthy 2011c, ch. 7.
140. According to Duncan Gallie, among those responding to a mid-1990s survey in various European Union countries, semi-skilled and non-skilled workers were less likely than higher-skilled workers to report being in jobs in which they could "definitely learn new things or exercise significant influence over the way things are done" (Gallie 2002, p. 100). Surveys from a variety of affluent countries suggest an increase in work intensity and work effort in the 1980s and 1990s (Gallie 2002; Green 2006; Kalleberg 2011). Interestingly, in the mid-1990s EU survey there was no difference across skill groupings in the likelihood of experiencing heightened work pressure. But Gallie points out that "there is now a wide body of research that points to the fact that the long-term health effects of increased pressure are likely to be particularly severe among the low-skilled. This is because the impact of work pressure is mediated by the degree of control that employees can exercise over the work task. Where people are allowed initiative to take decisions themselves about how to plan and carry out their work, they prove to be substantially more resilient in the face of high levels of work pressure. It is jobs that combine high demand with low control that pose the highest health risks" (Gallie 2002, p. 105–106).
141. O'Toole and Lawler 2006.
142. Gallie 2003. Although not to quite the same extent, Finland's government and interest group organizations also have encouraged greater attention to these issues among employers. Francis Green has examined survey data on employee discretion and influence over their work tasks in the United Kingdom and Finland, the only two countries for which there are comparable data over a number of years. He finds evidence of decreased worker discretion in the UK but increased discretion in Finland. See Green 2006, ch. 5.
143. Gallie 2002, pp. 120–122.
144. Presser 2003.
145. Presser 2003, ch. 9.
146. Esping-Andersen 1999, 2009; Esping-Andersen et al. 2002; Andersson, Holzer, and Lane 2005; Fitzgerald 2006.
147. Steensland 2007.

148. Van Parijs 2001; Murray 2006. For more, see Wright 2010; Widerquist 2013.
149. Van Parijs 2001, pp. 3, 19.
150. Moffitt 1981.
151. Kenworthy 2008a.
152. See Galston 2001.
153. Bergmann 2006.
154. Ackerman and Alstott 1999; Sherraden 2007; Boshara 2009; Cramer and Newville 2009.
155. *Economist* 2013a.
156. Barr 2012.
157. Wooldridge 2013.
158. Alesina and La Ferrara 2005; Alesina, Harnoss, and Rapoport 2013; Kenworthy 2013c. Moreover, the Nordic countries are not as homogenous as is sometimes assumed. For instance, though United States' foreign-born share is larger than Denmark's, it is lower than Sweden's.
159. Lindert 2004; Baumol, Litan, and Schramm 2007.

CHAPTER 5

1. Lipset 1996.
2. Micklethwait and Woolridge 2004, pp. 382, 303.
3. See also Brooks and Manza 2007.
4. Pew Research Center, ABC/*Washington Post*, CBS/*New York Times*, *Los Angeles Times*, reported in Pew Research Center 2011a, pp. 109–110. "Depends" and "don't know" responses omitted.
5. Gallup 2011. "No opinion" responses omitted.
6. Pew Research Center 2011a, p. 147.
7. National Election Study, sda.berkeley.edu/archive.htm.
8. General Social Survey, sda.berkeley.edu/archive.htm, series conlegis and confed.
9. General Social Survey, sda.berkeley.edu/archive.htm, series natfarey, nateduc, natheal, and natsoc.
10. Reported in the data set for Page and Jacobs 2009, series qhc2.
11. Pew Research Center 2011b, p. 24.
12. Data set for Page and Jacobs 2009, series qtaxl.
13. Data set for Page and Jacobs 2009, series qtaxm.
14. Data set for Page and Jacobs 2009, series qjob4.
15. General Social Survey, sda.berkeley.edu/archive.htm, series natfare.
16. Gilens 1999.
17. Wilentz 2008.
18. Manza, Heerwig, and McCabe 2012; Kenworthy 2013b.
19. Page and Shapiro 1983.
20. Gilens 2012.
21. Erikson, MacKuen, and Stimson 2002.
22. Newman and Jacobs 2010.

23. Ibid., p. 7.
24. Ibid., p. 5.
25. Pierson 1994.
26. Hirschman 1991.
27. "Republican Hopefuls Deny Global Warming," *Guardian*, September 14, 2010; "House Repubs Vote That Earth Is Not Warming," *Scientific American*, March 16, 2011.
28. Kenworthy, Barringer, Duerr, and Schneider 2007, using General Social Survey data.
29. Larry Bartels finds no decline in the share of whites in the bottom income third that voted Democratic in presidential elections between 1952 and 2004. But in eight of those fourteen elections a majority of this group voted for the Republican candidate, so it can't really be considered to have been the electoral base of the Democrats. See Bartels 2008; Kenworthy 2010c.
30. Teixeira 2011; Teixeira and Halpin 2012.
31. Inglehart 1977; Inglehart and Abramson 1994.
32. Judis and Teixeira 2002. See also Browne, Halpin, and Teixeira 2011.
33. Hibbs 2009; Bartels 2013.
34. Bartels and Zaller 2000; Fair 2012; Silver 2012; Sides and Vavreck 2013.
35. Hibbs 2012; McGhee 2012.
36. Bai 2012.
37. Center for Responsive Politics, "Outside Spending," www.opensecrets. org.
38. Bai 2012.
39. McGregor 2012; Starr 2012; Moser 2013.
40. Jacobs et al. 2004; Drutman 2012.
41. Feingold 2013.
42. Keith Poole, "Party Polarization: 1879–2010," polarizedamerica.com/ Polarized_America.htm, 2013.
43. Schattschneider 1960; Ferguson and Rogers 1986; Domhoff 1990; Hacker and Pierson 2010.
44. Ferguson and Rogers 1986; Vogel 1989; Krugman 2007a; Hacker and Pierson 2010.
45. Blank 1997; Garfinkel, Rainwater, and Smeeding 2010; Ben-Shalom, Moffitt, and Scholz 2011; Edelman 2012; Meyer and Sullivan 2012.
46. Gilens 1999.
47. See also Meyer and Sullivan 2012.
48. Huber, Ragin, and Stephens 1993; Tsebelis 1995; Amenta 1998. There is the additional possibility of veto by the judicial branch. Lobbying, too, plays a role in minimizing policy change; see Baumgartner et al. 2009.
49. Baldassarri and Gelman 2008; Bartels 2008.
50. Poole and Hare 2012.

51. On top of ideological purification, the leadership in both parties has taken to using an array of rewards and punishments—from allocation of committee positions to backing of reelection campaigns—to get back-benchers to vote the party line.
52. Mann and Ornstein 2012, pp. 57–58.
53. Keith Poole, "Party Unity Scores," pooleandrosenthal.com/party_unity.htm, 2013.
54. Grunwald 2012, p. 67.
55. Douthat and Salam 2008; Frum 2008; Brooks 2012; Murray 2012a; Ponnuru 2013.
56. Skocpol and Williamson 2012.
57. See "The Tortoise and the Hare," one of Aesop's fables.

CHAPTER 6

1. Emigration from the United States may well increase as the rest of the world develops economically and language barriers ease, though it likely will remain a small-scale phenomenon.
2. Helle Thorning-Schmidt, speech at the conference on Progressive Governance: Towards Growth and Shared Prosperity, organized by Policy Network and Global Progress, Copenhagen, April 11–12, 2013.
3. See, for instance, the 2011 executive order "Improving Regulation and Regulatory Review."

Bibliography

Aaron, Henry. 2013. "Progressives and the Safety Net." *Democracy*,
   Winter: 68–79.
Aaronson, Daniel and Bhashkar Mazumder. 2008. "Intergenerational
   Economic Mobility in the U.S., 1940 to 2000." *Journal of Human
   Resources* 43: 139–172.
Aber, Larry et al. 1994. "Welfare and Out-of-Wedlock Births: Research
   Summary." Unpublished paper.
Acemoglu, Daron, James Robinson, and Thierry Verdier. 2012. "Can't We
   All Be More Like Scandinavians? Asymmetric Growth and Institutions
   in an Interdependent World." Working Paper 12–22. Cambridge,
   MA: Department of Economics, Massachusetts Institute of Technology.
Ackerman, Bruce and Anne Alstott. 1999. *The Stakeholder Society*. New
   Haven, CT: Yale University Press.
Acs, Gregory, Pamela Loprest, and Austin Nichols. 2009. "Risk and
   Recovery: Understanding the Changing Risks to Family Incomes."
   Washington, DC: Urban Institute.
Adema, Willem. 1997. "What Do Countries Really Spend on Social Policies?
   A Comparative Note." *OECD Economic Studies* 28: 153–167.
Adema, Willem. 2001. "Revisiting Real Social Spending across
   Countries: A Brief Note." *OECD Economic Studies* 30: 191–197.
Adema, Willem and Maxime Ladaique. 2009. "How Expensive Is
   the Welfare State? Gross and Net Indicators in the OECD Social
   Expenditure Database (SOCX)." Social, Employment, and Migration
   Working Paper 92. Paris: Organisation for Economic Cooperation and
   Development (OECD).
Alesina, Alberto, Edward Glaeser, and Bruce Sacerdote. 2005. "Work
   and Leisure in the U.S. and Europe: Why So Different?" *NBER
   Macroeconomics Annual* 20: 1–100.

Alesina, Alberto and Eliana La Ferrara. 2005. "Ethnic Diversity and Economic Performance." *Journal of Economic Literature* 43: 762–800.

Alesina, Alberto and George-Marios Angeletos. 2005. "Corruption, Inequality, and Fairness." *Journal of Monetary Economics* 52: 1227–1244.

Alexander, Karl L., Doris R. Entwisle, and Linda Steffel Olson. 2007. "Lasting Consequences of the Summer Learning Gap." *American Sociological Review* 72: 167–180.

Alexina, Alberto, Johann Harnoss, and Hillel Rapoport. 2013. "Birthplace Diversity and Economic Prosperity." Working Paper 18699. Cambridge, MA: National Bureau of Economic Research.

Allegretto, Sylvia A. 2011. "The State of Working America's Wealth, 2011." Briefing Paper 292. Washington, DC: Economic Policy Institute.

Amable, Bruno. 2003. *The Diversity of Modern Capitalism*. Oxford: Oxford University Press.

Amenta, Edwin. 1998. *Bold Relief: Institutional Politics and the Origins of Modern American Social Policy*. Princeton, NJ: Princeton University Press.

Anderson, Martin. 1978. *Welfare*. Stanford, CA: Hoover Institution.

Anderson, Robert, James Curtis, and Edward Grabb. 2006. "Trends in Civic Association Activity in Four Democracies: The Special Case of Women in the United States." *American Sociological Review* 71: 376–400.

Andersson, Fredrik, Harry J. Holzer, and Julia I. Lane. 2005. *Moving Up or Moving On: Who Advances in the Low-Wage Labor Market*. New York: Russell Sage Foundation.

Anrig, Greg, Jr. 2006. "Creating a Softer Economic Cushion." Washington, DC: The Century Foundation.

Apollo Alliance. 2008. "Creating Green-Collar Jobs in America's Cities." Washington, DC and Madison, WI: Center for American Progress and Center on Wisconsin Strategy.

Arum, Richard and Josipa Roksa. 2011. *Academically Adrift: Limited Learning on College Campuses*. Chicago: University of Chicago Press.

Atkinson, Anthony B. 1999. *The Economic Consequences of Rolling Back the Welfare State*. Cambridge, MA: MIT Press.

Atkinson, Anthony, Thomas Piketty, and Emmanuel Saez. 2011. "Top Incomes in the Long Run of History." *Journal of Economic Literature* 49: 3–71.

Attanasio, Orazio, Erik Hurst, and Luigi Pistaferri. 2012. "The Evolution of Income, Consumption, and Leisure Inequality in the US, 1980–2010." Working Paper 17982. Cambridge, MA: National Bureau of Economic Research.

Attewell, Steven. 2012. "Competing Visions of the Past: Learning from History for the Future of American Social Policy." Washington, DC: New America Foundation.

Auguste, Byron, Paul Kihn, and Matt Miller. 2010. "Closing the Talent Gap: Attracting and Retaining Top-Third Graduates to Careers in Teaching." McKinsey and Company.

Autor, David H. 2010. "The Polarization of Job Opportunities in the U.S. Labor Market." Washington, DC: Center for American Progress and The Hamilton Project.

Autor, David H. and Mark Duggan. 2010. "Supporting Work: A Proposal for Modernizing the U.S. Disability Insurance System." Washington, DC: Center for American Progress and The Hamilton Project.

Avent, Ryan. 2011. *The Gated City*. Amazon Digital Services.

Bai, Matt. 2012. "How Much Has Citizens United Changed the Political Game?" *New York Times*, July 17.

Bailey, Martha and Susan Dynarski. 2011. "Gains and Gaps: A Historical Perspective on Inequality in College Entry and Completion." Pp. 117–131 in *Whither Opportunity? Rising Inequality, Schools, and Children's Life Chances*. Edited by Greg J. Duncan and Richard J. Murnane. New York: Russell Sage Foundation and Spencer Foundation.

Baker, Dean. 2011. *The End of Loser Liberalism: Making Markets Progressive*. Washington, DC: Center for Economic and Policy Research.

Baker, Tom and David Moss. 2009. "Government as Risk Manager." Pp. 87–109 in *New Perspectives on Regulation*. Edited by David Moss and John Cisternino. Cambridge, MA: The Tobin Project.

Bakija, Jon. 2012. "Economic Effects of Taxation: Some Stylized Facts." Unpublished paper.

Baldassarri, Delia and Andrew Gelman. 2008. "Partisans without Constraint: Political Polarization and Trends in American Public Opinion." *American Journal of Sociology* 114: 408–446.

Barnett, W. Steven. 2013. "Getting the Facts Right on Pre-K and the President's Pre-K Proposal." New Brunswick, NJ: National Institute for Early Education Research.

Barnett, W. Steven, Megan E. Carolan, Jen Fitzgerald, and James H. Squires. 2011. *The State of Preschool 2011*. New Brunswick, NJ: National Institute for Early Education Research.

Barr, Michael S. 2012. *No Slack: The Financial Lives of Low-Income Americans*. Washington, DC: Brookings Institution Press.

Barr, Nicholas. 2001. *The Welfare State as Piggy Bank*. Oxford: Oxford University Press.

Barro, Robert J. 2011. "How to Really Save the Economy." *New York Times*, September 10.

Bartels, Larry. 2008. *Unequal Democracy*. Princeton, NJ: Princeton University Press.

Bartels, Larry. 2013. "Obama Toes the Line." *The Monkey Cage*, January 8.

Bartels, Larry and John Zaller. 2000. "Presidential Vote Models: A Recount." Unpublished paper.

Barth, Erling and Karl Ove Moene. 2009. "The Equality Multiplier." Working Paper 15076. Cambridge, MA: National Bureau of Economic Research.

Bartlett, Bruce. 2012a. *The Benefit and the Burden*. New York: Simon and Schuster.

Bartlett, Bruce. 2012b. "Tax Reform That Works: Building a Solid Fiscal Foundation with a VAT." Washington, DC: New America Foundation.

Baumgartner, Frank R., Jeffrey M. Berry, Marie Hojnacki, David C. Kimball, and Beth L. Leech. 2009. *Lobbying and Policy Change*. Chicago: University of Chicago Press.

Baumol, William J. 1967. "Macroeconomics of Unbalanced Growth: The Anatomy of Urban Crisis." *American Economic Review* 57: 415–426.

Baumol, William J. 2012. *The Cost Disease*. New Haven, CT: Yale University Press.

Baumol, William J., Alan S. Blinder, and Edward N. Wolff. 2003. *Downsizing in America*. New York: Russell Sage Foundation.

Baumol, William J., Robert E. Litan, and Carl J. Schramm. 2007. *Good Capitalism, Bad Capitalism, and the Economics of Growth and Prosperity*. New Haven, CT: Yale University Press.

Ben-Galim, D. and A. Sachraida Dal, eds. 2009. *Now It's Personal: Learning from Welfare-to-Work Approaches Around the World*. Washington, DC: Institute for Public Policy Research.

Ben-Shalom, Yonatan, Robert Moffitt, and John Karl Scholz. 2011. "An Assessment of the Effectiveness of Anti-Poverty Programs in the United States." Unpublished paper.

Bergh, Andreas and Magnus Henrekson. 2011. "Government Size and Growth: A Survey and Interpretation of the Evidence." *Journal of Economic Surveys* 25: 872–897.

Bergh, Andreas and Martin Karlsson. 2010. "Government Size and Growth: Accounting for Economic Freedom and Globalization." *Public Choice* 142: 195–213.

Bergmann, Barbara R. 2006. "A Swedish-Style Welfare State or Basic Income: Which Should Have Priority?" Pp. 130–142 in *Redesigning Redistribution*. Edited by Erik Olin Wright. London: Verso.

Berman, Sheri. 2006. *The Primacy of Politics*. Cambridge, UK: Cambridge University Press.

Bernstein, Jared and Dean Baker. 2003. *The Benefits of Full Employment*. Washington, DC: Economic Policy Institute.

Blair, Tony. 2010. *A Journey: My Political Life*. New York: Knopf.

Blanchard, Olivier. 2004. "The Economic Future of Europe." *Journal of Economic Perspectives* 18(4): 3–26.

Blank, Rebecca M. 1997. *It Takes a Nation: A New Agenda for Fighting Poverty*. New York and Princeton, NJ: Russell Sage Foundation and Princeton University Press.

Blank, Rebecca M. 2010. "Middle Class in America." Washington, DC: US Department of Commerce.

Blinder, Alan S. 2009a. "How Many U.S. Jobs Might Be Offshorable?" *World Economics* 10(2): 41–78.

Blinder, Alan S. 2009b. "Stop the World (and Avoid Reality)." *New York Times*, January 6.

Block, Fred. 2011. "Crisis and Renewal: The Outlines of a Twenty-First Century New Deal." *Socio-Economic Review* 9: 31–57.

Bloome, Deirdre and Bruce Western. 2011. "Cohort Change and Racial Differences in Educational and Income Mobility." *Social Forces* 90: 375–395.

Boeri, Tito and Pierre Cahuc. 2008. *Working Hours and Job Sharing in the EU and USA*. Oxford: Oxford University Press.

Boix, Carles. 2000. "Partisan Governments, the International Economy, and Macroeconomic Policies in Advanced Nations, 1960–1993." *World Politics* 53: 38–73.

Boshara, Ray. 2009. "Combating Poverty by Building Assets." *Pathways,* Spring: 19–23.

Boushey, Heather, Chauna Brocht, Bethney Gundersen, and Jared Bernstein. 2001. *Hardships in America*. Washington, DC: Economic Policy Institute.

Bowen, William G. and Derek Bok. 1998. *The Shape of the River*. Princeton, NJ: Princeton University Press.

Bowen, William G., Matthew M. Chingos, and Michael S. McPherson. 2009. *Crossing the Finish Line: Completing College at America's Public Universities*. Princeton, NJ: Princeton University Press.

Broda, Christian and John Romalis. 2008. "Inequality and Prices: Does China Benefit the Poor in America?" Unpublished paper.

Brooks, Clem and Jeff Manza. 2007. *Why Welfare States Persist: The Importance of Public Opinion in Democracies*. Chicago: University of Chicago Press.

Brooks, David. 2012a. "The Party of Work." *New York Times*, November 8.

Brooks, David. 2012b. "The Talent Society." *New York Times*, February 20.

Browne, Matt, John Halpin, and Ruy Teixeira. 2011. "Building a Progressive Center: Political Strategy and Demographic Change in America." Washington, DC: Center for American Progress.

Brynjolfsson, Eric and Andrew McAfee 2011. *Race against the Machine*. Digital Frontier Press.

Bureau of Labor Statistics. 2011. "Highlights of Women's Earnings in 2010." Washington, DC.

Bureau of Labor Statistics. 2012a. "Employment by Major Occupational Group, 2010 and Projected 2020, and Median Annual Wage, May 2010." Washington, DC.

Bureau of Labor Statistics. 2012b. "Selected Paid Leave Benefits." Washington, DC.

Burgoon, Brian and Phineas Baxandall. 2004. "Three Worlds of Working Time: The Partisan and Welfare Politics of Work Hours in Industrialized Countries." *Politics and Society* 32: 439–473.

Burkhauser, Richard V. and Mary C. Daly. 2012. "Social Security Disability Insurance: Time for Fundamental Change." *Journal of Public Policy Analysis and Management* 31: 454–461.

Burkhauser, Richard V., Jeff Larrimore, and Kosali I. Simon. 2011. "A 'Second Opinion' on the Economic Health of the American Middle Class." Working Paper 17164. Cambridge, MA: National Bureau of Economic Research.

Burtless, Gary and Timothy M. Smeeding. 2001. "The Level, Trend, and Composition of Poverty." Pp. 27–68 in *Understanding Poverty*. Edited by Sheldon Danziger and Robert Haveman. New York and Cambridge, MA: Russell Sage Foundation and Harvard University Press.

Campbell, Andrea Louise. 2011. "The 10 Percent Solution." *Democracy*, Winter: 54–63.

Campbell, John L. and Ove K. Pedersen. 2007. "The Varieties of Capitalism and Hybrid Success: Denmark in the Global Economy." *Comparative Political Studies* 40: 307–332.

Caner, Asena and Edward Wolff. 2004. "Asset Poverty in the United States, 1984–1999." *Challenge* 47(1): 5–52.

Carasso, Adam, Gillian, Reynolds, and C. Eugene Steurle. 2008. "How Much Does the Federal Government Spend to Promote Economic Mobility and for Whom?" Washington, DC: Economic Mobility Project.

Carlin, Wendy. 2012. "A Progressive Economic Strategy: Innovation, Redistribution, and Labour-Absorbing Services." London: Policy Network.

Carpenter, Dick M., Lisa Knepper, Angela E. Erickson, and John K. Ross. 2012. *License to Work: A National Study of the Burdens from Occupational Licensing*. Arlington, VA: Institute for Justice.

Castles, Francis G., Stephan Leibfried, Jane Lewis, Herbert Obinger, and Christopher Pierson, eds. 2010. *The Oxford Handbook of the Welfare State*. Oxford: Oxford University Press.

Causa, Orsetta. 2008. "Explaining Differences in Hours Worked among OECD Countries: An Empirical Analysis." Economics Department Working Paper 596. Paris: OECD.

Census Bureau. 2011. "Income, Poverty, and Health Insurance Coverage in the United States: 2010." Washington, DC.

Center for Research on Education Outcomes. 2013. "Charter School Growth and Replication." Stanford, CA.

Center for Retirement Research. 2009. "Workers with Pension Coverage, by Pension Type, 1983, 1995, and 2007." Boston.

Cherlin, Andrew J. 2009. *The Marriage-Go-Round*. New York: Knopf.

Chetty, Raj and Amy Finkelstein. 2013. "Social Insurance: Connecting Theory to Data." Pp. 111–193 in *Handbook of Public Economics*. Volume 5. Edited by Alan J. Auerbach, Raj Chetty, Martin Feldstein, and Emmanuel Saez. Amsterdam: Elsevier.

Chetty, Raj, John N. Friedman, and Jonah E. Rockoff. 2011. "The Long-Term Impacts of Teachers: Teacher Value-Added and Student Outcomes in Adulthood." Working Paper 17699. Cambridge, MA: National Bureau of Economic Research.

Clinton, Bill. 1995. "What Good Is Government?" *Newsweek*, April 10.

Collier, Paul. 2007. *The Bottom Billion*. Oxford: Oxford University Press.

Conger, Rand D., Katherine J. Conger, and Monica J. Martin. 2010. "Socioeconomic Status, Family Processes, and Individual Development." *Journal of Marriage and the Family* 72: 685–704.

Congressional Budget Office (CBO). 2008. "Recent Trends in the Variability of Individual Earnings and Household Income." Washington, DC.

Congressional Budget Office (CBO). 2010. "Average Federal Tax Rates and Income, by Income Category, 1979–2007." Washington, DC.

CONSAD Research Corp. 2009. "An Analysis of Reasons for the Disparity in Wages Between Men and Women." Pittsburgh.

Cowen, Tyler. 2011. *The Great Stagnation*. New York: Penguin.

Cox, W. Michael and Richard Alm. 1999. *Myths of Rich and Poor*. New York: Basic Books.

Cramer, Reid and David Newville. 2009. "Children's Savings Accounts." Washington, DC: New America Foundation.

Currie, Janet. 2006. *The Invisible Safety Net*. Princeton, NJ: Princeton University Press.

Currie, Janet. 2011. "Inequality at Birth: Some Causes and Consequences." *American Economic Review* 101 (Papers and Proceedings): 1–22.

Davis, Karen, Cathy Schoen, and Kristof Stremikis. 2010. "Mirror, Mirror on the Wall: How the Performance of the U.S. Health Care System Compares Internationally." Washington, DC: Commonwealth Fund.

DeLong, J. Bradford. 2008. "Free Trade and Fair Trade." SIEPR 2008 Economic Summit Conference, Stanford, CA.

DeLong, J. Bradford. 2009. "Slow Income Growth and Absolute Poverty in the North Atlantic Region." Unpublished paper.

DeLong, J. Bradford. 2012. "The Changing Structure of Prices since 1960." *Grasping Reality with Both Invisible Hands*, December 8.

DeLuca, Stefanie and Peter Rosenblatt. 2010. "Does Moving to Better Neighborhoods Lead to Better Schooling Opportunities? Parental School Choice in an Experimental Housing Voucher Program." *Teachers College Record* 112: 1443–1491.

DeParle, Jason. 2004. *American Dream*. New York: Penguin.

DeParle, Jason. 2012. "Welfare Limits Left Poor Adrift as Recession Took Hold." *New York Times*, April 7.

Dertouzos, Michael L., Lester C. Thurow, Robert M. Solow, and the MIT Commission on Industrial Productivity. 1989. *Made in America*. Cambridge, MA: MIT Press.

Diamond, Peter A. and Peter Orszag. 2004. *Saving Social Security: A Balanced Approach*. Washington, DC: Brookings Institution Press.

Domhoff, G. William. 1990. *The Power Elite and the State*. New York: Aldine de Gruyter.

Douthat, Ross and Reihan Salam. 2008. *Grand New Party*. New York: Doubleday.

Downey, Douglas B., Paul T. von Hippel, and Beckett A. Broh. 2004. "Are Schools the Great Equalizer? Cognitive Inequality during the

Summer Months and the School Year." *American Sociological Review* 69: 613–635.

Drutman, Lee. 2012. "Why Money Still Matters." *The Monkey Cage*, November 14.

Duncan, Greg J. and Jeanne Brooks-Gunn, eds. 1999. *Consequences of Growing Up Poor*. New York: Russell Sage Foundation.

Duncan, Greg J., Aletha C. Huston, and Thomas S. Weisner. 2007. *Higher Ground: New Hope for the Working Poor and Their Children*. New York: Russell Sage Foundation.

Duncan, Greg J. and Richard J. Murnane, eds. 2011. *Whither Opportunity? Rising Inequality, Schools, and Children's Life Chances*. New York: Russell Sage Foundation and Spencer Foundation.

Duncan, Greg J., Kathleen M. Ziol-Guest, and Ariel Kalil. 2010. "Early-Childhood Poverty and Adult Attainment, Behavior, and Health." *Child Development* 81: 306–325.

Dynan, Karen. 2010. "The Income Rollercoaster: Rising Income Volatility and Its Implications." *Pathways*, Spring: 3–6.

Dynan, Karen E., Douglas W. Elmendorf, and Daniel E. Sichel. 2012. "The Evolution of Household Income Volatility." *B.E. Journal of Economic Analysis and Policy* 12.

Dynarski, Susan and Judith Scott-Clayton. 2013. "Financial Aid Policy: Lessons from Research." Working Paper 18710. Cambridge, MA: National Bureau of Economic Research.

Earles, Kimberly. 2011. "Swedish Family Policy: Continuity and Change in the Nordic Welfare State Model." *Social Policy and Administration* 45: 180–193.

Easterbrook, Gregg. 2003. *The Progress Paradox*. New York: Random House.

Eberstadt, Nicholas. 2008. "The Poverty of the Official Poverty Rate." Washington, DC: American Enterprise Institute.

Eberstadt, Nicholas. 2012. *A Nation of Takers: America's Entitlement Epidemic*. West Conshohocken, PA: Templeton Press.

Economic Mobility Project. 2012. "Pursuing the American Dream: Economic Mobility Across Generations." Washington, DC: Pew Charitable Trusts.

Economic Security Index. 2012. "Economic Security Index." New Haven, CT.

Economist. 2008. "The Trouble with Pensions." June 12.

Economist. 2013a. "Finance and the American Poor." February 16.

Economist. 2013b. "Special Report on Outsourcing and Offshoring." January 19.

Edelman, Peter. 2012. *So Rich, So Poor*. New York: New Press.

Edin, Kathryn and Maria J. Kefalas. 2005. *Promises I Can Keep: Why Poor Women Put Motherhood Before Marriage*. Berkeley: University of California Press.

Edin, Kathryn and Laura Lein. 1997. *Making Ends Meet*. New York: Russell Sage Foundation.

Edsall, Thomas B. 2012. "Cash and Carry." *Campaign Stops. New York Times Online*, February 26.

Ehrenreich, Barbara. 2001. *Nickel and Dimed: On (Not) Getting By in America*. New York: Henry Holt and Company.

Ellwood, David T. 1988. *Poor Support*. New York: Basic Books.

Ellwood, David T. and Christopher Jencks. 2004. "The Uneven Spread of Single-Parent Families: What Do We Know? Where Do We Look for Answers?" Pp. 3–77 in *Social Inequality*. Edited by Kathryn M. Neckerman. New York: Russell Sage Foundation.

Emanuel, Ezekiel. 2013. "We Can Be Healthy and Rich." *New York Times*, February 3.

Emanuel, Ezekiel, et al. 2012. "A Systemic Approach to Containing Health Care Spending." *New England Journal of Medicine*. DOI: 10.1056/NEJMsb1205901.

England, Paula and Kathryn Edin, eds. 2009. *Unmarried Couples with Children*. New York: Russell Sage Foundation.

England, Paula, Elizabeth McClintock, and Emily Fitzgibbons Shafer. 2012. "Birth Control Use and Early, Unintended Births: Evidence for a Class Gradient." Pp. 21–49 in *Social Class and Changing Families in an Unequal America*. Edited by Marcia Carlson and Paula England. Stanford, CA: Stanford University Press.

England, Paula, Lawrence L. Wu, and Emily Fitzgibbons Shafer. 2012. "Cohort Trends in Premarital First Births: What Roles for Premarital Conceptions and the Retreat from Preconception and Postconception Marriage?" Unpublished paper.

Erikson, Robert S., Michael B. MacKuen, and James A. Stimson. 2002. *The Macro Polity*. Cambridge, UK: Cambridge University Press.

Ermisch, John, Markus Jäntti, and Timothy Smeeding, eds. 2012. *From Parents to Children: The Intergenerational Transmission of Advantage*. New York: Russell Sage Foundation.

Esping-Andersen, Gøsta. 1990. *The Three Worlds of Welfare Capitalism*. Princeton, NJ: Princeton University Press.

———. 1999. *Social Foundations of Postindustrial Economies*. Oxford: Oxford University Press.

———. 2003. "Why No Socialism Anywhere? A Reply to Alex Hicks and Lane Kenworthy." *Socio-Economic Review* 1: 63–70.

———. 2004. "Unequal Opportunities and the Mechanisms of Social Inheritance." Pp. 289–314 in *Generational Income Mobility in North America and Europe*. Edited by Miles Corak. Cambridge, UK: Cambridge University Press.

———. 2009. *The Incomplete Revolution*. Cambridge, UK: Polity.

———. 2011. "The Social Democratic Road to Equality." Unpublished paper.

Esping-Andersen, Gøsta, with Duncan Gallie, Anton Hemerijck, and John Myles. 2002. *Why We Need a New Welfare State*. Oxford: Oxford University Press.

Esping-Andersen, Gøsta and John Myles. 2009. "Economic Inequality and the Welfare State." Pp. 639–664 in *The Oxford Handbook of Economic Inequality*. Edited by Wiemer Salverda, Brian Nolan, and Timothy M. Smeeding. Oxford: Oxford University Press.

Esping-Andersen, Gøsta and Sandra Wagner. 2012. "Asymmetries in the Opportunity Structure: Intergenerational Mobility Trends in Europe." *Research in Social Stratification and Mobility* 30: 473–487.

Fair, Ray. 2012. *Predicting Presidential Elections and Other Things*. 2nd ed. Stanford, CA: Stanford University Press.

Families USA. 2009. "Americans at Risk: One in Three Uninsured." Washington, DC.

Farber, Henry S. 2010. "Job Loss and the Decline in Job Security in the United States." Pp. 223–262 in *Labor in the New Economy*. Edited by Katharine G. Abraham, James R. Spletzer, and Michael Harper. Chicago: University of Chicago Press.

Feingold, Russ. 2013. "Building a Permanent Majority for Reform." *Democracy*, Winter: 45–49.

Ferguson, Thomas and Joel Rogers. 1986. *Right Turn: The Decline of the Democrats and the Future of American Politics*. New York: Hill and Wang.

Ferrarini, Tommy and Ann-Zofie Duvander. 2010. "Earner-Carer Model at the Cross-Roads: Reforms and Outcomes of Sweden's Family Policy in Comparative Perspective." *International Journal of Health Services* 40: 373–398.

Firebaugh, Glenn and Matthew B. Schroeder. 2009. "Does Your Neighbor's Income Affect Your Happiness?" *American Journal of Sociology* 115: 805–831.

Fischer, Claude S. 2010. *Made in America*. Chicago: University of Chicago Press.

Fischer, Claude S., Michael Hout, Martin Sanchez Jankowski, Samuel R. Lucas, Ann Swidler, and Kim Voss. 1996. *Inequality by Design*. Princeton, NJ: Princeton University Press.

Fishback, Price V. 2010. "Social Welfare Expenditures in the United States and the Nordic Countries: 1900–2003." Working Paper 15982. Cambridge, MA: National Bureau of Economic Research.

Fishman, Charles. 2012. "The Insourcing Boom." *Atlantic*, December.

Fitzgerald, Joan. 2006. *Moving Up in the New Economy: Career Ladders for U.S. Workers*. Ithaca, NY: ILR Press.

Fletcher, Michael A. 2013. "401(k) Breaches Undermining Retirement Security for Millions." *Washington Post*, January 15.

Fligstein, Neil and Taek-Jin Shin. 2003. "The Shareholder-Value Society." *Indicators*, Fall: 5–43.

Florida, Richard and Martin Kenney. 1990. *The Breakthrough Illusion*. New York: Basic Books.

Fölster, Stefan and Magnus Henrekson. 2001. "Growth Effects of Government Expenditure and Taxation in Rich Countries." *European Economic Review* 45: 1501–1520.

Frank, Robert H. 2008. "Progressive Consumption Tax." *Democracy*,
    Spring: 21–23.
Freeman, Richard B. and James L. Medoff. 1984. *What Do Unions Do?*
    New York: Basic Books.
Friedman, Benjamin M. 2005. *The Moral Consequences of Economic
    Growth*. New York: Knopf.
Friedman, Milton. 1962. *Capitalism and Freedom*. Chicago: University of
    Chicago Press.
Friedman, Milton and Rose Friedman. 1979. *Free to Choose*. San Diego:
    Harcourt Brace Jovanovich.
Frum, David. 2008. "The Vanishing Republican Voter." *New York Times*,
    September 7.
Furstenberg, Frank R. 2008. "Cause for Alarm? Understanding Recent
    Trends in Teenage Childbearing." *Pathways*, Summer: 3–6.
Galbraith, James. 2007. "Why Populists Need to Rethink Trade." *The
    American Prospect*, May 9.
Gallie, Duncan. 2002. "The Quality of Working Life in Welfare Strategy."
    Pp. 96–129 in Gøsta Esping-Andersen et al., *Why We Need a New
    Welfare State*. Oxford: Oxford University Press.
Gallie, Duncan. 2003. "The Quality of Working Life: Is Scandinavia
    Different?" *European Sociological Review* 19: 61–79.
Gallup. 2011. "In U.S., Fear of Big Government at Near Record Level."
    Washington, DC.
Galston, William A. 2001. "What About Reciprocity?" Pp. 29–33 in *What's
    Wrong with a Free Lunch?* Edited by Joshua Cohen and Joel Rogers.
    Boston: Beacon Press.
Gangl, Markus. 2006. "Scar Effects of Unemployment: An Assessment
    of Institutional Complementarities." *American Sociological Review*
    71: 986–1013.
Gangl, Markus and Andrea Zielfle. 2012. "The Making of a Good
    Woman: Motherhood, Leave Entitlements, and Women's Work
    Attachment." Unpublished paper.
Gans, Herbert J. 2011. "Long-Range Policies for the U.S. Economy."
    Challenge, May-June: 80–94.
Garfinkel, Irwin, Lee Rainwater, and Timothy Smeeding. 2010. *Wealth and
    Welfare States*. Oxford: Oxford University Press.
Gawande, Atul. 2011. "Cowboys and Pit Crews." *New Yorker*, May 26.
Gawande, Atul. 2012. "Big Med." *New Yorker*, August 13.
Ghilarducci, Teresa. 2008. *When I'm Sixty-Four*. Princeton, NJ: Princeton
    University Press.
Giddens, Anthony. 1998. *The Third Way*. Cambridge, UK: Polity.
Giddens, Anthony. 2000. *The Third Way and Its Critics*. Cambridge,
    UK: Polity.
Gilbert, Neil. 2010. "Comparative Analyses of Stateness and State
    Action: What Can We Learn from Patterns of Expenditure?" Pp.
    133–150 in *United in Diversity? Comparing Social Models in Europe*

and America. Edited by Jens Alber and Neil Gilbert. Oxford: Oxford University Press.

Gilder, George. 1981. *Wealth and Poverty*. New York: Basic Books.

Gilens, Martin. 1999. *Why Americans Hate Welfare*. Chicago: University of Chicago Press.

Gilens, Martin. 2012. *Affluence and Influence*. Princeton, NJ: Princeton University Press.

Glaeser, Edward. 2011. *Triumph of the City*. London: Penguin.

Gleason, Philip, Melissa Clark, Christina Clark Tuttle, and Emily Dwoyer. 2010. "The Evaluation of Charter School Impacts." Princeton, NJ: Mathematica Policy Research.

Goodin, Robert E., Bruce Headey, Ruud Muffels, and Henk-Jan Dirven. 1999. *The Real Worlds of Welfare Capitalism*. Cambridge, UK: Cambridge University Press.

Gordon, Robert, Thomas J. Kane, and Douglas O. Staiger. 2008. "Identifying Effective Teachers Using Performance on the Job." Pp. 189–225 in *Path to Prosperity*. Edited by Jason Furman and Jason E. Bordoff. Washington, DC: Brookings Institution Press.

Gordon, Robert J. 2010. "The Demise of Okun's Law and of Procyclical Fluctuations in Conventional and Unconventional Measures of Productivity." Unpublished paper.

Gordon, Robert J. 2012. "Is US Economic Growth Over? Faltering Innovation Confronts the Six Headwinds." Policy Insight 63. London: Centre for Economic Performance.

Gornick, Janet C. and Marcia K. Meyers. 2003. *Families That Work*. New York: Russell Sage Foundation.

Gosselin, Peter. 2008. *High Wire*. New York: Basic Books.

Gosselin, Peter and Seth Zimmerman. 2008. "Trends in Income Volatility and Risk, 1970–2004." Washington, DC: Urban Institute.

Gottschalk, Peter. 1998. "The Impact of Changes in Public Employment on Low-Wage Labor Markets." Pp. 72–101 in *Generating Jobs: How to Increase Demand for Less-Skilled Workers*. Edited by Richard B. Freeman and Peter Gottschalk. New York: Russell Sage Foundation.

Gough, Ian. 1996. "Social Welfare and Competitiveness." *New Political Economy* 1: 209–232.

Gould, Elise, Hilary Hething, Natalie Sabadish, and Nicholas Finio. 2013. "What Families Need to Get By." Issue Brief 368. Washington, DC: Economic Policy Institute.

Graetz, Michael J. and Jerry L. Mashaw. 1999. *True Security: Rethinking American Social Insurance*. New Haven, CT: Yale University Press.

Green, Francis. 2006. *Demanding Work: The Paradox of Job Quality in the Affluent Economy*. Princeton, NJ: Princeton University Press.

Grunwald, Michael. 2012. *The New New Deal*. New York: Simon and Schuster.

Hacker, Jacob. 2002. *The Divided Welfare State*. Cambridge, UK: Cambridge University Press.

Hacker, Jacob. 2006. *The Great Risk Shift*. New York: Oxford University Press.

Hacker, Jacob. 2011. "Working Families at Risk: Understanding and Confronting the New Economic Insecurity." Pp. 31–70 in *Old Assumptions, New Realities: Economic Security for Working Families in the 21st Century*. Edited by Robert D. Plotnick, Marcia K. Meyers, Jennifer Romich, and Steven Rathgeb Smith. A West Coast Poverty Center volume. New York: Russell Sage Foundation.

Hacker, Jacob S. and Elizabeth Jacobs. 2008. "The Rising Instability of American Family Incomes, 1969–2004." Washington, DC: Economic Policy Institute.

Hacker, Jacob S. and Paul Pierson. 2006. *Off Center: The Republican Revolution and the Erosion of Democracy*. New Haven, CT: Yale University Press.

Hacker, Jacob S. and Paul Pierson. 2010. *Winner-Take-All Politics*. New York: Simon and Schuster.

Hacker, Jacob S., Philipp Rehm, and Mark Schlesinger. 2010. "Standing on Shaky Ground." New Haven, CT: Economic Security Index.

Hall, Peter A. and Daniel W. Gingerich. 2004. "Varieties of Capitalism and Institutional Complementarities in the Macroeconomy: An Empirical Analysis." Discussion Paper 04/5. Max Planck Institute for the Study of Societies. Cologne, Germany.

Hall, Peter A. and Daniel W. Gingerich. 2009. "Varieties of Capitalism and Institutional Complementarities in the Political Economy: An Empirical Analysis." *British Journal of Political Science* 39: 449–482.

Hall, Peter A. and David Soskice. 2001. "An Introduction to Varieties of Capitalism." Pp. 1–68 in *Varieties of Capitalism*. Edited by Peter A. Hall and David Soskice. Oxford: Oxford University Press.

Hanushek, Eric A. 2010. "The Economic Value of Higher Teacher Quality." Working Paper 16606. Cambridge, MA: National Bureau of Economic Research.

Harding, David J., Christopher Jencks, Leonard M. Lopoo, and Susan E. Mayer. 2005. "The Changing Effect of Family Background on the Incomes of American Adults." Pp. 100–144 in *Unequal Chances: Family Background and Economic Success*. Edited by Samuel Bowles, Herbert Gintis, and Melissa Osborne Groves. New York and Princeton, NJ: Russell Sage Foundation and Princeton University Press.

Harrison, Bennett and Maryellen R. Kelley. 1991. "The New Industrial Culture: Journeys Toward Collaboration." *The American Prospect*, Winter: 54–61.

Haskins, Ron and Isabel V. Sawhill. 2009. *Creating an Opportunity Society*. Washington, DC: Brookings Institution Press.

Hauser, Robert M., John Robert Warren, Min-Hsiung Huang, and Wendy Y. Carter. 2000. "Occupational Status, Education, and Social Mobility in the Meritocracy." Pp. 179–229 in *Meritocracy and Economic Inequality*.

Edited by Kenneth Arrow, Samuel Bowles, and Steven Durlauf. Princeton, NJ: Princeton University Press.

Hays, Sharon. 2003. *Flat Broke with Children*. New York: Oxford University Press.

Heckman, James J. 2008. "Schools, Skills, and Synapses." Working Paper 14064. Cambridge, MA: National Bureau of Economic Research.

Heckman, James J. and Paul A. LaFontaine. 2007. "The American High School Graduation Rate: Trends and Levels." Working Paper 13670. Cambridge, MA: National Bureau of Economic Research.

Heclo, Hugh. 1974. *Modern Social Politics in Britain and Sweden*. New Haven, CT: Yale University Press.

Heller, Richard. 2001. "The New Face of Swedish Socialism." *Forbes*, March 19.

Hemerijck, Anton. 2012. *Changing Welfare States*. Oxford: Oxford University Press.

Herzenberg, Stephen A., John A. Alic, and Howard Wial. 1998. *New Rules for a New Economy*. A Century Fund book. Ithaca, NY: ILR Press.

Heymann, Jody, Hye Jin Rho, John Schmitt, and Alison Earle. 2009. "Contagion Nation: A Comparison of Sick Leave Policies in 22 Countries." Washington, DC: Center for Economic and Policy Research.

Hibbs, Douglas. 2009. "The Bread and Peace Model Applied to the 2008 US Presidential Election." www.douglas-hibbs.com.

Hibbs, Douglas. 2012. "The Partisan Division of House Seats in 2012: Implications of the 'Bread and Incumbency' Model." www.douglas-hibbs.com.

Hicks, Alexander and Lane Kenworthy. 2003. "Varieties of Welfare Capitalism." *Socio-Economic Review* 1: 27–61.

Hills, John. 2011. "The Changing Architecture of the UK Welfare State." *Oxford Review of Economic Policy* 4: 589–607.

Hirschman, Albert O. 1991. *The Rhetoric of Reaction*. Cambridge, MA: Harvard University Press.

Howard, Christopher. 1997. *The Hidden Welfare State*. Princeton, NJ: Princeton University Press.

Howard, Christopher. 2007. *The Welfare State Nobody Knows*. Princeton, NJ: Princeton University Press.

Hout, Michael. 2009. "Rationing College Opportunity." *The American Prospect*, November: A8–A10.

Hoxby, Caroline. 2003. "Our Favorite Method of Redistribution: School Spending Equality, Income Inequality, and Growth." Unpublished paper.

Huang, Chye-Ching. 2012. "Recent Studies Find Raising Taxes on High-Income Households Would Not Harm the Economy." Washington, DC: Center on Budget and Policy Priorities.

Huber, Evelyne, Charles Ragin, and John D. Stephens. 1993. "Social Democracy, Christian Democracy, Constitutional Structure and the Welfare State." *American Journal of Sociology* 99: 711–749.

Huo, Jingjing, Moira Nelson, and John Stephens. 2008. "Decommodification and Activation in Social Democratic Policy: Resolving the Paradox." *Journal of European Social Policy* 18: 5–20.

Inglehart, Ronald. 1977. *The Silent Revolution: Changing Values and Political Styles among Western Publics*. Princeton, NJ: Princeton University Press.

Inglehart, Ronald and Paul R. Abramson. 1994. "Economic Security and Value Change." *American Political Science Review* 88: 336–354.

Immervoll, Herwig and David Barber. 2006. "Can Parents Afford to Work? Childcare Costs, Tax-Benefit Policies, and Work Incentives." Discussion Paper 1932. Bonn: Institute for the Study of Labor (IZA).

Immervoll, Herwig and Mark Pearson. 2009. "A Good Time for Making Work Pay? Taking Stock of In-Work Benefits and Related Measures Across the OECD." Social, Employment, and Migration Working Paper 81. Paris: OECD.

Irons, John S. 2010. Testimony before the National Commission on Fiscal Responsibility and Reform. June 30. Washington, DC.

Isaacs, Julia B. 2008. "Economic Mobility of Families Across Generations." Pp. 15–26 in Julia B. Isaacs, Isabel V. Sawhill, and Ron Haskins, *Getting Ahead or Losing Ground: Economic Mobility in America*. Washington, DC: Brookings Institution.

Isaacson, Walter. 2011. *Steve Jobs*. New York: Simon and Schuster.

Isen, Adam and Betsey Stevenson. 2010. "Women's Education and Family Behavior: Trends in Marriage, Divorce, and Fertility." Unpublished paper.

Jacobs, Jerry A. and Kathleen Gerson. 2004. *The Time Divide*. Cambridge, MA: Harvard University Press.

Jacobs, Lawrence R. and Robert Y. Shapiro. 2000. *Politicians Don't Pander*. Chicago: University of Chicago Press.

Jacobs, Lawrence R. et al. 2004. "American Democracy in an Age of Rising Inequality." *Perspectives on Politics* 2: 651–666.

Jacoby, Melissa. 2012. "Financial Fragility, Medical Problems, and the Bankruptcy System." Unpublished paper.

Jaimovich, Nir and Henry Siu. 2012. "The Trend Is the Cycle: Job Polarization and Jobless Recoveries." Working Paper 18334. Cambridge, MA: National Bureau of Economic Research.

Jäntti, Markus, Bernt Bratsbert, Knut Røed, Oddbjørn Rauum, Robin Naylor, Eva Österbacka, Anders Björklund, and Tor Eriksson. 2006. "American Exceptionalism in a New Light: A Comparison of Intergenerational Earnings Mobility in the Nordic Countries, the United Kingdom, and the United States." Discussion Paper 1938. Bonn: Institute for the Study of Labor (IZA).

Jencks, Christopher. 1992. *Rethinking Social Policy*. Cambridge, MA: Harvard University Press.

Jencks, Christopher. 2005. "What Happened to Welfare?" *New York Review of Books*, December 15.

Jencks, Christopher. 2009. "The Graduation Gap." *The American Prospect*, November.

Jencks, Christopher and Susan Mayer. 1990. "The Social Consequences of Growing Up in a Poor Neighborhood." Pp. 111–186 in *Inner-City Poverty in the United States*. Edited by Laurence Lynn and Michael McGeary. Washington, DC: National Academy Press.

Jencks, Christopher, Marshall Smith, Henry Acland, Mary Jo Bane, David Cohen, Herbert Gintis, Barbara Heyns, and Stephan Michelson. 1972. *Inequality*. New York: Basic Books.

Jensen, Shane T. and Stephen H. Shore. 2008. "Changes in the Distribution of Income Volatility." Unpublished paper.

Johnson, David S. 2004. "Using Expenditures to Measure the Standard of Living in the United States: Does It Make a Difference?" Pp. 27–47 in *What Has Happened to the Quality of Life in the Advanced Industrialized Nations?* Edited by Edward N. Wolff. Cheltenham, UK: Edward Elgar.

Jones, Charles I. 1995. "Time Series Tests of Endogenous Growth Models." *Quarterly Journal of Economics* 110: 495–525.

Judis, John B. and Ruy Teixeira. 2002. *The Emerging Democratic Majority*. New York: Scribner.

Judt, Tony. 2010. *Ill Fares the Land*. New York: Penguin.

Kahlenberg, Richard. 1995. "Class, Not Race." *New Republic*, April 3.

Kahneman, Daniel. 2011. *Thinking, Fast and Slow*. New York: Farrar, Straus, and Giroux.

Kalleberg, Arne. 2011. *Good Jobs, Bad Jobs*. New York: Russell Sage Foundation.

Katz, Lawrence F. 1998. "Wage Subsidies for the Disadvantaged." Pp. 21–53 in *Generating Jobs: How to Increase Demand for Less-Skilled Workers*. Edited by Richard B. Freeman and Peter Gottschalk. New York: Russell Sage Foundation.

Kaus, Mickey. 1992. *The End of Equality*. New York: Basic Books.

Kemmerling, Achim. 2009. *Taxing the Working Poor*. Cheltenham, UK: Edward Elgar.

Kenworthy, Lane. 1995. *In Search of National Economic Success*. Thousand Oaks, CA: Sage.

———. 2004. *Egalitarian Capitalism*. New York: Russell Sage Foundation.

———. 2006. "Institutional Coherence and Macroeconomic Performance." *Socio-Economic Review* 4: 69–91.

———. 2008a. *Jobs with Equality*. Oxford: Oxford University Press.

———. 2008b. "Why Embrace Economic Change?" *Consider the Evidence*, April 6.

———. 2009a. "How Progressive Are Our Taxes? Follow-up." *Consider the Evidence*, January 8.

———. 2009b. "Reducing Inequality: Boosting Incomes in the Bottom Half." *Consider the Evidence*, April 16.

————. 2009c. "Who Should Care for Under-Threes?" Pp. 193–207 in Janet Gornick, Marcia Meyers, et al., *Gender Equality: Transforming Family Divisions of Labor*. London: Verso.

————. 2010a. "Institutions, Wealth, and Inequality." Pp. 399–420 in *The Oxford Handbook of Comparative Institutional Analysis*. Edited by Glenn Morgan, John L. Campbell, Colin Crouch, Ove Kaj Pedersen, and Richard Whitley. Oxford: Oxford University Press.

————. 2010b. "Labor Market Activation." Pp. 435–447 in *The Oxford Handbook of the Welfare State*. Edited by Francis G. Castles, Stephan Leibfried, Jane Lewis, Herbert Obinger, and Christopher Pierson. Oxford: Oxford University Press.

————. 2010c. "Why Don't Low-Income Whites Love the Democrats?" *The Monkey Cage*, December 6.

————. 2011a. "Are Progressive Income Taxes Fair?" *Consider the Evidence*, April 2.

————. 2011b. "How Should We Measure the Poverty Rate?" *Consider the Evidence*, August 14.

————. 2011c. *Progress for the Poor*. Oxford: Oxford University Press.

————. 2011d. "Step Away from the Pool." *Newsletter of the American Political Science Association Organized Section for Qualitative and Multi-Method Research*, Fall: 26–28.

————. 2011e. "Taxes and Work." *Consider the Evidence*, May 9.

————. 2011f. "The Great Decoupling." *Consider the Evidence*, January 31.

————. 2011g. "The Late American Jobs Machine." *Consider the Evidence*, September 13.

————. 2011h. "Were the Bush Tax Cuts Worse for Progressivity or for Revenues?" *Consider the Evidence*, November 2.

————. 2011i. "When Does Economic Growth Benefit People on Low-to-Middle Incomes—and Why?" Commission on Living Standards. London: Resolution Foundation.

————. 2012a. "Is Decoupling Real?" *Consider the Evidence*, March 12.

————. 2012b. "It's Hard to Make It in America: How the United States Stopped Being the Land of Opportunity." *Foreign Affairs*, November-December: 97–109.

————. 2012c. "Two and a Half Cheers for Education." Pp. 111–123 in *After the Third Way: The Future of Social Democracy in Europe*. Edited by Olaf Cramme and Patrick Diamond. A Policy Network book. London: I.B. Tauris.

————. 2013a. "Rising Incomes and Modest Inequality: The High-Employment Route." Pp. 31–43 in *The Squeezed Middle: The Pressure on Ordinary Workers in America and Britain*. Edited by Sophia Parker. Bristol, UK: Policy Press.

————. 2013b. "What Do Americans Want?" Unpublished paper.

————. 2013c. "Why Do Some Rich Countries Grow Faster Than Others?" Unpublished paper.

Kenworthy, Lane, Sondra Barringer, Daniel Duerr, and Garrett Andrew Schneider. 2007. "The Democrats and Working-Class Whites." Unpublished paper.

Kessler, Jim. 2011. "Mr. President, Say This on Tuesday Night." *The Caucus. New York Times Online,* January 21.

Kim, Anne, Adam Solomon, Bernard L. Schwartz, Jim Kessler, and Stephen Rose. 2007. "The New Rules Economy: A Policy Framework for the 21st Century." Washington, DC: ThirdWay.

Kim, Hwanjoon. 2000. "Anti-Poverty Effectiveness of Taxes and Income Transfers in Welfare States." *International Social Security Review* 53(4): 105–129.

Klein, Ezra. 2007. "The Health of Nations." *The American Prospect,* May.

Kletzer, Lori G. and Robert E. Litan. 2001. "A Prescription to Relieve Worker Anxiety." Policy Brief 01-2. Washington, DC: Peterson Institute for International Economics.

Kliff, Sarah. 2012. "The Problem for Premium Support: Seniors Don't Always Choose the Best Plan." *Wonkblog. Washington Post Online,* October 17.

Kling, Jeffrey R. 2008. "Fundamental Restructuring of Unemployment Insurance: Wage-Loss Insurance and Temporary Earnings Replacement Accounts." Pp. 29–62 in *Path to Prosperity.* Edited by Jason Furman and Jason E. Bordoff. Washington, DC: Brookings Institution Press.

Kochan, Thomas A. 2005. *Restoring the American Dream: A Working Families Agenda for America.* Cambridge, MA: MIT Press.

Konczal, Mike. 2012. "No Discount: Comparing the Public Option to the Coupon Welfare State." Washington, DC: New America Foundation.

Korpi, Walter and Joakim Palme. 1998. "The Paradox of Redistribution and Strategies of Equality: Welfare State Institutions, Inequality, and Poverty in the Western Countries." *American Sociological Review* 63: 661–687.

Kozol, Jonathan. 1991. *Savage Inequalities: Children in America's Schools.* New York: Crown.

Kristensen, Peer Hull and Kari Lilja, eds. 2011. *Nordic Capitalisms and Globalization.* Oxford: Oxford University Press.

Kristof, Nicholas. 2009. "Where Sweatshops Are a Dream." *New York Times,* January 14.

Kristof, Nicholas. 2012. "The New Haven Experiment." *New York Times,* February 15.

Krueger, Alan B. 2009. "A Future Consumption Tax to Fix Today's Economy." *Economix. New York Times Online,* January 12.

Krugman, Paul. 2007a. *The Conscience of a Liberal.* New York: W. W. Norton.

Krugman, Paul. 2007b. "Divided over Trade." *New York Times,* May 14.

Kruse, Douglas, Richard Freeman, and Joseph Blasi. 2008. "Do Workers Gain by Sharing? Employee Outcomes under Employee Ownership,

Profit Sharing, and Broad-Based Stock Options." Working Paper 14233. Cambridge, MA: National Bureau of Economic Research.

Kuttner, Robert. 1989. "Managed Trade and Economic Sovereignty." Washington, DC: Economic Policy Institute.

LaLonde, Robert J. 2007. "The Case for Wage Insurance." New York: Council on Foreign Relations.

Lareau, Annette. 2003. *Unequal Childhoods*. Berkeley: University of California Press.

Layard, Richard. 2005. *Happiness*. London: Penguin.

Layard, Richard, Guy Mayraz, and Stephen Nickell. 2009. "Does Relative Income Matter? Are the Critics Right?" Discussion Paper 918. London: Centre for Economic Performance.

Lebergott, Stanley. 1976. *The American Economy*. Princeton, NJ: Princeton University Press.

Lee, Chul-In and Gary Solon. 2009. "Trends in Intergenerational Income Mobility." *Review of Economics and Statistics* 91: 766–772.

Lesmerises, Monica. 2007. "The Middle Class at Risk." Washington, DC: Century Foundation.

Lindert, Peter. 2004. *Growing Public: Social Spending and Economic Growth since the Eighteenth Century*. 2 vols. Cambridge, UK: Cambridge University Press.

Lipset, Seymour Martin. 1996. *American Exceptionalism*. New York: W. W. Norton.

Luxembourg Income Study (LIS). 2012. Luxembourg Income Study Database. www.luxembourgdata-center.org.

MacLeod, Jay. 2009. *Ain't No Makin' It*. 3rd ed. Boulder, CO: Westview.

Madrick, Jeff. 2009. *The Case for Big Government*. Princeton, NJ: Princeton University Press.

Magaziner, Ira and Robert B. Reich. 1982. *Minding America's Business*. New York: Vintage.

Mahler, Vincent and David Jesuit. 2006. "Fiscal Redistribution in the Developed Countries: New Insights from the Luxembourg Income Study." *Socio-Economic Review* 4: 483–511.

Mandel, Michael. 2000. "The New Economy." *BusinessWeek*, January 31.

Mandel, Michael. 2012. "Beyond Goods and Services: The (Unmeasured) Rise of the Data-Driven Economy." Washington, DC: Progressive Policy Institute.

Mann, Thomas E. and Norman J. Ornstein. 2012. *It's Even Worse Than It Looks*. New York: Basic Books.

Manza, Jeff, Jennifer A. Heerwig, and Brian J. McCabe. 2012. "Public Opinion in the 'Age of Reagan.'" Pp. 117–145 in *Social Trends in American Life*. Edited by Peter V. Marsden. Princeton, NJ: Princeton University Press.

Marmor, Theodore R., Jerry L. Mashaw, and Philip L. Harvey. 1990. *America's Misunderstood Welfare State*. New York: Basic Books.

Marx, Ive, Lina Salanauskaite, and Gerlinde Verbist. 2012. "The Paradox of Redistribution Revisited." Unpublished paper.

Marx, Ive and Gerlinde Verbist. 2008. "Combating In-Work Poverty in Europe: the Policy Options Assessed." Pp. 273–292 in *The Working Poor in Europe*. Edited by Hans-Jürgen Andreß and Henning Lohmann. Cheltenham, UK: Edward Elgar.

Mayer, Susan E. 1999. *What Money Can't Buy*. Cambridge, MA: Harvard University Press.

Mayer, Susan E. and Christopher Jencks. 1993. "Recent Trends in Economic Inequality in the United States: Income versus Expenditures versus Material Well-being." Pp. 121–203 in *Poverty and Prosperity in the USA in the Late Twentieth Century*. Edited by Dimitri B. Papadimitriou and Edward N. Wolff. New York: St. Martin's Press.

McCall, Leslie. 2013. *The Undeserving Rich*. New York: Cambridge University Press.

McGhee, Eric. 2012. "Forecasting House Elections." *The Monkey Cage*, September 17.

McGregor, Richard. 2012. "Inside Obama's HQ." *Financial Times*, September 16.

McKenzie, Brian and Melanie Rapino. 2011. "Commuting in the United States: 2009." Washington, DC: Census Bureau.

McLanahan, Sara. 2001. "Life without Father: What Happens to the Children?" Princeton, NJ: Center for Research on Child Wellbeing.

McLanahan, Sara and Gary Sandefur. 1994. *Growing Up with a Single Parent*. Cambridge, MA: Harvard University Press.

Mendes, Elizabeth. 2012. "More Than Three in 10 in U.S. Put Off Treatment Due to Cost." Washington, DC: Gallup.

Mettler, Suzanne. 2011. *The Submerged State*. Chicago: University of Chicago Press.

Meyer, Bruce D. and James X. Sullivan. 2011. "The Material Well-Being of the Poor and the Middle Class Since 1980." Working Paper 2011–04. Washington, DC: American Enterprise Institute.

Meyer, Bruce D. and James X. Sullivan. 2012. "Dimensions of Progress: Poverty from the Great Society to the Great Recession." Presented at the fall 2012 Brookings Panel on Economic Activity. Washington, DC.

Milanovic, Branko. 2011. *The Haves and the Have-Nots*. New York: Basic Books.

Miller, David. 2005. "What Is Social Justice?" Pp. 3–20 in *Social Justice: Building a Fairer Britain*. Edited by Nick Pearce and Will Paxton. Washington, DC: Institute for Public Policy Research.

Miller, Matthew. 2003. *The Two Percent Solution*. New York: PublicAffairs.

Mishel, Lawrence, Josh Bivens, Elise Gould, and Heidi Shierholz. 2012. *The State of Working America*. 12th ed. Washington, DC: Economic Policy Institute.

Mishel, Lawrence and Heidi Shierholz. 2013. "A Lost Decade, Not a Burst Bubble: The Declining Living Standards of Middle-Class Households in the US and Britain." Pp. 17–30 in *The Squeezed Middle: The Pressure on Ordinary Workers in America and Britain*. Edited by Sophia Parker. Bristol, UK: Policy Press.

Moffitt, Robert A. 1981. "The Negative Income Tax: Would It Discourage Work?" *Monthly Labor Review*, April: 23–27.

Moffitt, Robert A. and John Karl Scholz. 2009. "Trends in the Level and Distribution of Income Support." Working Paper 15488. Cambridge, MA: National Bureau of Economic Research.

Morel, Nathalie, Bruno Palier, and Joakim Palme, eds. 2012. *Towards a Social Investment Welfare State?* Bristol, UK: Policy Press.

Morgan, Kimberly J. 2013. "America's Misguided Approach to Social Welfare: How the Country Could Get More for Less." *Foreign Affairs*, January-February: 153–164.

Morgan, Kimberly J. and Andrea Louise Campbell. 2011. *The Delegated Welfare State*. New York: Oxford University Press.

Morgan, Kimberly J. and Kathrina Zippel. 2003. "Paid to Care: The Origins and Effects of Care Leave Policies in Western Europe." *Social Politics* 10: 49–85.

Morgen, Sandra, Joan Acker, and Jill Weigt. 2010. *Stretched Thin: Poor Families, Welfare Work, and Welfare Reform*. Ithaca, NY: Cornell University Press.

Moser, Bob. 2013. "What We Lost in 2012." *The American Prospect*, January-February.

Moss, David A. 2002. *When All Else Fails: Government as the Ultimate Risk Manager*. Cambridge, MA: Harvard University Press.

Munnell, Alicia H. 2012. "Bigger and Better: Redesigning Our Retirement System in the Wake of the Financial Collapse." Pp. 204–228 in *Shared Responsibility, Shared Risk*. Edited by Jacob S. Hacker and Ann O'Leary. Oxford: Oxford University Press.

Murray, Charles. 1984. *Losing Ground: American Social Policy, 1950–1980*. New York: Basic Books.

———. 2006. *In Our Hands: A Plan to Replace the Welfare State*. Washington, DC: AEI Press.

———. 2009. *Real Education*. New York: Random House.

———. 2012a. *Coming Apart: The State of White America, 1960–2010*. New York: Crown Forum.

———. 2012b. "Narrowing the New Class Divide." *New York Times*, March 7.

Myles, Gareth D. 2000. "Taxation and Economic Growth." *Fiscal Studies* 21: 141–168.

Myles, Gareth D. 2009. "Economic Growth and the Role of Taxation: Aggregate Data." Economics Department Working Paper 714. Paris: OECD.

National Center for Education Statistics. 2012. *The Condition of Education*. Washington, DC: US Department of Education.

National Commission on Higher Education Attainment. 2013. "An Open Letter to College and University Leaders: College Completion Must Be Our Priority." Washington, DC: American Council on Education.

Nelson, Timothy J. and Kathryn Edin. 2013. *Doing the Best I Can: Fathering in the Inner City*. Berkeley: University of California Press.

Newman, Katherine S. 1999. *No Shame in My Game: The Working Poor in the Inner City*. New York: Vintage Books and Russell Sage Foundation.

Newman, Katherine S. 2006. *Chutes and Ladders: Navigating the Low-Wage Labor Market*. New York and Cambridge, MA: Russell Sage Foundation and Harvard University Press.

Newman, Katherine S. and Elisabeth S. Jacobs. 2010. *Who Cares? Public Ambivalence and Government Activism from the New Deal to the Second Gilded Age*. Princeton, NJ: Princeton University Press.

Noah, Timothy. 2012. "The Mobility Myth." *New Republic*. February 8.

Nolan, Brian and Ive Marx. 2009. "Economic Inequality, Poverty, and Social Exclusion." Pp. 315–341 in *The Oxford Handbook of Economic Inequality*. Edited by Wiemer Salverda, Brian Nolan, and Timothy M. Smeeding. Oxford: Oxford University Press.

North, Douglass C. 1990. *Institutions, Institutional Change, and Economic Performance*. Cambridge, UK: Cambridge University Press.

Nussbaum, Martha C. 2011. *Creating Capabilities*. Cambridge, MA: Harvard University Press.

OECD (Organization for Economic Cooperation and Development). 2001. "Balancing Work and Family Life: Helping Parents into Paid Employment." Pp. 129–166 in *OECD Employment Outlook*. Paris: OECD.

———. 2006. *Starting Strong II: Early Childhood Education and Care*. Paris: OECD.

———. 2007. "Financing Social Protection: The Employment Effect." Pp. 157–206 in *OECD Employment Outlook*. Paris: OECD.

———. 2008. *Growing Unequal?* Paris: OECD.

———. 2010. *Education at a Glance 2010*. Paris: OECD.

———. 2011. *Health at a Glance 2011*. Paris: OECD.

———. 2012. "Country Note: United States." *Education at a Glance 2012*. Paris: OECD.

Ohanian, Lee, Andrea Raffo, and Richard Rogerson. 2007. "Work and Taxes: Allocation of Time in OECD Countries." *Federal Reserve Bank of Kansas City Economic Review* 92(3): 37–58.

Osborne, David. 1987. "Economic Competitiveness: The States Take the Lead." Washington, DC: Economic Policy Institute.

Osterman, Paul. 1999. *Securing Prosperity*. Princeton, NJ: Princeton University Press.

O'Toole, James and Edward E. Lawler III. 2006. *The New American Workplace*. New York: Palgrave Macmillan.

Page, Benjamin and Lawrence Jacobs. 2009. *Class War? What Americans Really Think about Economic Inequality*. Chicago: University of Chicago Press.

Page, Benjamin I. and Robert Y. Shapiro. 1983. "Effects of Public Opinion on Policy." *American Political Science Review* 77: 175–190.

Parlapiano, Alicia. 2012. "Unmarried Households Are Increasingly the Norm." *New York Times*, July 14.

Paulus, Alari, Holly Sutherland, and Panos Tsakloglou. 2009. "The Distributional Impact of In-Kind Public Benefits in European Countries." *Journal of Policy Analysis and Management* 29: 243–266.

Pessoa, João Paolo and John Van Reenen. 2012. "Decoupling of Wage Growth and Productivity Growth: Myth and Reality." Commission on Living Standards. London: Resolution Foundation.

Pew Research Center. 2011a. "The Generation Gap and the 2012 Election." Washington, DC.

Pew Research Center. 2011b. "Public Wants Changes in Entitlements, Not Changes in Benefits." Washington, DC.

Pierce, Justin R. and Peter K. Schott. 2012. "The Surprisingly Swift Decline of U.S. Manufacturing Employment." Working Paper 18655. Cambridge, MA: National Bureau of Economic Research.

Pierson, Paul. 1994. *Dismantling the Welfare State? Reagan, Thatcher, and the Politics of Retrenchment*. Cambridge, UK: Cambridge University Press.

Piore, Michael J. and Charles F. Sabel. 1984. *The Second Industrial Divide*. New York: Basic Books.

Polanyi, Karl. (1944) 1957. *The Great Transformation*. Boston: Beacon Press.

Ponnuru, Ramesh. 2013. "Reaganism after Reagan." *New York Times*, February 17.

Pontusson, Jonas. 2005. *Inequality and Prosperity*. Ithaca, NY: Cornell University Press.

Pontusson, Jonas. 2011. "Once Again a Model: Nordic Social Democracy in a Globalized World." Pp. 89–115 in *What's Left of the Left?* Edited by James Cronin, George Ross, and James Shoch. Durham, NC: Duke University Press.

Poole, Keith T. and Christopher Hare. 2012. "An Update on Political Polarization (through 2011)." *Voteview*, January 30.

Prescott, Edward C. 2004. "Why Do Americans Work So Much More Than Europeans?" *Federal Reserve Bank of Minneapolis Quarterly Review* 28(1): 2–13.

Presser, Harriet. 2003. *Working in a 24/7 Economy*. New York: Russell Sage Foundation.

Przeworski, Adam. 1985. *Capitalism and Social Democracy*. Cambridge, UK: Cambridge University Press.

Putnam, Robert D. 1993a. *Making Democracy Work: Civic Traditions in Modern Italy*. Princeton, NJ: Princeton University Press.

Putnam, Robert D. 1993b. "The Prosperous Community: Social Capital and Public Life." *The American Prospect*, Spring: 35–42.

Putnam, Robert D. 2000. *Bowling Alone: The Collapse and Revival of American Community*. New York: Simon and Schuster.

Quiggin, John. 2007. "The Risk Society: Social Democracy in an Uncertain World." Sydney: Centre for Policy Development.

Rank, Mark, 2004. *One Nation, Underprivileged*. New York: Oxford University Press.

Rank, Mark and Thomas A. Hirschl. Forthcoming. *Chasing the American Dream: Understanding the Dynamics That Shape Our Fortunes*. New York: Oxford University Press.

Ratcliff, Caroline and Signe-Mary McKernan. 2010. "Childhood Poverty Persistence: Facts and Consequences." Washington, DC: Urban Institute.

Rawls, John. 1971. *A Theory of Justice*. Cambridge, MA: Harvard University Press.

Ray, Rebecca and John Schmitt. 2007. "No-Vacation Nation." Washington, DC: Center for Economic and Policy Research.

Reardon, Sean. 2011. "The Widening Academic-Achievement Gap between the Rich and the Poor: New Evidence and Possible Explanations." Pp. 91–115 in *Whither Opportunity? Rising Inequality, Schools, and Children's Life Chances*. Edited by Greg J. Duncan and Richard J. Murnane. New York: Russell Sage Foundation and Spencer Foundation.

Rector, Robert. 2007. "How Poor Are America's Poor?" Backgrounder 2064. Washington, DC: Heritage Foundation.

Reich, Robert B. 1983. *The Next American Frontier*. New York: Penguin.

———. 1991. *The Work of Nations*. New York: Vintage.

———. 1999. "We Are All Third-Wayers Now." *The American Prospect*, March.

———. 2007. *Supercapitalism*. New York: Knopf.

———. 2010. *Aftershock*. New York: Knopf.

Reid, T. R. 2009. *The Healing of America*. New York: Penguin.

Reno, Virginia P. and Lisa D. Ekman. 2012. "Social Security Disability Insurance: Essential Protection When Work Incapacity Strikes." *Journal of Public Policy Analysis and Management* 31: 461–469.

Reskin, Barbara F. 1998. *The Realities of Affirmative Action in Employment*. Washington, DC: American Sociological Association.

Roemer, John E. 1998. *Equality of Opportunity*. Cambridge, MA: Harvard University Press.

Rogers, Joel. Forthcoming. *Productive Democracy*.

Rønsen, Marit. 2001. "Market Work, Child Care, and the Division of Household Labour: Adaptations of Norwegian Mothers Before and After the Cash-for-Care Reform." Report 2001/3. Statistics Norway.

Rønsen, Marit and Marianne Sundstrom. 2002. "Family Policy and After-Birth Employment Among New Mothers: A Comparison of

Finland, Norway, and Sweden." *European Journal of Population* 18: 121–152.

Rose, Stephen J. 2010. *Rebound*. New York: St. Martin's Press.

Rose, Stephen J. and Scott Winship. 2009. "Ups and Downs: Does the American Economy Still Promote Upward Mobility?" Washington, DC: Economic Mobility Project.

Rothstein, Bo. 1998. *Just Institutions Matter: The Moral and Political Logic of the Universal Welfare State*. Cambridge, UK: Cambridge University Press.

Rothstein, Bo. 2011. *The Quality of Government*. Chicago: University of Chicago Press.

Ruffing, Kathy A. 2011. "What the 2011 Trustees' Report Shows about Social Security." Washington, DC: Center on Budget and Policy Priorities.

Ruhm, Christopher and Jane Waldfogel. 2011. "Long-Term Effects of Early Childcare and Education." Discussion Paper 6149. Bonn: Institute for the Study of Labor (IZA).

Saez, Emmanuel, Joel Slemrod, and Seth H. Giertz. 2012. "The Elasticity of Taxable Income with Respect to Marginal Tax Rates: A Critical Review." *Journal of Economic Literature* 50: 3–50.

Salam, Reihan. 2011. "Vouchertopia." *The Agenda. National Review Online*, July 27.

Samuelson, Robert J. 1995. *The Good Life and Its Discontents*. New York: Times Books.

Sawhill, Isabel V. 2002. "Is Lack of Marriage the Real Problem?" *The American Prospect*, April 8.

Scharpf, Fritz W. 2000. "The Viability of Advanced Welfare States in the International Economy: Vulnerabilities and Options." *Journal of European Public Policy* 7: 190–228.

Schattschneider, E. E. 1960. *The Semisovereign People*. New York: Holt, Rinehart, and Winston.

Schneider, Martin R. and Mihai Paunescu. 2012. "Changing Varieties of Capitalism and Revealed Comparative Advantages from 1990 to 2005: A Test of the Hall and Soskice Claims." *Socio-Economic Review* 10: 731–754.

Schultze, Charles L. 1977. *The Public Use of Private Interest*. Washington, DC: Brookings Institution.

Schwartz, Christine R., and Robert D. Mare. 2005. "Trends in Educational Assortative Marriage from 1940 to 2003." *Demography* 42: 621–646.

Seidman, Laurence. 2013. "Medicare for All: An Economist's Case." *Challenge*, January-February: 88–115.

Sejersted, Francis. 2011. *The Age of Social Democracy*. Princeton, NJ: Princeton University Press.

Sen, Amartya 1999. *Development as Freedom*. Oxford: Oxford University Press.

Shaefer, H. Luke and Marci Ybarra. 2012. "The Welfare Reforms of the 1990s and the Stratification of Material Well-being among Low-Income Households with Children." *Children and Youth Services Review* 34: 1810–1817.

Sherraden, Michael. 2007. "Assets for All: Toward Universal, Progressive, Lifelong Accounts." Pp. 151–164 in *Ending Poverty in America.* Edited by John Edwards, Marion Crain, and Arne L. Kalleberg. New York: New Press.

Shiller, Robert J. 2003. *The New Financial Order.* Princeton, NJ: Princeton University Press.

Sides, John and Lynn Vavreck. 2013. *The Gamble: Choice and Chance in the 2012 Presidential Election.* Princeton, NJ: Princeton University Press.

Silver, Nate. 2012. "Measuring the Effect of the Economy on Elections." *FiveThirtyEight. New York Times Online*, July 5.

Simon, William E. 1978. *A Time for Truth.* New York: Reader's Digest Press.

Skocpol, Theda. 1992. *Protecting Soldiers and Mothers.* Cambridge, MA: Harvard University Press.

Skocpol, Theda. 2003. *Diminished Democracy: From Membership to Management in American Civic Life.* Norman: University of Oklahoma Press.

Skocpol, Theda and Vanessa Williamson. 2012. *The Tea Party and the Remaking of Republican Conservatism.* New York: Oxford University Press.

Slemrod, Joel and Jon Bakija. 2008. *Taxing Ourselves.* 4th ed. Cambridge, MA: MIT Press.

Soltas, Evan. 2012. "What Paul Ryan, and His Critics, Can Learn from Canada." *The Ticker. Bloomberg Online*, August 19.

Sperling, Gene. 2005. *The Pro-Growth Progressive.* New York: Simon and Schuster.

Starr, Paul. 2012. "America on the Brink of Oligarchy." *New Republic*, September 13.

Steensland, Brian. 2007. *The Failed Welfare Revolution: America's Struggle over Guaranteed Income Policy.* Princeton, NJ: Princeton University Press.

Stiglitz, Joseph E. 1989. "On the Economic Role of the State." Pp. 11–85 in *The Economic Role of the State.* Edited by Arnold Heertje. Oxford: Basil Blackwell.

Stiglitz, Joseph E. 2006. *Making Globalization Work.* New York: W. W. Norton.

Stiglitz, Joseph E. 2009. "Regulation and Failure." Pp. 11–23 in *New Perspectives on Regulation*, Edited by David Moss and John Cisternino. Cambridge, MA: The Tobin Project.

Stokey, Nancy L. and Sergio Rebelo. 1995. "Growth Effects of Flat Tax Rates." *Journal of Political Economy* 103: 519–550.

Surowiecki, James. 2010. "Soak the Very, Very Rich." *New Yorker*, August 16.

Tanzi, Vito. 2011. *Government versus Markets*. Cambridge, UK: Cambridge University Press.

Teixeira, Ruy. 2011. "The White Working Class: The Group That Will Likely Decide Obama's Fate." *New Republic*, June 20.

Teixeira, Ruy and John Halpin. 2012. "The Obama Coalition in the 2012 Election and Beyond." Washington, DC: Center for American Progress.

Teles, Steven M. 2012. "Kludgeocracy: The American Way of Policy." Washington, DC: New America Foundation.

Thiebaud Nicoli, Lisa. 2012. "Half a Loaf: Generosity in Cash Assistance to Single Mothers Across U.S. States, 1911–1996." PhD dissertation. Department of Sociology, University of Arizona.

Thurow, Lester. 1984 "Building a World-Class Economy." *Society* 16(1): 16–29.

de Tocqueville, Alexis. 1840. *Democracy in America*. www.gutenberg.org.

Toder, Eric and Joseph Rosenberg. 2010. "Effects of Imposing a Value-Added Tax to Replace Payroll Taxes or Corporate Taxes." Washington, DC: Tax Policy Center.

Toder, Eric, Marjery Austin Turner, Katherine Lim, and Liza Getsinger. 2010. "Reforming the Mortgage Interest Deduction." Washington, DC: Urban Institute and Tax Policy Center.

Tsebelis, George. 1995. "Decision Making in Political Systems." *British Journal of Political Science* 25: 289–325.

Tyson, Laura D'Andrea. 1992. *Who's Bashing Whom?* Washington, DC: Institute for International Economics.

Uchitelle, Louis. 2006. *The Disposable American*. New York: Knopf.

US Senate Committee on Health, Education, Labor, and Pensions. 2012. "The Retirement Crisis and a Plan to Solve It." Washington, DC.

Van Parijs, Philippe. 2001. "A Basic Income for All." Pp. 3–26 in *What's Wrong with a Free Lunch?* Edited by Joshua Cohen and Joel Rogers. Boston: Beacon Press.

Vandell, Deborah Lowe and Barbara Wolfe. 2000. "Child Care Quality: Does It Matter and Does It Need to Be Improved?" Special Report 78. Institute for Research on Poverty, University of Wisconsin–Madison.

Vedder, Richard, Christopher Denhart, Matthew Denhart, Christopher Matgouranis, and Jonathan Robe. 2010. "From Wall Street to Wal-Mart: Why College Graduates Are Not Getting Good Jobs." Washington, DC: Center for College Affordability and Productivity.

Vogel, David. 1989. *Fluctuating Fortunes: The Political Power of Business in America*. New York: Basic Books.

Waldfogel, Jane. 2006. *What Children Need*. Cambridge, MA: Harvard University Press.

Waldfogel, Jane. 2009. "The Role of Family Policies in Antipoverty Policy." *Focus* 26(2): 50–55.

Waldfogel, Jane. 2010. *Britain's War on Poverty*. New York: Russell Sage Foundation.

Waldfogel, Jane and Elizabeth Washbrook. 2011. "Income-Related Gaps in School Readiness in the United States and the United Kingdom." Pp. 175–207 in *Persistence, Privilege, and Parenting: The Comparative Study of Intergenerational Mobility*. Edited by Timothy M. Smeeding, Robert Erickson, and Markus Jäntti. New York: Russell Sage Foundation.

Wang, Chen and Koen Caminada. 2011. "Disentangling Income Inequality and the Redistributive Effect of Social Transfers and Taxes in 36 LIS Countries." Working Paper 567. Luxembourg Income Study.

Wanniski, Jude. 1978. *The Way the World Works*. New York: Basic Books.

Warren, Elizabeth and Amelia Warren Tyagi. 2003. *The Two-Income Trap*. New York: Basic Books.

Weeden, Kim A. 2002. "Why Do Some Occupations Pay More Than Others? Social Closure and Earnings Inequality in the United States." *American Journal of Sociology* 108: 55–101.

Weidenbaum, Murray L. et al. 1980. "On Saving the Kingdom." *Regulation*, November-December: 14–35.

Weitzman, Martin L. 1984. *The Share Economy*. Cambridge, MA: Harvard University Press.

Weller, Christian. 2012. "Unburdening America's Middle Class." *Challenge*, January-February: 23–52.

Western, Bruce. 2006. *Punishment and Inequality in America*. New York: Russell Sage Foundation.

Western, Bruce. 2012. "Crime and Punishment." *Boston Review*, March-April: 5–6.

Western, Bruce, Dierdre Bloome, Benjamin Sosnaud, and Laura Tach. 2012. "Economic Insecurity and Social Stratification." *Annual Review of Sociology* 38: 341–359.

Western, Bruce and Jake Rosenfeld. 2011. "Unions, Norms, and the Rise in U.S. Wage Inequality." *American Sociological Review* 76: 513–537.

Whiteford, Peter. 2008. "How Much Redistribution Do Governments Achieve? The Role of Cash Transfers and Household Taxes." Chapter 4 in *Growing Unequal?* Paris: OECD.

Whiteford, Peter. 2009. "Transfer Issues and Directions for Reform: Australian Transfer Policy in Comparative Perspective." Kensington, Australia: Social Policy Research Center.

Wider Opportunities for Women (WOW). 2011. "Living Below the Line: Economic Insecurity and America's Families." Washington, DC.

Widerquist, Karl. 2013. "Is Universal Basic Income Still Worth Talking About?" Pp. 568–584 in *The Economics of Inequality, Poverty, and Discrimination in the 21st Century*. Edited by Robert Rycroft. New York: Praeger.

Wilensky, Harold L. 1975. *The Welfare State and Equality*. Berkeley: University of California Press.

Wilensky, Harold L. 2002. *Rich Democracies*. Berkeley: University of
    California Press.
Wilentz, Sean. 2008. *The Age of Reagan*. New York: HarperCollins.
Wilson, William Julius. 1978. *The Declining Significance of Race*.
    Chicago: University of Chicago Press.
Wilson, William Julius. 1987. *The Truly Disadvantaged*. Chicago:
    University of Chicago Press.
Wilson, William Julius. 1996. *When Work Disappears*. New York: Vintage.
Wilson, William Julius. 2009. *More Than Just Race*. New York: W. W.
    Norton.
Wilson, William Julius and Sylvia Laurent 2012. "Can the Newly Reelected
    Obama Save the American Public School?" *Pathways*, Fall: 28–32.
Winship, Scott. 2012. "Bogeyman Economics." *National Affairs*,
    Winter: 3–21.
Winship, Scott. 2013. "The Dream Abides: Economic Mobility in America
    from the Golden Age to the Great Recession." Policy Brief. Washington,
    DC: Brookings Institution.
Wolff, Edward N. 2011. *The Transformation of the American Pension
    System*. Kalamazoo, MI: Upjohn Institute.
Wolff, Edward N. 2012. "The Asset Price Meltdown and the Wealth of the
    Middle Class." Unpublished paper.
Womack, James P., Daniel T. Jones, and Daniel Roos. 1990. *The Machine
    That Changed the World*. New York: Rawson Associates.
Wood, Robert G., Sheena McConnell, Quinn Moore, Andrew Clarkwest, and
    JoAnn Hsueh. 2012. "The Effects of Building Strong Families: A Healthy
    Marriage and Relationship Skills Education Program for Unmarried
    Parents." *Journal of Policy Analysis and Management* 31: 228–252.
Wright, Erik Olin. 2010. *Envisioning Real Utopias*. London: Verso.
Wright, Erik Olin and Rachel Dwyer. 2003. "The Patterns of Job
    Expansions in the United States: A Comparison of the 1960s and 1990s."
    Socio-Economic Review 1: 289–325.
Yglesias, Matthew. 2011. "The Era of Big Government." *ThinkProgress*,
    January 22.
Yglesias, Matthew. 2012. *The Rent Is Too Damn High*. New York: Simon
    and Schuster.
Yglesias, Matthew. 2013. "Balanced Budget Amendment with 18 Percent
    Spending Cap Encourages Inefficient Regulatory Mandates." *MoneyBox*.
    Slate, February 11.
Zingales, Luigi. 2012. *A Capitalism for the People*. New York: Basic Books.
Zysman, John. 1983. *Governments, Markets, and Growth*. Ithaca, NY:
    Cornell University Press.

Index